The ...

BERKSHIRE

BERKSHIRE

THE LITTLE GUIDES

WINDSOR CASTLE

BERKSHIRE

By

F. G. BRABANT, M.A.

*With Illustrations by Edmund H. New
and from Photographs*

"Thames along the silent level
Streaming thro' his osier'd aits."
TENNYSON.

"The Kennet swift, for silver eels renowned,
The Loddon slow, with verdant alders crowned."
POPE.

LONDON
METHUEN & CO. LTD.
36 *Essex St. Strand*

First Published in 1911

PREFACE

THIS little work is composed on a plan similar to that of the other Little Guides. It differs only in one point from my former guides to Sussex and Oxfordshire—namely that, as Berkshire is smaller in extent, and, comparatively speaking, less rich in material, I have been able to make the descriptions longer and more detailed. In the case of Windsor Castle alone I have aimed at compression, lest the account should run to a length disproportioned to the size of the book. My labours on the county, though interrupted at intervals by other work, now date back several years, during which I have penetrated, so to speak, every corner of it, carefully observed the varieties of scenery, and investigated every old church and almost every ancient building.

I have to make the customary acknowledgments to my predecessors in the same field, without whose labours such a work as the present would be impossible. I am much indebted to many of the local antiquaries, among whom I may mention Mr J. H. Parker, Rev. P. H. Ditchfield, Mr Walter Money, Mr C. E. Keyser, Dr J. C. Cox, Mr J. Meade Faulkner, Rev. F. T. Wethered, Dr J. B. Hurry, and Mr W. H. Dixon. I have made considerable use of the "Victoria History of Berkshire," and *The Berks Archæological Journal*, to both of which many of the above authorities have been contributors. I have also again found the *National Dictionary of Biography* invaluable. I have again to thank Dr A. A. Rambaut for placing the records of the Radcliffe Observatory at my service; also the owners of many historic houses, who have kindly permitted me to inspect them. Finally, I think I have even better reason than on previous occasions for thanking my illustrator, Mr E. H. New.

22 MUSEUM ROAD, OXFORD
    March 1911

CONTENTS

vii

CONTENTS

LIST OF ILLUSTRATIONS, MAPS
AND PLANS

BERKSHIRE

LIST OF ILLUSTRATIONS

INTRODUCTION

I. Size and Extent

BERKSHIRE may be called the most northerly of the counties of S.E. England which lie S. of the Thames. It is bounded on the N. by Oxfordshire and Buckinghamshire, and also by a very little bit of Gloucestershire at the N.W. corner; Wiltshire lies to the W., Hampshire to the S., and Surrey to the E.— that is, so far as the points of the compass can strictly be applied to a county of so irregular a shape. This irregularity is due to the serpentine windings of the Thames, which forms the N. boundary-line for nearly 110 m. The other boundaries are comparatively regular. The W. boundary has a distinct S.E., and the E. boundary a S.W., trend, so that the S. boundary is narrower than the N. one. It runs first along the River Enborne, then turns along the line of the Devil's Highway till it reaches the Blackwater, which stream forms the rest of the S. boundary-line. The shape of the county, which has been compared to a lute and to a slipper, is in many details curiously like that of Oxfordshire. The longest line which can be drawn from E. to W. across the county is 41 m. By taking a direction from about W.N.W. to E.S.E. a line of about 45 m. can be drawn. The extreme E. and W. points of the county are about 50 m.

A   1

apart, but the straight line connecting them passes into Oxfordshire. The county is broader in the W. part, the maximum breadth from N. to S. being 31 m., on a line nearly coincident with the Oxford to Newbury road. Toward the E. it narrows in remarkable fashion, so that at Reading it is only 7 m. broad. In the E. part it broadens again to a maximum of 16 m. The most N. point is at King's Weir on the Thames, about $3\frac{1}{2}$ m. N.W. of Oxford. The most W. point is on the Cole, $1\frac{1}{2}$ m. before it flows into the Thames near Lechlade. The most southerly point is at the S.W. corner, 2 m. S.W. of Combe, on the S. side of Inkpen Beacon, and the most easterly point on the Thames between Windsor and Old Windsor. The county contains 722 square m., or 462,367 acres, and is the thirty-third in size among the counties of England.

II. Physical Features and Scenery

For scenery Berkshire holds a high place among our S.E. counties. It is far more beautiful than Oxfordshire, and in its best parts hardly yields to Surrey and Sussex. It contains the chief beauties of the Thames, including the whole of its passage through the chalk gorge, between Streatley and Maidenhead. The Berkshire Downs are a chalk range very little inferior in beauty and interest to the South Downs, and some of the loveliest villages to be found in England nestle under their N. slopes. The valleys of the Lambourn and the Pang are full of a delicate miniature beauty, and the loveliness of the Kennet Valley, with its bounding commons and forests, has hardly yet been adequately recognized. Finally, in the E. there is the Forest District, a sand plateau covered with mile after mile of pine woods. In fine churches and ancient mansions the county is, it must be confessed, comparatively deficient, but there is abundance of historical and antiquarian interest, chiefly in connexion with the towns of Windsor, Reading, Wallingford, Abingdon, Faringdon and Newbury.

Geographically Berkshire may be called a section of the S. basin of the Thames, comprising roughly the basins of four of its tributaries, the Ock, the Pang, the Kennet and the Loddon. The last two tributaries rise outside the county, but the greater part of their courses lies within it. But we shall get a clearer idea of the build of the county by calling to our aid the sister science of Geology. The characteristics of Berkshire chiefly depend on the lie of the chalk strata. The great chalk plateau which covers nearly the whole of Wiltshire divides into two portions as it passes eastward. The N. escarpment of the S. part forms the Inkpen Beacon range of Downs, which lies entirely in Hampshire, except, curiously enough, at Inkpen Beacon itself—the highest point—where the Berkshire boundary makes a sudden sweep southwards to include it. The other part, of which the Berkshire Downs form the N. escarpment, trends N.E., passing through the middle of the county, of which it may be said to form the backbone. In the neighbourhood of Streatley it leaves Berkshire for Oxfordshire, where it forms the Chiltern Hills. More to the N.E., the strange northward curve of the Thames between Reading and Maidenhead brings another small portion of this chalk belt within the limits of the county. Between these two belts the chalk dips underground to form a large wedge-shaped basin filled with tertiary strata. The point of the wedge is near Hungerford, and at first this district coincides with the Valley of the

Kennet and its boundary hills, nearly all of which are part of Berkshire. But, near the point where the Kennet runs into the Thames, the wedge has grown broader, and presently expands far beyond the limits of the county, forming in fact the basin of the Lower Thames, in which London lies. Thus the part of Berkshire which lies E. of the Loddon, though composed of the same strata as the Kennet Valley, may fairly be considered a different part of the county. N. of the central chalk range, between the Downs and the Thames, there lies another region of Berkshire, composed of strata older than the chalk. Most of this belongs to the Vale of the White Horse, which name may conveniently be given to the whole district.

Berkshire then may be divided into four parts, which, according to the antiquity of the strata composing them, are : (1) the Vale of the White Horse, including all the country between the Thames and the Downs ; (2) the Chalk Belt ; (3) the Valley of the Kennet with the hills which bound it ; (4) the district E. of the Loddon. As a fifth division may be added the Thames Valley, which deserves separate treatment. Such a classification, though rough and arbitrary, gives much help in understanding the scenery.

1. The S. bank of the Thames as far as Oxford is bounded by flat meadows due to a narrow strip of Oxford clay. Directly S. of this there is a sharp rise of 150 to 200 feet to the *Berkshire Ridge,* composed of coral rag. This forms the N. boundary of the *Vale of the White Horse,* into which it gently slopes on the S. side. The ridge is well wooded, with good views, and contains several interesting villages. It starts on the W. with Badbury Hill and Faringdon

4

VALE OF THE WHITE HORSE

Clump, and rises E. to Cumnor Hurst and Boar's Hill, the country beloved of Matthew Arnold. All these four hills are capped with the Lower Greensand. Wytham Hill is a detached part of the ridge in which the coral rag rises as high as 583 ft. The Vale itself is broad and flat, the N. part, through which the quiet Ock flows to join the Thames at Abingdon, being formed of the Kimmeridge Clay, the S. part of Gault. The absence of any Lower Greensand strata brings the two clays together, thus making a wide belt of flat country. To the W. of the Vale there is a band of Lower Greensand stretching from Uffington nearly to Faringdon, and forming the watershed separating the Ock from the Cole. A thin band of the Upper Greensand runs just in front of the Downs, but widens in the E. part of the Vale into a low plateau, usually known as the fruit-bearing country, on which stand many pleasant villages which are continued in a string all along under the face of the Downs.

2. The *Chalk Belt* which runs across the county culminates northward in the line of beautiful *Downs*, which descend steeply into the Vale of the White Horse, forming, with the line of villages beneath, one of the most attractive parts of Berkshire. The villages must never be left out of the picture, for the abundant trees in which they shelter are well set off by the bare slopes of the Downs behind, treeless, but for the occasional beech-clumps which crown the summits. The grandest part of the range is on the W., where *White Horse Hill* (856 ft.), the highest point of all, from which the valley is named, displays its steep, grassy sides, deep-set combes and fine sky-line. All the Downs on the W. sink directly to the Vale with one downward sweep. But a few miles farther E. the main ridge recedes some distance to the S., and leaves

in front a lower chalk plateau about two miles broad, which then slopes by a second descent to the Vale. The villages nestle under the lower slope, which is often trenched with deep-set wooded ravines, from which the clear streams issue. Though this arrangement shows less grandeur than that on the W. part of the range, yet it lends both beauty and variety to the central Downs, especially when the Greensand plateau branches out, thus forming a third step downwards before the valley level is reached. The three steps are very well marked on the Abingdon to Newbury road. Farther E., beyond the point where the Didcot and Newbury railway crosses the Downs, the main ridge disappears altogether. From this point until the Thames is reached the Downs are low, but breaking up, as they do, into groups of rounded hills separated by deep-seated " bottoms," they retain, or even increase, their fascination. The only point to regret about this beautiful line of hills is that so much of their slopes has been given over to cultivation. When this is remunerative, æsthetic considerations must, of course, give way, but the real pity is that land once broken up and afterwards abandoned (see p. 23) does not easily recover the characteristic surface of smooth turf in which the Down-lover rejoices. It is in the central part that this cultivation extends highest up the slopes ; at the E. and W. ends there is abundance of open Down-land. An ancient grass track, known as the *Ridgeway*, runs along the main summit from end to end, from which there are a series of grand views northward over the Vale.

The rest of the chalk country is not so interesting as the Downs themselves. The main chain throws out some fine lateral ridges to the S., some of which are bare, others clothed with beech woods. Those which converge on Lambourn are perhaps the best. But, generally speaking, cultivation reasserts itself very soon, as the plateau descends gradually towards the Kennet Valley. The main interest is in the clear-cut valleys of two delightful chalk streams, the Lambourn, which flows S.E. to join the Kennet near Newbury, and the Pang, which after a very circular course falls into the Thames at Pangbourne.

3. The *Tertiary Strata*, of which the rest of Berkshire is composed, belong to three formations : (1) Reading Beds ; (2) London Clay ; (3) Bagshot Sands. Of these the London Clay may be dismissed for the present, since it hardly affects the scenery of the Kennet Valley at all. Speaking roughly, the Bagshot Sands may be said to form the hills on the S. side of the Kennet Valley, and the Reading Beds those on the N. side ; also the flat valley strath, so far as it is not alluvial. But the main point to notice is that the Reading Beds, though more gravelly than the Bagshot Sands, yet form essentially the same type of scenery—*i.e.* sand hills, covered with furzy and heathery commons, alternating with thick forests, in which the pine-trees predominate. These features are to be seen all along both sides of the Kennet, and it is hard to say which of the two sides is the more beautiful. To appreciate the full charm it is best not to keep to the valley—indeed a cyclist along the Bath Road might be at a loss to understand why the valley is so highly praised—but to take the roads on either side which lead over the commons. The traveller who has gone past Aldermaston to Crookham and Greenham commons, or from Bradfield uphill to Bucklebury Common and then onward to Cold Ash, will pass through scenery hardly to be equalled in the famous commons of Surrey and Sussex. A grand background to every southward view is given by the chalk range of Inkpen Beacon,

rising over the thick forests of the sand hills. Nor must the Kennet itself, with its osier banks and poplars, be neglected. Streams which rise on the sand have mostly scanty and discoloured waters, such as the Enborne, tributary of the Kennet on the S., and the Blackwater, the principal tributary of the Loddon. But the Kennet itself rises in the chalk plateau of Wiltshire, and therefore has the clear and abundant waters characteristic of chalk streams, in which the spotted trout, and possibly the " silver eels " too, may be plainly observed swimming about.

4. The last division of Berkshire was described as that E. of the Loddon. But first it is necessary to say a few words about the valley of the Loddon itself, which does not fall exactly under either division. The Loddon rises in the chalk district of Hampshire, near Basingstoke, and reaches Berkshire at its narrowest part. From thence its course is almost entirely along the flat London Clay, which forms the least interesting part of the county. Its quiet stream, bordered by its characteristic alders, has found two panegyrists, Pope and Miss Mitford.

The part of *Berkshire E. of the Loddon* is really very much diversified in character. To the N. the sweeping curve of the Thames between Reading and Maidenhead brings, as we have already said, the Chalk Belt again within the county. This is chiefly remarkable for three prominent hills, Crazey, Bowsey (454 ft.) and Ashley hills, all of which are thickly covered with wood, and capped by outliers of the London Clay. The N.E. prolongation of this range forms the Quarry Woods, which turn an almost precipitous side to the Thames. Windsor Castle also stands on a chalk bluff, which is an inlier rising from the middle of the Tertiary Strata. S. of the chalk there is a thin belt of the Reading Beds, passing by Twyford and the two Walthams to Bray. It is, however, too narrow to affect the scenery much. Then comes the wider belt of the London Clay, which gives a flatter but not unpleasing country, on which many villages stand. Finally, in the S.E. corner of the county, is the *Forest District* proper—*i.e.* the well-wooded plateau formed by the Bagshot Sands, and stretching from a little S. of Windsor to Sandhurst. The central part is East-hampstead Plain, which rises to 423 ft. The forests are almost entirely pine woods, with occasional stretches of heather and gorse. It is remarkable to find so wild a tract of country so close to London. Several inroads have been made into it both by private villas and public institutions, the latter being tempted by the cheapness of the land. But the central part is still marvellously lonely, and it is quite easy to lose one's way hopelessly among the straight grass paths which intersect the pine woods.

5. The last part of Berkshire to be described is the course of the *Thames*, at once its N. boundary and most striking natural feature. Its remarkably tortuous course falls naturally into four divisions :

1. Between Lechlade and Oxford it is known as the " Upper River " and flows in an E. and N.E. course over the Oxford Clay.

2. Between Oxford and Streatley it flows mainly S. through an undulating country, where flat meadows and low hills alternate.

3. Between Streatley and Maidenhead it cuts a deep gorge through the chalk.

4. After Maidenhead the rest of its course is over the flatter Tertiary Strata.

When it enters the county a little below Lechlade,

the " stripling Thames " of Matthew Arnold is already a broad stream, whose apparent width is lessened by the numerous beds of reeds and rushes, the haunt of the moor-hen. Its E. course is determined by the low Berkshire ridge, which stretches E. from Faringdon. When this broadens out into the Cumnor and Wytham hills, the river is deflected northward and sweeps round them in a semicircular course to Oxford. After Buscot and Eaton Hastings are passed no more villages border the river, the utter loneliness of which is most striking. It passes two old bridges, Radcot and New Bridge, and a few hamlets. Presently, just below Swinford Bridge, it skirts for a moment the beautiful hanging woods of Eynsham, and then wanders away again into the flats *en route* for Oxford. Below Oxford, though its broadening stream makes every view of it attractive, the most beautiful parts are those where a low wooded hill rises from one bank. It is very characteristic of the Thames that in such cases the other bank is usually flat meadow land. For some time Berkshire has to be content with flat meadows, until, some way below Abingdon, the detached chalk hills called the Wittenham or Dorchester clumps come close to the stream on the S. After rounding them the Thames flows S. awhile, past Wallingford and Moulsford, until at Streatley Goring Gap is reached, where the river enters the chalk district, with the Berkshire Downs R. and the Chilterns L. The loveliest part of the Thames now follows. The chalk hills descend into the valley on both sides, and usually a steep wooded bluff rises from one of the banks. The charm of the river is much increased by the weirs, and by the numerous eyots or aits, covered with willows, which interrupt the current. On the Berkshire side we have first Pangbourne, where overbuilding has partly impaired the picturesqueness, then the beautiful Purley Woods. The river keeps discreetly aloof from busy Reading, of which nevertheless there is a long story to be told, and turns northward to continue its windings among the chalk hills. Next come the pretty riverside villages of Sonning and Wargrave, after which the steep bluff descending from Park Place forms one of the most attractive parts of the river. On the N. part of the great bend we pass the historic villages of Hurley and Bisham. The magnificent Quarry Woods come next, the last time in Berkshire where chalk hills border the Thames. At Cookham the beauty of the river is at its greatest, but, when we reach Cliefden Woods, all the beauty is on the Buckinghamshire side and Berkshire contributes only flat meadow. At Maidenhead, the flatter portion of the Thames Valley begins, and we pass by Bray on to royal Windsor, which gives us one more grand river view. When the limits of Windsor Park are reached, we have also come to the boundary of Berkshire.

III. CLIMATE

Berkshire, like Oxfordshire, shows few marked peculiarities in climate. It is not so central, yet it is almost as far from the sea, and its elevation is moderate.

1. *Rainfall.*—Berkshire forms part of the central plain of England, which has a moderate rainfall, averaging from 25 to 30 in. yearly. The rain-bearing winds from the W. and S.W. part with most of their moisture on the mountainous region to the W. before reaching the central plain, which is therefore much drier than the W. or S. districts, but not so dry as the E. coast, on many portions of which the rainfall is as

little as 25 to 20 in. Berkshire, however, lies in the S. part of this central region, and closely adjoins the wetter belt lying to the S. of it, where the rainfall is from 30 to 35 in. Accordingly the S. part of the county is somewhat wetter than the N., and in the S.W. parts, especially in the higher stations, which are usually the wetter, the rainfall shows a tendency to rise above 30 in. It will be convenient to take Oxford as a standard of comparison, because the average rainfall has been calculated there for a long term of years, and ascertained to be 26·10 in. In the Thames Valley in Berkshire the rainfall varies very little from this either way. Reading has about the same rainfall as Oxford. At Abingdon and Wallingford it is about 1 in. less, at Cookham and Maidenhead about ½ in. more. The flatter parts of the Vale of the White Horse are also about ½ in. wetter than Oxford, and the sand plateau in the S.E. from 1 to 2½ in. wetter. The wettest stations are on the chalk plateau in the S.W. At Welford, for instance, the average (calculated for a period of 40 years) is 30·63 in. At Farnborough, 700 ft. high on the chalk, the average for the last seven years is as high as 33·39 in. This is the wettest station in Berkshire, but it has been under observation for too short a period for its average to be exactly ascertained.[1]

2. *Temperature.*—No data exist for determining the relative temperatures of different parts of Berkshire. These are now recorded for Reading and Maidenhead, but have only been under regular observation recently. The general climatic conditions, however, of the county can be readily ascertained. The temperature of any place in England is mainly determined by : (1) the heat

[1] The rainfall of Oxford is taken from the records of the Radcliffe Observatory. The other figures and conclusions are based upon the data in " British Rainfall."

of the sun, which is a matter of latitude and season ; (2), its elevation above sea-level (temperature diminishing as a rule 1° for every 270 ft. in altitude) ; and (3), the warm waters and winds from the Atlantic, which affect all England, but are not felt so much in the inland regions. From this it may be readily inferred that Berkshire has a climate a good deal warmer than the N. of England, but colder than the country lying S., and also than most of the W. coast and parts adjacent to it. The least elevated parts of the county (such as the Lower Thames Valley), from about 75 to 150 ft. above sea-level, have an average yearly temperature of about 50°. The higher parts will be on an average 1° or 2° colder than this. Such peculiarities as the climate has are due to the absence of the moderating influence of the sea. Thus in summer Berkshire is hotter than the S. coast, and the E. part comes very close to the region of greatest summer temperature in England, which is about 64°, and embraces London and the Lower Thames Valley. The winter, on the other hand, is colder than on the S. and N. coasts.[1]

3. The amount of sunshine in a given place depends mainly upon the power of the sun, which is mostly a question of latitude, but also on the comparative absence of the conditions which form clouds and rain. Thus the sea-coast is usually sunnier than the inland parts, and in Great Britain the wet country to the W. is generally less sunny than the drier regions to the E.

[1] These results depend upon the tables and maps of Dr Buchan, who states that the mean average temperature of Great Britain ranges from about 46° on the N. of Scotland to 52½° in the Scilly Isles. He has given no definite figures for Berkshire, but the conditions closely resemble those of Oxfordshire, except that the lower parts of the county are nearer sea-level, and that its more southerly position will make it somewhat warmer.

Berkshire will therefore be sunnier than the N. of England and somewhat sunnier than Oxfordshire, but less sunny than the S. and E. coasts. Unfortunately there are no records of sunshine for Berkshire, but it will probably be fairly correct to say that it enjoys about 200 hours' sunshine a year less on an average than the South Coast, the sunniest part of England.

IV. FLORA AND FAUNA

The great authority for the flora of Berkshire, as well as of Oxfordshire, is Mr G. C. Druce. The subject is so vast that to give any idea of it in two or three pages is impossible. All that can be done here is to indicate by a few extracts from his work some of the characteristic and rarer plants in four or five of the most typical districts.

1. The Coralline Plateau of N. Berkshire has a few species entirely confined to it, such as *Rosa Agrestis* and the two species of *Sedum Dasyphyllum* and *Cotyledon umbilicus*, which are found on old village walls. Among the rarer plants which are found locally on or near this formation are the ivy-leaved bell-flower and *Calamintha Parviflora*, which grow in Bagley Wood, *Polygonum dumetorum* and *Lathyrus sylvestris* (wild everlasting pea), which grow on the hedges of Tubney Wood; *Daphne Mezereum*, near Appleford and Frilsham, and *Onopordon* (Cotton Thistle), which is native at Frilford, but found elsewhere on the oolite. A wood near Pusey is full of *Impatiens Parviflora* (Russian Balsam), and there is a rich growth of *Lilium Martagon* at Kingston Bagpuize.

2. The Vale of the White Horse is too much cultivated to be a good botanical district. But in some fields near Marcham there is a salt spring, which results in

some maritime or semi-maritime plants, such as *Buda marina, Juncus Gerardi, Scirpus maritimus* and *Zannichellia pedunculata.*

3. The Downs and Chalk Plateau are remarkable for the number of bright-hued flowering plants. Common flowers on the open Downs are the rock-rose, the milk-wort and the horseshoe vetch, the blue and yellow of the last two flowers well contrasting. There are two species of purple gentian, one of which, *Gentiana Germanica,* is rare and principally found in Letcombe Castle. Also several orchises, the pyramidal, the bee, the frog, the dwarf and the musk orchis (the last very rare). The Pasque flower (*Anemone Pulsatilla*) is rather local, and *Galium Sylvestre* a rare plant only found in the meadow near Sulham. In the chalk woods the hairy violet, butcher's broom and deadly nightshade are common. Another group of orchises is found, the fly, the butterfly, the smaller butterfly, the bird's nest and the yellow bird's nest. The rare monkey and soldier orchises are probably now extinct in Berkshire. Several beautiful flowers are more local. Solomon's seal, which is rare in Oxfordshire, is a conspicuous ornament of the central woods in Berkshire. The white-flowered Helleborine is also found in many of the woods. But the spiked star of Bethlehem (*Ornithogalum pyrenaicum*) is confined to the district near Ilsley, and the wood forget-me-not is found only in Riever Wood, on the slopes of the Inkpen Beacon range. Ploughed fields on the chalk are often overgrown with yellow mustard, locally called " charlock." Here also are three species of *Fumaria,* one of which (*F. Vaillantii*) is very rare, and found chiefly near Lowbury Hill.

4. The district of the Bagshot Sands affords a very interesting flora, including many species which are not

found in other parts of the county. In the ponds near Sandhurst and Wellington College are found many rare species, including *Illecebrum Verticillatum*, and two species of *Elatine* (*E. Hydropiper* and *E. Hexandra*), all three exceedingly scarce; also *Potentilla Palustris* and *Pilularia globulifera*. In other parts of the heathy and woody plateaux are found *Epilobium lanceolatum*, *Gentiana Pneumonanthe*, *Viola lactea*, *Capnoides claviculata*, *Hypochoeris glabra*, *Sagina subulata*, *Agrostis setacea*, *Myrica Gale*, *Narthecium ossifragum*, and *Ranunculus Lenormandii*. *Pyrola minor*, which is fairly common in the Chiltern Woods, is absent from Berkshire, except in two places on the Bagshot Sands. *Arnoseris pusilla* is a rare and interesting plant, found on sandy cornfields reclaimed from heath. The *Osmunda regalis* is sparingly found in boggy spots in shady woods, and the *beech fern* has also been discovered near Mortimer, but both are very rare.

5. The last region to consider is that of the river valleys, especially the Thames, Kennet and Loddon, with their adjacent meadows and ditches. The beauty of the Thames largely depends on the following characteristic flowers: the comfrey, with its bell-shaped blossoms, ranging in hue from white to deep purple; the spiked purple loosestrife; the somewhat less common yellow loosestrife, which belongs to a different genus; the hairy willow herb, which borders the stream in parts with rich masses of purple colour, and is equally effective when the seed pods have opened in the late autumn; the yellow iris; the arrow-head (*Sagittaria Sagittifolia*), which both in leaves and flowers is one of our prettiest aquatic plants; the flowering rush (*Butomus umbellatus*), a " gem among watering-plants," occurring in the river at intervals. Both the white and yellow water-lily are often found in quiet places, both in the

Thames and the Loddon; also the fringed water-lily. On the river meadows the two most remarkable flowers are the snakeshead fritillary, which grows in great abundance in the meadows between Iffley and Kennington, and is also found on the lower courses of the Kennet and the Loddon; and the summer snowflake, found at intervals from Iffley downwards, but especially beautiful on the lower reaches of the Loddon, where the flowers are called Loddon lilies. Other characteristic water plants are the water violet, the water parsnip, the sweet flag, and the frogbit. Mr Druce's own discovery of the Loddon pondweed (*Potamogeton Drucei*), which he calls the most beautiful pondweed in England, must be chronicled. *Oenanthe crocata* is very rare on the Upper Thames, but common on the Kennet and the Loddon. *Geum rivale* is plentiful on the Kennet and the Pang, but not found on the other rivers. *Teucrium Scordium* seems to be extinct in Berkshire.

Distribution of Trees.—Along the course of the rivers willows and poplars are chiefly found. The alder is also very conspicuous on the banks of the Loddon and Blackwater, but hardly at all found near the other rivers. In the lowlands the dominant tree is the elm. Oaks are also found all over the county, but are mainly conspicuous in the woods and parks, such as Windsor Park and Bagley Wood. On the chalk beech woods and hazel copses are conspicuous. Many juniper bushes are found on the part of the Downs overhanging Moulsford and Streatley. Ash-trees are common enough in all parts except the sandy districts, as indeed local names such as Ashbury, Ashampstead and Cold Ash bear witness. On the sand hills S. and S.E. of the county extensive pine forests are found, often interspersed with patches of birch-trees. In many of the grand hanging woods on the Thames the beech may be said to form the ground plan, but the effect is produced by the admixture of a great variety of other trees.

The *Wild Animals* of Berkshire present hardly any distinctive features. Stoats and weasels are not very common, but badgers survive more than is usually supposed. A polecat was seen in Wittenham Woods as late as 1896. The otter is common in the Thames and its tributaries, and Windsor Park is full of squirrels.

On the *Birds* of Berkshire there seems to be no detailed work. The appended facts are extracted from the article by Mr Heatley Noble in the " Victoria History." The county, owing to its inland position, is stated not to be rich in birds. The number of species is 216, of which about one-third are residents, one-sixth migrants which stay to breed, and a good half other migrants and occasional visitors. During the last century some species have become extinct, such as the Great Bustard, and probably the Little Bustard as well, the Marsh Harrier, the Bearded Tit or Reedling, and the Red Kite. On the whole, however, the number of species has increased, owing to the new feeding-grounds gained by the extension of gardens and plantations, and the greater protection now afforded to birds generally. In some ways this might well be increased ; for instance, the Hobby would breed in the county in greater numbers if it were not so regularly destroyed. Also beautiful birds like the Hoopoe and the Golden Oriole would breed, if their conspicuous appearance did not make them the regular prey of the gunner. Among the rarer residents may be mentioned the Dartford Warbler, the Cirl Bunting, the Woodlark, the Long-eared Owl, the Water-rail and the Buzzard (the latter being very scarce). The Goldfinch is disappearing owing to the large numbers taken by bird-catchers. The Reel-bird or Grasshopper Warbler is somewhat local in distribution. The Reed-warbler is common, and its nest is often selected by the cuckoo to deposit an intrusive egg.

Of the migrants there seems little to say of general interest. The distribution of the Red-start is noticed as unaccountably local; the Wood-wren is stated to be rather rare, and the Quail less plentiful than formerly. The Golden Plover is a regular winter visitor of the fields between Newbury and Thatcham. The Brambling, hardly ever entirely absent, sometimes appears in flocks to feed on the beech-mast. The Dotterel is curiously local. It seems generally to keep on the line of the Downs when migrating, but habitually takes a short cut from the Berkshire Downs to the Chilterns by way of Childrey and Wallingford. On the comparative rarity of the occasional visitors it is difficult to make decided statements, for the records mainly come from four centres of observation only—Reading, Newbury, Radley College and Wellington College. One interesting case of a rare visitor is that of the Dipper, which is reported to have nested and reared its young in 1899 in the masonry of Mapledurham Weir. But, as in the case of the neighbouring Oxfordshire, the large number of sea-birds found among its casual visitors is a remarkable feature. Occasionally flocks of birds such as the Herring-gull are seen flying overhead. Occasionally storm-driven wanderers, such as the Manx Shearwater and the Storm Petrel, are found, and even picked up in an exhausted or dying condition. A more common case is that of gulls, terns and other sea-fowl, who have been driven inland in bad weather for food and shelter, and have been tempted to rest awhile by the Berkshire waterways. For instance, Sandwich Terns were in 1895 seen swimming on the Thames at Maidenhead. Mr Noble comments on the fact that the Great Northern

Diver, which breeds in Iceland, is fairly often found in the Thames, while the Red-throated Diver, which breeds in Scotland, is an exceedingly rare visitor. He also mentions that out of the forty-three British species of *Anatidæ* as many as twenty-five have visited Berkshire. "Hardly a winter passes," says another authority, "without one or other of the wild geese visiting us in greater or lesser numbers."

V. DISTRIBUTION OF POPULATION

Berkshire, being an agricultural county, is in the main somewhat sparsely populated. The total population in 1901 was 256,480, very little more than that of Bristol. The only important centre of population is the one manufacturing town, Reading, which contains 72,214 inhabitants. Next, but after a considerable interval, come Windsor, which, including the adjacent suburb of Clewer, has about 20,000, and Maidenhead and Newbury, which have about 13,000 and 11,000 respectively. Abingdon follows next with 6480. The other towns are but small, Wantage, Wokingham and Cookham having between 4000 and 3000, and Faringdon, Hungerford, Wallingford, Lambourn and Thatcham between 3000 and 2000. The villages are scattered about the county fairly evenly, except that they are rarer on the chalk plateau and in the Forest District. The distribution of population, with the single exception of Reading, is determined mainly by the consideration whether the neighbourhood is residential or not. The residential parts, which are mainly the Thames Valley between Streatley and Maidenhead, and the edges of the Forest District, are the most densely populated. Next, after an interval, comes the Valley of the Kennet, while on the chalk plateau and in the Vale of the White Horse the population is mostly sparse. There is, however, the usual string of villages at the foot of the Downs.

In 1801 the population was 110,752, so that in the century there is an increase of 145,728. Of this the growth of Reading accounts for quite two-fifths, and the rest is mainly explained by the exodus of the well-to-do into the fairer parts of the county, which has sown the Thames Valley and the borders of the pine forests thick with new villas, turned Windsor and Maidenhead into considerable towns, and largely increased the riverside and forest villages. This increase is almost all in the E. part of the county. It is true that most of the towns in the W., such as Newbury, Abingdon, Wantage, Wallingford and Faringdon, show also a rise in numbers. But, on the other hand, the villages remain much where they were, and many of them are actually smaller than they were a century ago. Towards the middle of last century all the villages had increased considerably in population. But for the last thirty years they have been greatly on the decline. The causes are the too familiar ones, which have had the same effects in the neighbouring county of Oxford, agricultural depression, the introduction of machinery and the attractions of the towns. A very plain tale is told by the figures of 1901 as compared with those of 1891. All the parishes which show rising figures are more or less residential—*i.e.* they belong to the riverside, the Forest District and the Kennet Valley. But all the agricultural villages, and most of the towns as well, show a decided decline.

VI. Communications

1. *Roads.*—The principal thoroughfare of the county, both historically and at the present day, is the Bath Road, still called by that name in Berkshire. This crosses the Thames and enters the county at Maidenhead, whence it runs by Twyford to Reading, and then up the Kennet Valley to Speenhamland, close to Newbury, leaving the county near Hungerford. At Maidenhead and Speenhamland there used to be great coaching inns. In 1752 "flying coaches" took twelve hours to go from Newbury to London (57 m.). The place in Berkshire where highwaymen were most apprehended was Maidenhead Thicket. The Bath Road in the old coaching days is the scene of many incidents in Stanley Weyman's romances—*e.g.* in "Chipping." At the present day the road is well kept, and excellent for cycling. At Reading there diverges a riverside road by Wallingford to Oxford, also very good. A third road diverges from this at Streatley, the ancient Port Way, which runs along the foot of the Downs. For a road which is on or near the chalk the whole time it is quite good, though rather up and down. The Wantage to Faringdon road is also good. Of the roads which diverge from Oxford the Faringdon road is first rate, but the other two, the Wantage and Hungerford road, and the Abingdon and Newbury road, are apt to be greasy when crossing the Vale, and loose upon the chalk plateau. The cross-roads in the Vale and on the chalk are usually bad and circuitous, but S. of the Kennet and in the Forest District they are quite good, except that many of them are rather loose, and that the cycle often gets powdered with the local sand.

2. *Railways.*—Most of the county is served by the

G.W.R., whose main line enters it at Maidenhead and runs to Reading. Reading is an important railway junction, from which one branch runs S. to join the L. & S.W.R. at Basingstoke, and a second up the Kennet Valley to Newbury and Hungerford. The third is the main line, which keeps to the Thames Valley until Didcot, another important junction. Here it divides into two, one branch running to Oxford, the other W. to Swindon. A third branch runs S. to Newbury. Wallingford, Abingdon and Faringdon are all on short branch lines, a fact which has retarded their development. From Newbury a light railway runs up the Lambourn Valley to Lambourn. The Forest District is served by the S.E.R. line from Reading to Guildford, and two branches of the L. & S.W.R., which diverge at Ascot to Wokingham and Camberley respectively.

3. *Canals.*—The Kennet and Avon canal runs from the Thames at Reading up the Kennet Valley to Hungerford. The Berks and Wilts canal, starting from Abingdon, traverses the Vale, but it is no longer used, and its bed is dry. The whole course of the Thames in this county is navigable by barges.

VII. Industries

1. *Agriculture.*—One of the most interesting facts about Berkshire agriculture is that, if we go back to the beginnings of history, the first part of the county to be cultivated was the Downs. This phenomenon is found in Sussex and Surrey as well, and is due to the same causes—*i.e.* the comparative safety of the Downs, where the hill forts provided refuge, and the fact that the uncleared lowlands were still a tangled mass of wood and underwood. Traces of this early period

are still shown by the "lynchets," as they are called in Wiltshire—*i.e.* the well-marked parallel terraces left by ancient cultivation, which in many places may be seen running along the side of the Downs. When the valleys began to be tilled, cultivation spread upwards only as far as the lower slopes. But during the last century, before the repeal of the Corn Laws, when the high price of corn resulted in the breaking up of forest and pasture lands all over the country, the "margin of cultivation" crept upward nearly to the top of the Downs, and the grass slopes gave way to waving corn lands. During the last thirty years the importation of cheap corn has again changed the scene. The Berkshire farmers have been very hard hit, and even in the more fertile valleys much of the corn land has been changed to pasture. Consequently the "margin" has again subsided, though a great deal of wheat is still grown on the lower chalk slopes. Much wheat is also to be found in the Vale of the White Horse, which is considered one of the most fertile parts of England. But a great deal of it has been lately turned into pasture land, and the successors of wheat-growing farmers are content to live by supplying London with milk. In the Vale of the Kennet there is much arable and meadow land, and also on the London Clay, but the S. and E. of the county have large tracts of common land and pine forest. The Thames Valley is pasture land, but the corn lands often fringe its slopes.

Perhaps, however, the most characteristic industry of Berkshire is sheep farming. On the wilder and grass-grown parts of the Downs in particular, the sheep have it all their own way. The number reared is less than in the last generation, but East Ilsley sheep fair is still the largest in the S. of England. The true

Berkshire breed of sheep, the "Berkshire Nott," is believed to be extinct, but the Hampshire breed is largely reared. Berkshire sheep are not allowed to run wild over the Downs, but pass an existence of careful penning and tending. The Berkshire hog is of a famous breed which keeps up its reputation and commands high prices, both at home and abroad.

Other industries akin to agriculture may be noticed. (1) *Fruit-growing* is common on the Upper Greensand to the E. of the Vale, in a triangular district between the Thames and the Downs. Most of the trees are cherry and plum. (2) *Vegetable-growing* is carried on largely near Reading and Newbury. (3) *Osier-cutting* is practised on the islands and about the backwaters of the Thames and Kennet. (4) The open Downs afford great facilities for the *training of racehorses*, especially about E. Ilsley and Lambourn, where there are famous training-stables, which are the cause of a good deal of local prosperity. Races have been lately instituted in Newbury.

2. *Manufactures.*—In the Middle Ages Berkshire was known for its manufacture of cloth. The principal centres of the industry were Reading, Newbury, Abingdon, Wallingford and E. Hendred. The annals of all these towns supply many important illustrations, and in particular the fall of E. Hendred into an insignificant village, when the cloth trade left it, is worthy of note. The decay of the trade seems due to the fact that agriculture was found more profitable, especially when the competition of the N. of England became formidable. At present Abingdon alone has a small cloth factory. It also has a carpet factory, which has been thriving of late. Reading is the one great manufacturing town in the county. The biscuit factories of Huntley & Palmer, the seed establishment

of Sutton & Co., and the "Reading Sauce" of Messrs Cocks, are so well known that they need only be simply referred to. Modern Reading, however, stands quite by itself in Berkshire as a strange industrial centre in the heart of a purely agricultural county. The one widely extended industry not agricultural is malting and brewing, which is carried on at Abingdon, Aldermaston, Maidenhead, Reading, Wallingford, Windsor and other places. Boat-building is also an industry in many of the riverside villages.

VIII. History

The events which connect Berkshire with English History mainly concern the towns of Windsor, Reading, Wallingford, Abingdon and Newbury, whose early importance is military, and due to their command of the fords of the Thames and the Kennet. The history of these places is given elsewhere in detail, but it will be useful here to string the facts together into a connected narrative.

At the time of the Roman Conquest Berkshire was mainly inhabited by the Atrebates, who seem to have defended the line of the Downs from the great earthen forts still existing on the top of them, and the more advanced one of Sinodun. There are no details of the Roman occupation, which was probably quite peaceful, and occurred in the third or fourth year of the Conquest. Thenceforward the British became rapidly civilized, though no large Romano-British towns exist in Berkshire. Silchester (*Calleva Atrebatum*) is just over the border; Speen (*Spinae*) was probably little more than a Roman station, and the claims of Wallingford to have been a Roman town are doubtful.

In the 6th cent. Berkshire was conquered by the West Saxons, who, after subduing Wiltshire, turned E. down the Thames Valley. Thenceforth it became part of Wessex, and for a long time its history is concerned with the eternal duel between Wessex and Mercia, when each kingdom strove to push the other back from the frontier of the Thames. When Wessex was driven back it found a second and usually successful line of defence in " Ashdown "—*i.e.* the line of the Downs. This was vigorously maintained, for instance, by the Prince Cuthred against Penda. The next Mercian invader, Wulfhere, proved more successful, and defeated the West Saxons at Biedenheaford, which may possibly be Beedon. Ethelbald also had power in Abingdon and the adjoining parts of Berkshire, until he was overthrown at Burford. Lastly Offa seized the whole Vale of the White Horse, and drove Wessex back to the old frontier of the Downs ; until Ecgberht in turn drove the Mercians for the last time over the Thames.

The next invaders were the Danes, but Alfred, the hero-king, who was to subdue them, had already been born in the *Villa regia* at Wantage in 849. In 871 he was just of age, and acting as lieutenant for his brother, King Ethelred. The Danes had seized and fortified Reading, but had been checked near Englefield by Ethelwulf, the Berkshire Ealdorman. On this the brothers besieged Reading, but were defeated and driven across the Loddon to Twyford. The Danes now marched out on to the Ridgeway on the Downs, but were attacked and defeated by Ethelred and Alfred at the famous battle of Ashdown. Of the site of this battle all that can be said for certain is that it was fought somewhere on the line of Downs to which the general name Ashdown was then given. In spite of his victory, the fighting was indecisive, and when

Alfred became king he was for a time driven out of
Berkshire into Wiltshire and Somerset, and not until
after the final victory of Ethandune in 878 was Berkshire regained for Wessex. During the second period
of Danish invasion the Danes again attacked Berkshire.
They came to Reading, sacked and burnt Wallingford
and Cholsey, and again turned up on to the Downs at
Scutchamore Knob (1006). But no brave Ethelred or
Alfred was now on the throne, only an incompetent
namesake of the former, so that the Danes retired safely
with their plunder and repeated their raid in following
years.

The story of Earl Godwin's death at Old Windsor
Palace is only a Norman slander. In 1066 William I
crossed the Thames at Wallingford, which was surrendered to him by the rich Saxon Wigod, whose
daughter married the powerful Norman noble, Robert
D'Oilly. Henceforward Wallingford becomes a place
of importance ; also Windsor, where William I. had
just built his castle.

With the Civil War of Stephen's reign Berkshire is
much connected. In 1127 the barons had sworn
fealty to Matilda at Windsor. The oath was faithfully
kept by Earl Brian of Wallingford, whose castle was
held for Matilda during the whole war (though Berkshire was mainly on Stephen's side), and twice provided
her a refuge after her sensational escapes from Winchester and Oxford. Finally it was at Wallingford
in 1153, that the treaty was made by which Henry II
secured the throne. There had also been sieges of
Newbury and Faringdon castles, in which Stephen
had been more successful. In Richard I.'s absence
Windsor was seized, first by William Longchamps,
then by John, who also seized Wallingford Castle. Both
castles were used by him to prosecute his treacherous

lans against his brother, but he was presently forced
o surrender them. In Henry III.'s reign William the
Marshal died at Caversham near Reading in 1219.
At the time of the Barons' War Richard, King of the
Romans, was in command of Wallingford Castle.
Simon de Montfort, however, captured both Wallingford
nd Windsor, and after his victory at Lewes sent the
King of the Romans prisoner to his own castle of Wallingford, together with Prince Edward. When Henry
ecovered his power, he gave back Wallingford to the
King of the Romans. In the troubles of Edward II.'s
eign Wallingford had again a large share. Piers
Gaveston held the castle, and his behaviour at a tournament there gave great offence. Afterwards the castle
was given to Queen Isabella, who held high festival
here, with Mortimer, at Christmas 1326, after they
had captured the unfortunate Edward. Edward III.'s
ame is closely connected with Windsor, where he
ounded the College of St George, with the Order of the
Garter, and revived the chivalry of Arthur's Round
Table. Here also he entertained two captive kings,
David of Scotland, and John of France. In 1387 oc-
urred the battle of Radcot Bridge, in which Richard II.'s
inister, the Duke of Ireland, was defeated by the
orces of the Lords Appellant. After the deposition
f Richard II., there occurred in 1400 the conspiracy of
he three Earls of Kent, Salisbury and Huntingdon.
ailing to murder Henry IV. at Windsor, they re-
reated by Maidenhead Bridge, Sonning, Wallingford,
nd Faringdon to Cirencester, where they were defeated
nd slain. In the Wars of the Roses, Berkshire was
mainly Lancastrian, but little occurred except a siege
t Newbury.

In Henry VIII.'s reign we have the romantic figure
f Jack of Newbury leading his clothiers to Flodden

Field and entertaining royalty. When the dissolution of the monasteries came Abingdon Abbey was surrendered quietly, but the last abbot of Reading refused to give way. and was hanged for treason before his own Abbey Gateway, after a mockery of a trial. Three martyrs were burnt by Henry at Windsor in 1543, and three at Newbury by Mary in 1556. In Elizabeth's reign the Jesuit Campion ventured from his hiding-place at Stonor to say mass at Lyford on the Ock, where he was betrayed and arrested. In the earlier part of the 17th cent. little occurred to connect Berkshire with English History.

The Great Civil War.—Here the history of Berkshire becomes of great importance, since, owing to the nearness of the county both to the Royalist headquarters at Oxford and the Parliamentary headquarters at London, it was the scene of much important fighting. The district of Windsor was disloyal to the King, and held by the Parliament throughout, but the rest of Berkshire was Royalist, and at the beginning of the war the fortified posts of Wallingford and Abingdon were held for the King. Reading also soon fell into his hands and received a strong garrison.

In 1643 Essex advanced from Windsor to Reading which he took after a twelve days' siege, and the failure of an attempt of Charles to relieve it. After this the theatre of the war was transferred awhile to Oxfordshire. Later in the year came the *First battle of Newbury.* The trained bands of London, led by Essex, were marching back after relieving Gloucester, when they were intercepted by Charles' army at Newbury, which barred the London road by which they had to retreat. After a severe day's fighting, in which Lord Falkland and other noblemen were killed, the Puritan army secured their retreat to London. They repulsed some attacks

of Rupert on their rearguard, and reached London
safely, though on their way they abandoned Reading,
which was recaptured by the Royalists. In 1644
Charles resolved to hold Berkshire strongly by a
cordon of forts, through which the Parliamentarians
would be unable to break. Accordingly not only were
Reading, Abingdon and Wallingford held as before,
but garrisons were also thrown into Donnington Castle
and Faringdon House. But this plan broke down at
once, for Reading was abandoned when Essex again
advanced, and ten days later the Governor of Abingdon
evacuated the town in a panic, so that both places fell
into the hands of the Parliament. Charles' position at
Oxford was now endangered, especially when Waller
forced the passage of the Thames at Newbridge,
but he retrieved it by a skilful retreat from Oxford,
followed shortly by the victory at Cropredy. Meanwhile Abingdon was maintained by the Puritans with
some difficulty. The garrison was so weak that they
were not able to prevent Sir Henry Gage from making
a skilful dash across Berkshire, relieving Basing House,
and retiring in safety. Later in the year came the
Second battle of Newbury. The Parliamentary leaders
had decided to make a combined attempt to crush
Charles. Accordingly Charles had just relieved
Donnington Castle when he found that the forces of his
enemies were within a day's march of him. But
Manchester, their commander, moved so slowly that
Charles had time to take up a strong defensive position
in which Speen Hill, Donnington Castle and Shaw
House were included. On this position a simultaneous
attack in both front and rear was planned by the
Puritans, but failed, mainly through Manchester's
want of energy. In the night Charles escaped, and
there was no effective pursuit. A fortnight later

Charles marched again to Donnington and successfully carried off his ammunition, which he had left behind. The result of this was the Self-denying Ordinance, and the formation of the New Model Army, which drilled continually in Windsor Park. Early in 1645 a daring attempt of Rupert to take Abingdon by a sudden assault on the bridge nearly succeeded. In it Sir Henry Gage was killed. In April Cromwell assailed Faringdon House unsuccessfully. After Naseby the only fighting was to subdue the three Royalist garrisons, all of which held out till 1646, Donnington surrendering in April, Faringdon in June, and finally Wallingford in July.

During the Revolution of 1688 Berkshire lay in the direct route of William of Orange from Torbay to London. He reached Hungerford on December 6th, and two days later received here three commissioners from James. At Reading about this time a smart skirmish took place, where about 250 of William's troops attacked 600 Irish, and, aided by the inhabitants, drove them in confusion from the town. During the last two centuries nothing of importance occurred. In 1836 Berkshire was made part of Oxford diocese. For 800 years it had belonged to the diocese of Salisbury.

IX. ANTIQUITIES

1. *Prehistoric.*—The so-called Grey Wethers, or Sarsen Stones, many of which are found in front of Ashdown House, are supposed by some to be ancient monuments. It is, however, more probable that they are indurated stones of the Bagshot and Reading beds, left by denudation on the top of the chalk. The Blowing Stone and the Imp Stone are really Sarsen Stones. Wayland Smith's Cave is a good cromlech, the

only one in Berkshire. Near it is the Great White Horse, cut out in the chalk, which is at least British, if not even older. The Ridgeway or Ickleton Street, which runs along the top of the Downs, is of immemorial antiquity. Of ancient hill camps there are fifteen in all, of which three of the most celebrated are on the line of the Downs—*i.e.* Uffington Castle, Letcombe Castle and Blewburton Camp. Walbury Camp, near Inkpen Beacon, is also worth mentioning for its size and height, and also Cherbury Camp, because it is strangely placed on level ground, in the Vale of the White Horse. There are several round barrows on the Downs, of which Scutchamore Knob and the " Seven Barrows " near Lambourn (there are really twenty) are the most famous. There are also three boundary ditches, all called Grim's Ditch. Two remarkable hoards of the Bronze Age have been discovered at Yattendon and Wallingford, and one of the Early Iron Age at Hagborne Hill.

2. *Romano-British.*—There are three Roman roads in Berkshire which are mentioned in the Itinerary of Antoninus : (1) That from *Londinium* to *Calleva Atrebatum* (Silchester). This crosses the Thames at *Pontes* (Staines), and proceeds through S. Berkshire, where it is known as the Devil's Highway. (2) That from *Calleva* W. to *Cunetio* (Marlborough), which passes through *Spinae* (Speen). A little W. of Silchester on this road is the Imp Stone, possibly a Roman mile-stone. (3) That from *Spinae* to *Corinium* (Cirencester). This is called Ermine Street, and runs over the high ground between the Kennet and the Lambourn. Speen is certainly *Spinae*, the station where the two roads diverge. Other probably Roman roads are that from Silchester to Dorchester, which passes by Theale, where Roman remains have been dis-

covered, and that from Besselsleigh to Wantage, which passes by a Roman villa at Frilford. This villa has been fully explored, also two at Letcombe Regis and Hampstead Norris. Six or seven other Roman villas have been found in the county. The hill forts were certainly occupied by the Romans, and one of them, on Lowbury Hill, may even have been constructed by them. There was possibly a Roman settlement at Wallingford, but the strange earthworks surrounding it are of unknown date. A Romano-British village was discovered in 1893 near Long Wittenham.

3. *Saxon*.—Berkshire is remarkable for the number of Anglo-Saxon cemeteries which have been discovered within it. Of these the most remarkable is near Long Wittenham. Others are at Frilford, Reading, Lockinge and East Shefford. From these many interesting objects have been unearthed. At Wallingford an important Saxon seal was found. In Mortimer church there is an ancient Saxon inscription to Ædelward, son of Kippyng.

4. *Churches*.—In respect of fine churches Berkshire cannot compare with its neighbour Oxfordshire. Except St George's Chapel Windsor, there is no large church of the first rank. Nevertheless there are many beautiful churches with strong features of interest. The best exploring ground for the church-lover is the string of villages lying just N. of the Downs, nearly every one of which has an interesting church. The best are Blewbury, E. Hagborne, Wantage, Childrey, Sparsholt, Uffington and Ashbury, but several other are nearly as interesting. If we add to these Cholsey, N. Moreton, W. Hanney, Stanford-in-the-Vale, in the Vale of the White Horse, and Lambourn, Beedon and Aldworth in the heart of the Downs a little S. w include most of the best churches in the county. O

the Berkshire ridge also are some interesting churches
—*i.e.* Cumnor, Fyfield, Longworth, Buckland and
Faringdon. In the Kennet Valley and the country
near it there are few churches of real interest. The
best are Aldermaston, Stanford Dingley, Newbury and
Avington. On the banks of the Thames the churches
have mostly been restored. The best are St Helen's,
Abingdon, Sutton Courtenay, Long Wittenham and
Hurley. In the E. part of the county restoration has
left few churches worth looking at. The only two
worth naming are Shottesbrook and Warfield.

Saxon remains are scanty. The church at Hurley
is probably largely pre-Conquest. Wickham has a good
Saxon tower, and Cholsey tower was in all probability
also originally Saxon. S. Moreton, Upton and Aston
Tirrold have Saxon doors.

Pure Norman work survives mainly in arcades,
doorways and fonts, when the rest of the church has
been altered. Avington is the best church entirely in
this style. Catmore, Frilsham, Padworth and Upton
are small Norman churches of some interest. (See also
Buckland and Cholsey naves and Bisham tower.)

Transition-Norman is well represented in some of
the larger churches, especially Blewbury and Lambourn. Other interesting churches are Cumnor, Stanford Dingley, Eaton Hastings and Beedon (late).
Of the latest stage of Transition-Norman (dated
c. 1200), which is hardly distinguishable from E.E.,
there are several good instances. About this period
a great access of wealth came to some of the villages
just N. of the Downs, so that their churches were
generally restored. Hence arcades of the period
are pretty common—*e.g.* at Ardington, Faringdon,
E. Hendred, Harwell and E. Hagborne ; also several
doorways—*e.g.* at Faringdon, Fyfield, Ardington and

St Lawrence, Reading. Two of these are in private houses, at Sutton Courtenay and Appleton.

The best *Early English* church is Uffington, and the smaller churches of Tidmarsh and Enborne deserve notice. There are several good E.E. chancels—*e.g.* at Faringdon, Chieveley, Baulking and Cholsey.

The *Decorated* work is mostly late. The principal churches showing earlier work are Wantage (arcades and tower), Ashbury (chancel), and N. Moreton (Stapleton Chapel, which is late Geometrical). Of Curvilinear work Shottesbrook is a fine example; Sparsholt, Steventon and Aldworth are almost entirely in this style, and there is also good work in Cumnor, Fyfield, W. Hanney (S. aisle), Stanford-in-the-Vale (chancel), Sutton Courtenay, Harwell (chancel) and Warfield.

The best *Perpendicular* work is found in St George's Chapel Windsor (a magnificent example) and in the parish churches of Newbury and Abingdon (St Helen's). Childrey is also mainly Perp. Of course Perp. windows and doors are quite common, but Perp. arcades are rare.

There are two Norman round towers at W. Shefford and Welford, the latter capped by a beautiful E.E. spire. Stone spires are very rare in the county. Uffington has an octogonal E.E. tower. Many of the smaller churches have belfries supported on internal wooden framework. In the E. part of the county there are several brick towers of the 17th and 18th centuries. There are leaden fonts at Long Wittenham, Childrey and Woolstone.

5. *Monastic Buildings.*—Three monasteries show considerable remains—*i.e.* those of Reading, Abingdon and Hurley. The two latter are interesting, the Reading ruins are extensive but featureless. There are two houses built on monastic sites, one of which,

ANTIQUITIES

Bisham Abbey, is interesting; the other, Sandleford
Priory, has little to show. At Brimpton is a chapel
once belonging to a Preceptory of the Templars.
Of Poughley Abbey a very few fragments are incorporated with a farmhouse. Of the cell at Coxwell
there only remains the splendid tithe barn. There
are hospitals with more or less ancient buildings
at Abingdon, Childrey, Donnington, Newbury and
Wallingford.

6. *Castles.*—Windsor Castle is of transcendent
interest. Almost every other castle has perished
utterly. Of Donnington there remain the two entrance
towers, of Wallingford the site and a few fragments,
of Beaumyss only the moat.

7. *Domestic Architecture.*—In this Berkshire is
comparatively poor, most ancient houses having been
pulled down and rebuilt. Among the oldest buildings
the most interesting are the three at Sutton Courtenay.
Appleton Manor has work of about A.D. 1200 ; Charney
Bassett a grange partly of 13th-century work. Attached
to E. Hendred House is a R.C. chapel of the 13th century.
Fyfield Manor shows some 14th-century work. Ockwells
and Wytham Abbey are the two principal mansions
dating from the 15th and 16th centuries, though some
Perp. details will also be found at Compton Beauchamp,
Ashbury, Southcote House, Denchworth and Shilling-
ford. Englefield House has been modernized. There
are two fine Elizabethan mansions—*i.e.* Shaw House and
Ufton Court (part of which is older), and smaller houses
will be found at Fawley and Lyford. The best Jacobean
mansions are at Ashdown and Coleshill.

BERKSHIRE

X. Celebrated Men

In the following list names already mentioned in the historical summary are not repeated, and no attempt has been made to state fully all the great men who have been connected with Windsor Castle.

Poets.—First comes Shakespeare, whose *Merry Wives* shows an accurate knowledge of Windsor and its neighbourhood. Chaucer also lived a year at Windsor Castle. The Chaucer connected with Donnington was Thomas, probably the poet's son. Earl Surrey composed many poems when a prisoner at Windsor. Pope was brought up at Binfield and in "Windsor Castle" sang of the Thames and its Berkshire tributaries. Gay is the author of a song connected with Wokingham. Pye, laureate of George III., lived at Faringdon. Shelley used to boat on the Thames near Bisham in 1817. Matthew Arnold has made the country of the Hinkseys and the Cumnor Hills classic ground.

The *Literary Associations*, though few, are brilliant. Scott, in "Kenilworth," has immortalized the stories of Cumnor Hall and Wayland Smith's cave. The Vale of the White Horse is enthusiastically described in the opening chapters of "Tom Brown." Newbury is apparently the "Whitbury" of Kingsley's "Two Years Ago," and Lambourn is the village described in the first part of Thomas Hardy's "Jude the Obscure." Miss Mitford's "Our Village" is Three Mile Cross, S. of Reading. Harrison Ainsworth's "Windsor Castle" may also be referred to. Other names known to literature are Swift, who was a guest at Bucklebury; Mrs Montagu, the "blue-stocking," who lived at Sandleford Priory; and Judge Talfourd, who was born at Reading.

The list of *Divines* might be indefinitely extended, but the following will be the best-known names. Birinus, the Apostle of Wessex, is stated to have preached to King Cynegils on Churn Knob. William of Wykeham had much to do with the rebuilding of Windsor Castle under Edward III. Bishop Jewel was vicar of Sunningwell, where he built a remarkable porch, and where Dr Fell of Christchurch lies buried. Dr Twiss, the famous Puritan divine, was rector of Newbury. Archbishop Laud was born at Reading, and always took an interest in his native place. John Bunyan was often in Reading, sometimes in the disguise of a carter. Bishop Ken was once rector of Woodhay, and afterwards was one of many non-juring divines who consorted at Shottesbrook. Bishop Butler, author of the "Analogy," was born at Wantage. John Wesley is, as usual, found in many place; in particular he paid many visits to Reading and Newbury. Dr Sewell was founder of Radley College.

Statesmen and Warriors.—To those already mentioned in the historical account many names may be added. Both William the Marshal, Earl of Pembroke, and the fierce Roger Bigod, Earl of Norfolk, have lived at Hampstead Marshall. We hear of three of Queen Elizabeth's knights, Sir Thomas and Sir Philip Hoby at Bisham, and Sir Henry Unton at Faringdon. The Earl of Leicester is implicated, at least in story, in Amy Robsart's tragic death at Cumnor. The Marquis of Winchester, the gallant defender of Basing House, ended his days at Englefield, and the equally gallant Earl of Craven had homes at Ashdown and Hampstead Marshall. Richard Lord Lovelace, a prominent supporter of William of Orange, lived at Hurley, and Francis Cherry, a prominent opponent, at Shottesbrook. Bolingbroke's country house was at Bucklebury. The Duke of Cumberland is connected with racing at Ascot and with training-stables at East Ilsley. Warren Hastings, when waiting for his trial, lived at Purley Court. Of modern heroes Lord Wantage, V.C., may be referred to, whose home was at Lockinge, where Lady Wantage still lives.

In conclusion it is worth remarking how very few of the old Berkshire families still exist. The Eystons of Hendred date back to the 15th century, and the connexion of the Cravens and the Lenthalls with the county begins with the 17th century. The Puseys of Pusey are not the original family. Fuller says that " the lands of Berkshire are skittish and apt to cast their owners," a remark which could be abundantly illustrated. The complete list of old county families still surviving would be a small one.

DESCRIPTION OF PLACES IN BERKSHIRE ARRANGED ALPHABETICALLY

NOTE.—The position of any place can be readily discovered from the map on the fly-leaf, which contains the names of the railway stations. If the place has no railway station, the distance by road from the nearest station is always given.

The following abbreviations are constantly used for the architectural styles :—

Trans. = Transition-Norman (*i.e.* about 1160-1200). E.E. = Early English (often called " thirteenth century," but really about 1200-1270). Dec. = Decorated (often called " fourteenth century," but really about 1270-1370). Early Dec. or Geometrical is from 1270-1315. Late Dec. or Curvilinear is from 1315-1370. Perp. = Perpendicular (often called " fifteenth century," but beginning about 1370 or 1380).

The styles overlap and run into one another so much that it is hardly practicable to date them exactly.

ABINGDON, one of the most important towns in Berkshire, lies just N. of the point where the Thames is joined by the little river Ock, and is at the end of a branch railway which diverges from the main G.W.R. at Radley. For many centuries the history of the town was identical with that of the great Abbey about which it sprang up. *Abingdon Abbey* was founded in 675 by Cissa, a subordinate prince of Wessex, a charter being granted by Ceadwalla, the King of Wessex. Ina, the next king, at first revoked the grant, but presently was led to change his mind, and the Abbey was completed, the first abbot being Hean, Cissa's nephew.

In the next century the Abbey fell into the power of Offa, King of Mercia, who in 777 defeated the West Saxons at Bensington and drove them S. of the line of the Thames. The monks patiently submitted to Offa's patronage, and obeyed the Mercian Bishop of Leicester. There is a story that Offa himself built a palace on Andersey island, which is formed by the Thames close to the Abbey, giving the monks in exchange the manor of Goosey, but that the royal huntsmen and falconers became such a nuisance to the Abbey that the abbot persuaded Offa's successor, Cynulf, to return Andersey, and take instead the manor of Sutton Courtenay. In the reign of Alfred the Abbey was destroyed by the Danes. The rebuilding was commenced in Edred's reign, and completed under Edgar, the great church being consecrated by St Dunstan. It had been splendidly adorned by St Ethelwold, who became the next abbot, and who also built the mills and the aqueduct. The Abbey now rose to great power and splendour and was visited by many kings, in particular Henry III. and Edward I. It, however, became involved in disputes about the valuable privilege of holding a market, which had been originally granted by Edward the Confessor. When this right was questioned by Henry I., the Abbot hastened to London and obtained its confirmation. In the reign of Henry II. the privilege was again disputed by the tradesmen of Oxford and Wallingford. The latter obtained an *ad interim* injunction and tried to stop the market by force. After a long wrangle the Abbey obtained a fresh confirmation of the privilege. The monopoly still caused much bad feeling in Abingdon itself, as well as in the neighbouring towns, and in 1327 a savage attack was made on the Abbey, in which Oxford and Abingdon tradesmen are said to have joined. The Abbey was plundered and many buildings burnt; the monks were partly killed and partly fled. After this disaster the Abbey was naturally for a time in financial straits. But it revived so completely that at the Dissolution the annual revenue was returned as £711 (representing perhaps about £14,000 of our present money). The last abbot, Thomas Rowland, was partly worried and partly terrified by Thomas Cromwell into an early surrender. The foulest charges were made against him, but were perhaps sufficiently refuted by the fact that he was allowed to retire to Cumnor with the handsome pension of £200 a year. The downfall of the proud abbot was prophesied in a remarkable passage in " The Vision of Piers Plowman ":

" And thanne shal the Abbot of Abyngdoun and alle his
    issu for euere
Haue a knokke of a kynge and incurable the wounde." [1]

A less serious reference to the Abbey will be found in the " Ingoldsby Penance," where the Prior of Abingdon (a Benedictine monk and next in authority to the abbot) is oddly described as " a barefooted friar " !

By this time Abingdon was a prosperous town, which sent a member to Parliament, a privilege which continued till 1832. It was the seat of a thriving cloth manufacture, and many of the great cloth merchants were substantial benefactors to the town (see later).

During the Great Civil War Abingdon was at first garrisoned for the King, but on the advance of the Parliamentary troops in 1644 it was abandoned in cowardly fashion by its governor, Wilmot. On this

[1] Skeat's edition, Bk. X. 326. Abingdon is only mentioned as a typical abbey. Another reading is " the abbot of England."

Waller seized it and fortified it for the Parliament, for whom it was successfully held during the rest of the war, though by a garrison so inefficient that Manchester once said that, if the King attacked it, it must surrender. The main attack came in January 1645, when the Royalists crossed Culhamford Bridge, and were half way across the causeway before the garrison met them. A sharp skirmish followed, ending in the repulse of the attack and the death of Sir Henry Gage.

The antiquities of Abingdon cluster round the two old churches of St Nicholas and St Helen. *St Nicholas'* stands E. of the market-place. Of the original Trans. church there remain two small lancet windows N. of nave, and the lower part of W. front, comprising a blind arcade with W. door, all much restored. Above is a large inserted Perp. window. S. of nave there are three Dec. windows and one Perp. The very late Perp. window N. of nave may be connected with the curious tombs to John and Jane Blackwall, 1625, standing in a shallow recess from which a dole of loaves is still distributed. The chancel is Perp. with a modern Dec. E. window. The W. tower is also Perp. and is curiously built on two stone pillars *inside* the W. end. Inside the porch there are a ruined stoup and a curious stone lantern-holder. On the N.W. side is a remarkable square turret, with a gable on the N. and small triangular arch. It contains a newel staircase leading to the " minstrels' gallery," W. of the nave, whence there is a good view of the fine timber roof. Note also (1) part of an old Perp. carving now built into the S. wall of chancel ; (2) triangular aumbry with bowl-shaped piscina below it ; (3) mutilated piscina near pulpit ; (4) Perp. font ; (5) brass plate, 1669.

All the remains of the *Abbey* lie S. and S.E. of the church. Exactly S. and leading out of the market-

Chimney of
Abbot's Lodg-
ing: Abingdon:

place is the fine Perp. gateway, the only part still kept in repair. It is vaulted and contains handsome restored windows, and a niche on the W., in which an image of the Virgin has been replaced. The remaining ruins belong to the Corporation. (*The key must be asked for at the first house on the R. just beyond the gateway.*) On the way to the ruins some arches and windows are seen on the L., but these are not *in situ*, and have nothing to do with the Abbey. The ruins are R. and consist of two continuous buildings, usually known as the Prior's House and the Guest House, though these names are little more than conjectural. The Prior's House rests on a groined undercroft, above which are two rooms, now reached by a ladder. The door and windows which face us are graceful Dec., but the original building is E.E. The principal features are the two doors which form a triangle with the outside door, a good E.E. door in one room, and a beautiful E.E. fireplace in the other, with side columns showing characteristic foliage and a beautifully quaint chimney, to be seen from outside, and which shows a triple lancet. Outside also are two good gabled buttresses. The Guest House is a plain rectangular building of two stories. It is Perp. in style and has several characteristic windows to the S., also some later ones with straight mullions, and a gateway leading to the Abbey mill. On the N. there are no windows, but a curious open brick and timber gallery to the upper story, by which access was gained to the several sleeping compartments. There is a good timber roof and two fireplaces. The Abbey church has entirely disappeared. The unique E.E. chimney is best seen from a lane which passes to the W. of it and leads to the river. (See illustration.)

The ancient Abbey gateway (to which we now return)

and the rooms to the W. of it are now used for the Corporation Buildings. No old windows remain, and the interiors are modernized. On the ground floor is the Police Court, formerly an old chapel. Above it there was built in Charles II.'s reign the Great Council room, a large handsome chamber, hung with portraits, of which those of Charles II. and James II. are copies of Lely ; while that of George III. and his queen is by Gainsborough. The " St Sebastian " has been falsely attributed to Vandyke. The little council-chamber is more to the S. It contains an old map of the town (c. Henry VI.). The Abbey buildings do not appear and are supposed to have been erased at the Diss oution. There is also a copy of Vicat Cole's view of Abingdon, and an old print of the Town Hall. In the corridor leading to the room over the tower are kept the standard measures of Queen Elizabeth, a valuable service of pewter belonging to the Corporation, and copies of royal addresses and other such documents. The Abbey room over the tower is handsomely fitted and contains the chairs of the Mayor and Corporation.

A little to the S. is the *Old Grammar School*. Entering from the street by passing under a gateway with an inscription on it we reach the quadrangle, to the E. of which is the ancient Jacobean schoolroom. It contains the inscription *Ingredere ut proficias,* and a tablet stating that it was endowed by John Roysse in 1563. The school had really existed for two centuries before, but John Roysse's munificence practically refounded it. The buildings are no longer used, the school having been removed in 1859 to new buildings in " the Park," the pleasant and tree-covered N.W. quarter of the town.

In the centre of the market-place is the handsome square *Town Hall*, with a tall and prominent lantern. It was built in 1677 and said to have been designed by

Inigo Jones. It stands on the site of Abingdon Cross,
destroyed by Waller in 1644. Facing it is the modern
brick Corn Exchange, and between them a Jubilee
Statue of Queen Victoria.

The other group of ancient buildings surrounds St
Helen's church, and is reached from the market-place
by going down East Street. The oldest part of St
Helen's is the tower (on the N.E. side), which has three
stories of good E.E. The basement has been restored.
On this is set the graceful Perp. spire with flying
buttresses which is so prominent in many views of the
town. The church has five parallel aisles, and is therefore broader than it is long. The central aisle and the
two to the S. are Perp., the outer aisle being dated 1539.
The inner N. aisle is also Perp., but the outer one has
Dec. windows, which however are unconvincing and
look modern. Apart from this the church is handsome
Perp., with two porches, four arcades, a central clerestory and several large windows. The chancel contains
a great deal of elaborate modern work, including a
reredos by Bodley. There is a Jacobean pulpit (1634),
a painted timber ceiling to N. aisle (c. Henry VI.), a
font cover (1636), and a chained Bible (1611). The
monuments include several memorials to the merchant
princes of Abingdon. The principal ones are (1) old
canopied niche with (modern) figure of St Birinus;
(2) half figure of Galfridus Barbour, mercator, 1417;
(3) tomb of John Roysse (founder of the Grammar
School), repaired in 1873, but with old plate—I.R.1571;
(4) plate to Thomas Mayott, twice mayor, 1627; (5)
square tomb of Richard Curtaine, 1643, with curious
epitaph; (6) brass plate to Tobias Garbrand, 1688. The

Near the church, in the angle between the Thames
and the Ock, are the old buildings of *Christ's Hospital*,
an interesting almshouse founded in 1553. Facing the

church is a long open wooden gallery with two projecting porches. Opening out of it are the doors of the living rooms, which show beautiful wood-carving. The main porch is enriched with paintings illustrative of texts. On the side facing the river there are four foliated windows and a picture of an old cross. At the back there is a delightful garden. On this side the building is all of ancient stone, except the chimneys, which are brick, and there are two old doorways. In the centre is the Governors' Hall or council-chamber, which has a fine mullioned oriel window, and is capped by a quaint and beautiful lantern, dated 1707. Inside it is panelled with dark oak and has an open stone fireplace, in which logs of wood may be still burnt on the " fire-dogs." In the centre is an old Elizabethan table, and round the walls hang the portraits of the benefactors of Abingdon, some of whom, as we have already seen, are also commemorated in the parish church. It is desirable at this point to refer more in detail to the history of the institution, that these worthies may be to us something more than names. Christ's Hospital really grew out of an earlier foundation, the Guild of the Holy Cross, whose duty was to keep in repair the Abingdon bridges and to maintain a priest for the service of travellers who crossed them. Before the bridges were built the traveller from the Oxfordshire side of the river had first to cross a backwater at Culhamford and then to traverse a mile of marshland, often flooded, to the ferry over the main stream. In flood-times carts had to be hired to cross the flats, and fatal accidents from drowning seem to have been frequent. Finally, " in the fourth year of King Henry V.," the important Burford Bridge, a handsome structure with all its arches pointed except the central one, was built over the Thames close to the town, and connected by a raised causeway, a mile

Christ's Hospital & St. Helen's Ch. Abingdon:

in length, with another bridge at Culhamford. All these particulars are referred to in some curious verses, very well worth reading, of which an illuminated copy on vellum hangs on the walls of the council-chamber. The King, as usual, seems to have taken all the credit for the good action, but the stone was given by Sir Peter Besils (v. *Besselsleigh*), and the workmen paid by Geoffrey Barbour, who also seems to have been the first to endow an almshouse in connection with the guild. In an old picture, also in the council-chamber, the building of the bridge is represented, with Barbour in the foreground paying money to John Stonehouse, apparently the contractor. In 1442 the guild was incorporated and endowed, and, in addition to its other functions, was given the duty of providing for thirteen aged poor. The first trustees were Thomas Chaucer (see *Donnington*) and Sir John Golafre (see *Fyfield*). At the Dissolution the guild shared in the fate of similar institutions, but, more fortunate than most, was re-founded and re-endowed in 1553 as Christ's Hospital, by Sir John Mason, a distinguished citizen of Abingdon, who gained Henry VIII.'s favour, became Ambassador to France and Chancellor of Oxford University, and was able to get part of the guild property restored.

In the window of the council-chamber there are the arms of Henry VI., who helped in the bridge-building, Edward VI., Sir John Golafre (1441), Sir John Mason, Thomas Tesdale, founder of Pembroke College, Oxford, who was a distinguished pupil of the Grammar School, Lionel Bostock (1600) and Richard Curtaine (1648), members of two famous families also commemorated in the parish church. There are also portraits of most of these, also of Maud Tesdale, John Curtaine and others.

Near to Christ's Hospital is Twitty's Hospital, founded 1707. It is built of brick with white-painted windows

D

and gables. Amongst the other great citizens of Abingdon may be mentioned Edmund Rich, afterwards Archbishop of Canterbury, and consecrated as St Edmund after his death. He was born in what is now St Edmund's Lane, where a chapel (now vanished) was built to commemorate him.

Beautiful views of the town and church may be had from Burford Bridge. The Ock is a small and quiet stream of little charm.

ALDERMASTON, one of the prettiest villages in the Kennet Valley, stands S. of the river just below the thickly-wooded sand hills which are so conspicuous a feature in this part of the county. The principal street of the well-built village slopes upwards to the picturesque lodge of Aldermaston Park, which is entered by a pair of very good wrought-iron gates. The extensive and irregular deer park is full of fine old trees of all sorts, including avenues of oak and lime, one of which opens out of the Mortimer Road. The manor-house is modern, but contains a few features preserved from the ancient Jacobean house, burnt down in 1843—*i.e.* the chimneys, carved oak staircase and some ancient glass. The principal lords of the manor were the Forsters, who dwelt here for more than three centuries, up till 1711, since which time the changes in ownership have been frequent. The interesting church is separated from the Park grounds by an old brick wall, which, backed by a number of fine yews and cedars, forms a striking background. Close at hand there is a fine view-point over the Kennet Valley. The architecture of the church is difficult to read accurately. The building is rectangular, but for a S. transeptal chapel, and the Trans. arch leading into this is the only one in the church, there being no aisles and no separation between nave and chancel. The church originally dates from the 12th cent., but the Norman details are scanty. The W. door is very fine Norman with cable moulding both round the arch and on the side pillars, and well-executed birds on the capitals. There are two plainer Norman doors, now blocked, one S. of the chancel, the other N. of the nave, with a head which has been reopened as a window. The chancel was rebuilt rather late in the E.E. period, and has a good lancet triplet at the E. end. The windows N. of chancel seem to have been modernized. There is no chancel arch, but two small windows, high up, mark the position of the rood-loft. One of these is round-headed, the other a slit. Below are two low-side windows, that on the S. round-headed, that on the N. Dec. (a cinq-foiled lancet). A third low-side window, also a cinq-foiled lancet, is more to the W., and there is another two-light window of the same kind. The other Dec. window N. of the nave is very late in the style and almost Perp. The tower and W. window are of the same date. The transeptal chapel has two foliated lancets E. and W., a late Dec. window S. and a Dec. piscina. It contains : (1) fine alabaster tomb of Sir George Forster (d. 1526) and his wife. Round the tomb are figures of twelve sons and eight daughters. He wears the S.S. collar and his feet rest on a hind. A little dog is pulling at the lady's robe ; (2) brass inscriptions to William Forster, 1574, and to the four daughters of Sir Humphrey Forster, 1638. The figures of these have disappeared ; (3) altar-tomb to Ralph Congreve, 1773, one of the owners of the manor.

The church is covered with modern painting, but there are also some old frescoes, in particular a St Christopher with figure of Christ in his hand, and a mermaid and a fish below, also a head surrounded with a halo under a canopy. There is some old glass N. of the nave, and an Elizabethan pulpit with sounding board. The font is modern. The church was restored in 1896 at the expense of Mr C. E. Keyser, who is the present occupier of the manor-house.

During the Civil War there were two skirmishes not far from Aldermaston, one in 1643, when Essex's army, retreating after Newbury fight, beat off an attack of Rupert's on their rearguard ; and the other in 1644, when Sir Henry Gage, on his way to relieve Basing House, cut to pieces a detachment of Parliamentary cavalry.

The railway station is nearly 2 m. N. of the valley. Close by it is *Aldermaston Wharf* on the canal, a picturesque scene which is worth seeing. Not far from the quay where the barges unload is a lock, just below which there is a sort of backwater of the canal, where it expands into a largish piece of ornamental water.

ALDWORTH (1½ m. E. of Compton station, 4 m. W. of Goring station) is a lonely village, beautifully situated on the top of the bare chalk Downs, between 500 and 600 ft. above sea-level. To appreciate its scenery rightly, it should be approached from Compton and left in the direction of Streatley and Goring. It has a remarkable well, 372 ft. deep, with a canopy. The churchyard contains one of the most famous yews in Berkshire, now growing very decrepit. The earliest part of the church is the W. tower (plain E.E.). The base mouldings of the font seem to indicate that it is of the same date, and the N. wall, which has no architectural features, may also belong to this period. The rest of the church is late Dec. The chancel is about twenty years earlier than the S. aisle, which was built c. 1340, but the Geometrical E. window is a modern insertion. There are two plain sill-sedilia, and a pretty Dec. piscina with shelf. The nave has an old wooden roof, some pews with good poppy-heads, a Jacobean pulpit, dated 1639, and a carved oak reading-desk. The S. arcade has octagonal pillars. The hood-mouldings over the arches show grotesque corbel heads, and there is a bracket-niche on the E. respond. The W. aisle, which is as broad as the nave, has three good windows of a reticulated pattern.

But the feature which usually attracts visitors to this church is the remarkable series of ancient tombs of the De la Beche family, who long held the manor here, and whose name still lingers in Beche Farm, S.E. of the church, where some encaustic tiles and a silver seal have been found. There are eight tombs in all, three under the N. wall, three under the S. wall, all six under Dec. canopies, and two containing three figures, between the nave and aisles. These monuments have long been celebrated. Queen Elizabeth, during one of her progresses, is said to have diverged to see them, riding on a pillion behind the Earl of Leicester. This visit is referred to by a Captain Symonds, in 1644, at the time of the Great Civil War. He heard from the vicar that at the time of the Queen's visit there was a genealogy of the De la Beche family written on parchment and hung up in the church as a guide to the tombs, but the Earl of Leicester took it down to show the Queen, and it was never brought back. Captain Symonds adds that the statue under an arch outside of the church was called John Everafraid, and that it was said he had promised his soul to the devil if he was buried in church or churchyard; accordingly he was buried in the church wall. The arch under which he rested is still visible outside the S. wall, but his effigy has disappeared. Three of the inside figures were afterwards dubbed locally John Long, John Strong and John Neverafraid; but now they are usually known as

53

the Giants. The figures are very mutilated and nearly all of them have lost two or more limbs. Those who wish to know how far they can be identified may study the genealogy to be found in the vestry, and compiled by the Rev. F. L. Lloyd, 1877. Although the general effect of so many stone figures is most extraordinary, the workmanship is bad and rude. The figures are usually carved in one block with the stone tombs, and have a very suspicious likeness. The Dec. canopies, which are very fine, are all of the same date. It looks as if all were carved at the same time, and the suggestion that a De la Beche of the 14th cent., probably Sir Nicholas (d. 1347), presented the church with a complete set of his ancestors, seems probable enough. The vestry contains also a green altar-cloth, dated 1705, and a carved figure with crossed arms and the inscription, " Jesus held his peace." Probably this stood on the bracket-niche already mentioned, at the foot of the tomb attributed to John De la Beche.

The walk or ride from Compton to Aldworth is a breezy ramble over high, bare downs, but the descent from Aldworth to Streatley is most fascinating. For 2 m. the road keeps on a high level, with a deep combe on either side, which runs far into the heart of the downs. The combe on the R. falls rapidly to a wooded bottom which winds round Streatley Hill into the Thames Valley near Basildon. At the far end there is a vista of the Thames Valley itself, with the level country beyond Reading as a background. Then we come to the brow of Streatley Hill, and one of the most famous river-views in the south of England is spread before us. The road descends rapidly by the most break-neck hill in the county, which is often chosen for hill-climbing competitions by cyclists and motorists.

Andersey. (See *Abingdon.*)

Appleford (3 m. N. of Didcot) is a village just S. of the Thames. Though the main G.W.R. from London to Oxford runs through it, half way between Culham and Didcot, there is no station, and the roads are so devious and intricate that it is a journey of several miles to reach the village from either of the places just mentioned. The church has been rebuilt, but a careful inspection reveals a few ancient features. There are two Norman doors, of which the S. one has been rebuilt, but the N. one still retains part of the old work. There is also a blocked Norman arch outside the N. wall. E.E. features are one lancet, which now lights the vestry, a blocked priest's door, and possibly the blocked low-side window, which is square. The Perp. window in the chancel is also partly original. There is a curiously shaped old font, which is E.E. (or possibly Trans.).

Appleton (7 m. S.E. of Oxford) is a pleasant village a little W. of the Besselsleigh Woods. The church has a fine row of Trans. pillars and arches (1180); otherwise it is mainly restored or churchwarden, and has no original windows. The tower is late Perp., also the S. porch, which has a stone roof, a dilapidated stoup, and a canopied niche above the outer door. There is a cylindrical Norman font with small cover, a shroud brass to John Goodrynton, 1518, and handsome Elizabethan tomb to Sir John Fettiplace, 1593. The old manor-house, where the Fettiplaces lived, and which they sold in 1600, contains three remarkable round-headed arches, which point clearly to the date 1200. The principal archway, which is the main door leading into the hall, shows stiff-stalk foliage and deeply-cut E.E. mouldings. The other two, which lead out of the hall on the L., are plainer, and show a grotesque head between them. Such remains of a private house in the time of King John are as rare as they are strange.

55

The hall has a timber roof-beam resting on oaken pillars. Some of the rooms are panelled, and one has a good Jacobean mantelboard.

Arborfield (3 m. W. of Wokingham) is a scattered village mostly grouped about Arborfield Cross, where five roads meet. The grounds of Arborfield Hall, which has old stables, built 1654, stretch to the Loddon. Here is also the old parish church, mainly in ruins, though the N. aisle was rebuilt in 1867 as a separate chapel, and the old porch tacked on to it. On the floor is a brass plate to Thomas Harwood, 1643, and under the altar plates to the Rev. — Hodgkinson and his wife, with a request that their ashes may never be removed. The church was originally Perp., but it is now so smothered in ivy and creeping plants that hardly a feature can be distinguished. A new church has been built a little way from the hall grounds.

ARDINGTON (2 m. E. of Wantage) is one of the pretty villages which lie S. of the Port Way, just before the chalk downs slope upward from the Upper Greensand plateau. It is a model village, consisting of well-built cottages embowered in trees. Many cottages are thatched and timber-built, but, though the effect is pleasing, none are really old. Lockinge Park bounds the village on the S. The fine church is almost entirely E.E., but well-meant rebuilding and restoration have largely spoilt it and confused its history. A new bay has been added W. of the nave ; the tower and spire have been rebuilt, also both of the side chapels ; while only three original windows have been left throughout the church. In spite of all this, much remains of interest. The E.E. work of the nave is very early ; indeed it can hardly be later than 1200. The beautiful N. door has a round arch, deeply-cut plain mouldings, and a row of dog-tooth. It may be safely dated 1200.

The stone porch is also E.E., but some later Dec. carvings have been subsequently built into it. W. of the door is one of the original windows, a very small and plain lancet. The S. arcade has good stiff-stalk foliage, but of a rudimentary character, and there is a little plain cup-piscina, very early-looking, in the E. respond.[1] The chancel is later E.E., and has an elaborate chancel arch, a piscina, and one original double lancet (S.), on the exterior moulding of which are some good corbel heads. The other two windows are Perp. insertions (the only ones in the church). The two side chapels seem to be still later E.E., but rebuilding has spoilt them in different ways. The S. chapel is now plain and clumsy, but retains a trefoil-headed squint and a segmental W. arch, resting on very elaborate corbels. Note also the old tiling and the monument to Edward Clarke. The N. chapel has been rebuilt in a pretentious and over-elaborate style, but retains very beautiful late E.E. (or Trans. to Dec.) piscina and squint, both trefoil-headed and with good hood-mouldings, and a bishop's head in the angle between them. There are also some remains of an old reredos, which may be early Dec. The original two-light window S. of nave is late E.E. The S. door and the font are good Dec., and both show ball-flower. The roof of nave is also Dec., and rests on good corbel heads. The pulpit is Jacobean. The rebuilt tower and spire were originally E.E., with a late Dec. N. window. S. of the church is the stump of an old cross. The cross to the N. is modern.

Ascot has long been celebrated for its horse-racing. The heath on which the races are held yearly every June is on high ground, fringed on all sides with trees,

[1] Ardington is one of a group of churches rebuilt c. 1200. See note on E. Hagborne.

in the beautiful country of the Bagshot Sands, and at the
S.W. corner of Windsor Park. When in 1813 the
Enclosure Act was passed, it was specially provided in
it that Ascot Heath " should be kept and continued as
a race-course for the public use." The original founder
of " Royal Ascot " was not, as it is often stated, the
Duke of Cumberland in 1757, but Queen Anne in 1711.
The first race was on August 11th in that year, as we
learn from a letter of Swift to Stella, confirmed by *The
London Gazette*. Since then the races have been continuous, though the Duke of Cumberland certainly
infused new life into them. In particular, he bred in
1764 the famous horse "Eclipse" (see *East Ilsley*), which
won a plate at Ascot in 1769. The Ascot Gold Cup
was first offered in 1807. In 1839 were built the white
buildings of the Grand Stand, S. of the heath and close
to the road, which are now thronged annually by all
London society from the King downwards. Behind
them a small town has sprung up quite recently, the
parish only having been founded in 1864. In 1897
another parish of South Ascot was formed. The many
houses and villas now dotted about the country have
a good deal damaged its picturesqueness.

Ashampstead (2½ m. E. of Hampstead Norris) is a
small village, high up on the central chalk plateau.
In the little church the original windows are all lancets,
but the thickness of the wall, and the fact that the
lancets are almost round-headed and deeply splayed,
make it probable that the work is before the close of
the 12th cent. The chancel is wholly original ; the
nave has two original lancets, but the S. side is modern.
There is no chancel arch, only a wooden beam. The
belfry is supported on a wooden framework. There
is a square piscina, also traces of frescoes on the N.
wall.

ASHBURY (2 m. S. of Shrivenham station) is a village in the extreme W. of the county, picturesquely built on the lower slopes of the chalk downs, which here rise steeply from the flat plain. Just beneath the houses are two steep-sided ravines, in which springs of clear water gush forth at the foot of the chalk. They are, as usual, utilized as watercress beds. The manor-house is the lowest in the village, and is now a large farm. It is a fine pile of 15th-cent. buildings. The front shows several two-light windows with mullions and foliations, and a gabled brick porch, on the door of which is an inscription with the dates 1488 and 1697. A moat is traceable on three sides. The beautiful cruciform church is in a commanding situation high up on the Downs. It is mainly Dec. and Perp., but there are interesting traces of an earlier Trans. structure, chiefly at the W. end. The S. door is early Trans. with elaborate zigzag. At the W. end of the present nave arcade may be seen the responds and spring of the arches of the original Trans. arcades. The deeply recessed and slightly pointed lancet on the W. side of the S. aisle is also of the same period, but the lower stage of the W. tower seems later—i.e. pure E.E. Next in date is the early Dec. work of the chancel (c. 1290), which has an intersecting E. window and Geometrical side windows. At the same time the upper stage of the tower was built, which has Geometrical windows similar to those in the chancel, and two plain contemporary windows were inserted in the N. aisle. The transepts are later Dec., of which there remain two windows in the N. and one in the S., transept. Early in the Perp. period the present nave arcades were sub-stituted for the original Trans. ones. They are of beautiful light work, and the roof of timber and plaster, resting on well-carved corbel heads, is also good. The Perp. arches leading from the transepts to the aisles look as if they had been set on earlier Dec. columns.[1] Other Perp. changes were the insertion of windows—*i.e.* those in the S. aisle, two in the S. transept, and the W. window of the tower; also the addition of a handsome N. porch with side windows, fan-vaulting and parvise. Near it, inside, is a hollow where a stoup may have stood. There is also a fine panelled Perp. font. The chancel arch and roof are modern. In the chancel there is a trefoiled piscina, and also a Dec. piscina in each of the transepts. In the S. transept there is a strange squint, full of Dec. tracery, leading from the S. aisle. Apparently it was to command a view of the altar to which the existing piscina was attached. There are also in the transept a large Dec. canopied niche and a stone coffin. There are three brasses, (1) Thomas de Buschbury, rector, 1409 ; (2) Wm. de Skelton, rector, 1448 ; (3) John de Walden.

Ashbury was the first parish in England where Sunday schools were held. They were started in the church in 1777 by the Rev. Thomas Stock, when curate. In 1778 he went to Gloucester, where he had a talk with Robert Raikes, the well-known pioneer of Sunday schools. The result was that the two arranged to start a school together, and two years afterwards Raikes opened one in his own parish.

ASHDOWN PARK (4½ m. S. of Shrivenham station, 3½ m. N.W. of Lambourn) is reached from the N. by way of Ashbury. The road first climbs the Downs, and then gradually drops into a beautiful upland valley, with

[1] Since writing the above I have read a description of the church by Mr C. E. Keyser. In the main it agrees with my account. He considers that three of the four arches leading into the transepts are Dec.

the long ridge of Odstone Down L. and the thick woods
of Ashdown Park R. In rather more than 2 m. after
leaving Ashbury the Park gates are reached. The
house was built by Webb, a pupil of Inigo Jones. It is
four-square, and commands a view in the direction of
the four points of the compass, the best being north-
wards up the long avenue leading through the woods.
On each side there are three stories with five windows
in each, and a fourth story with three gable windows.
Above are two huge chimneys and between them a
platform with a railing. In the centre is a cupola with
a golden ball at the top. This strange house was
built for William, the first Earl of Craven (see also
Hampstead Marshall). The traditional story is that
the founder of the house, when flying from the plague,
chose a site on the bare Downs with no other house in
view. This is singularly inapplicable to William
Lord Craven, who remained heroically in London
during the Great Plague and Fire, and did his best
to cope with the terrible situation. In 1688 he was
in command of the troops who were guarding James II.
in Whitehall Palace, when it was surrounded by the
soldiers of William of Orange. Macaulay sketches
his life and character in a few graphic touches: " The
Coldstream Guards were commanded by William Earl
of Craven, an aged man who more than fifty years before
had been distinguished in war and love, who had led
the forlorn hope at Creuznach with such courage that he
had been patted on the shoulder by the great Gustavus,
and who was believed to have won from a thousand
rivals the heart of the unfortunate Queen of Bohemia.
Craven was now in his eightieth year, but time had not
tamed his spirit." He was with difficulty induced to
forego a resistance which could have served no purpose.
In the house there are portraits of the Earl himself, of the

Queen of Bohemia, to whom he was chivalrously devoted throughout his life, and of her sons Prince Rupert and Prince Maurice. The family still possesses the estate, its present owner being the Countess of Craven.

In the meadow in front of the house are lying several so-called Sarsen (*i.e.* Saracen) Stones, otherwise Grey Wethers. They are really the remains of a tertiary stratum, left by denudation on the top of the chalk. We are here close on the borders of Wiltshire, with which county these curious stones are chiefly associated. A little to the west of the Ashdown Woods is Alfred's Camp, a rather small earthwork of the usual type, and only remarkable for being placed on comparatively level ground. Of course it is prehistoric, and only connected with Alfred by an unhistorical tradition. This seems the best place to refer to the celebrated *battle of Ashdown* or Æscesdun, fought in 871 by King Ethelred and his younger brother Alfred against the Danes. The battle certainly took place somewhere on these Downs, which were in those days called Ashdown as a whole, but to discover the exact site seems an insoluble puzzle. Inconsistent local traditions are connected with various parts of the range. One set points to the W. end which we are now describing, a second to Scutchamore Knob, a third to Aston Apthorpe and the heights above Blewbury, and others to other parts. There is little to associate the battle with the present site except the name, for the traditions connecting Alfred with Alfred's Camp, the Great White Horse and the Blowing Stone are untrustworthy. It seems more probable that the fight was nearer the E. end of the range, for the Danes had just left Reading and ascended the Downs to the Ridgeway, when the Saxons apparently climbed the steep N. front of the hill to assail them. The story is told by Alfred's historian, Asser, that Ethelred heard mass in his tent before the fight, and refused to engage before it was finished, while his impetuous younger brother Alfred could not wait, but sprang up the hill to the attack "like a wild boar," and was somewhat roughly handled till Ethelred came to his aid. The Danes had divided themselves into two bodies, one led by two kings, the other by the earls, of which the former was attacked by Ethelred, the latter by Alfred. The only local detail mentioned by Asser is a stunted thorn-tree, which does not give much help. The battle raged along the Downs all day, until at nightfall the Danes broke and fled back to Reading with the loss of a king and five earls. It may not be wholly superfluous to add the reminder that this was not the more celebrated battle in which Alfred, as king, thoroughly crushed the Danes. Alfred did not become king until the death of Ethelred later in the same year (871), and the check to the Danes caused by the victory of Ashdown was quite temporary. The final overthrow came seven years later at Ethandune.

Aston Tirrold (3½ m. from Cholsey station by a circuitous road) is one of two little villages which nestle under the E. side of Blewburton Hill. The church is of considerable interest, but has been a good deal spoiled. Into the wall of the modern N. aisle there has been built a very rude and ancient door, which seems to be Saxon. It is now blocked by a tombstone with a floreated cross. A small early Norman window has also been inserted in the W. side of the aisle. The S. door is plain Norman, and the rude circular font is at least early Norman, and may even be Saxon. The chancel is mainly E.E., with a pretty priest's door, a piscina and aumbry, two splayed lancets, and a low-side window, which is later in the style and has two lancets with circle above, under an arch which is nearly round. This window has been moved from its original position. The W. window is Dec., with an ogee arch. The windows in the S. transept are also Dec., and there is a square-headed Dec. window in the nave. The tracery of these windows indicates a late date in the style. The tower is Perp. There is an old timber roof in the nave, a small piece of screen at the W. end, and some oak-panelling built into the porch. The door of the rood-loft and some remains of a stoup are still to be seen, and there is an old Perp. pulpit. There is also in the village an old Independent Chapel, said to date from as early as 1670. If authentic, this is highly remarkable, for the Nonconformists would not have been allowed to worship at all at that date.

Aston Apthorpe is almost continouus with its sister village. The small church is very old, but is of little interest. On the N. side there are a plain Norman door and window, and an ivy-grown wooden porch. The E. and W. windows are Perp. and there is a blocked S. door. The font is Norman. There is a tradition that it was in Aston Apthorpe church that King Ethelred heard mass before the battle of Ashdown. But the story as told by Asser distinctly states that Ethelred heard mass in his *tent*. This rather implies that there was no church near at hand where mass could be duly celebrated, so that the tradition throws little light on the vexed question of the site of the battle (see under *Ashdown*).

AVINGTON (about 1 m. direct N.W. from Kintbury station, but 2 m. by road) consists of a small group of buildings close to the Kennet between Newbury and Hungerford, and a little S. of the Bath Road. It contains the most beautiful little Norman church in the county, and one still unspoiled. The edifice is a

Avington Church

rectangular building of five bays, each 15 ft. square, of which two belong to the chancel and three to the nave. The chancel bays were to have been vaulted, but the design was abandoned, probably because the walls were not strong enough. Between the bays are built a pair of side columns which support no arch, and the springers of the vaulting are seen starting in every corner. The ribs of the W. bay were to have been ornamented with beak-heads, those of the E. bay with a star ornament. At the E. end the springers rest on grotesque heads, possibly meant for a calf and a lion. The chancel arch is depressed and broken in two at the top, also the side walls visibly lean outwards. The arch has a triple line of zigzag, and the soffit arch a double row of beak-heads (an ornament rarely used except outside a church). There are three side columns on either side, of which the outer has arabesque carving. On the E. side there are no shafts, only plain imposts, which may have supported the rood. At the W. end there is a Norman triplet, a larger window between two very small ones. All the side windows in the church are round-headed Norman. There is a large Norman sedile, a square aumbry, and two Norman piscinæ, one in the nave, just S.W. of the chancel arch. The S. door of the nave is ornamented with zigzag and pellet. The font is cylindrical and has thirteen figures upon it, two on one panel. The suggestion is that the thirteenth is the devil tempting Judas, but the point is not plain, and some notes in the church talk of "two figures embracing and kissing," which points to a different explanation. Near the font is a Norman stoup, with fine enlaced work, which has been placed on a carved stone under a blocked Perp. arch. The only other parts of the church which are not pure Norman are : (1) low-side window ; (2) lancet in vestry ; (3) arch

leading into vestry; (4) priest's door. All of these
are E.E. The rebuilt S. porch is 16th cent. Close
to the church are the Rectory, and a modern house
on the site of an old mansion of the Chope family,
which was burnt in 1770. They are embowered
in trees and form a picturesque group by the riverside.

Bablockhythe (6½ m. W. of Oxford by a bad road
through Cumnor and Eaton, or about 5 m. by a bridle
path from Cumnor) is a ferry on the Upper Thames.
The course of the river is so devious that it has to run
12 m. from this point before reaching Oxford. The
banks are flat, and for the Thames the river view is
hardly first rate. The reference in Matthew Arnold's
"Scholar Gipsy" will be familiar to all:

> "Thee at the ferry Oxford riders blithe,
>   Returning home on summer nights, have met
>   Crossing the stripling Thames at Bablockhythe
>   Trailing in the cool stream thy fingers wet,
>   As the punt's rope chops round."

Badbury Castle. (See *Great Coxwell.*)

Bagley Wood covers the S. slopes of Cumnor Hill.
The greater part of it lies E. of the Oxford to Abingdon
road, between the second and third milestones. Its
beauties can be seen only from the road, for it is kept
strictly private by its owners, the fellows of St John's
College, Oxford. The result of this precaution is that it
is the nearest place to Oxford where primroses grow in
abundance. The persistent grubbing up of roots has
led to the entire disappearance of this flower in the
neighbourhood, except in private woods and gardens.
The profusion of oak-trees mingled with birch is
also unusual near Oxford, and the bluebells and
bracken are delightful in their respective seasons.

We are still in the haunts of the Scholar Gipsy, who was seen

> " In Autumn, on the skirts of Bagley Wood."

The name Thessaly referred to by Matthew Arnold seems to have disappeared. Was it beside the upper part of the wood, near Boar's Hill ?

Barkham (2 m. S.W. of Wokingham) is a pleasant village with numerous elm-trees. The church is modern, but retains in the porch a wooden effigy of a lady (14th cent.), conjectured to be Agnes Neville, the great lady of the parish at that date. Outside is a fine cedar-tree planted in 1788.

Basildon (2½ m. S. of Goring station) is a village on the road between Streatley and Pangbourne. S. of the road, in a commanding situation on the hill-slopes overlooking the Thames Valley, is the extensive and beautiful Basildon Park. The present house is on the site of an ancient one, but was only built in 1767. It now belongs to the Morrison family, and contains several good oil-paintings. The church is some way N. of the road, on the low ground close to the river. It has an E.E. S. door, but otherwise is good early Dec., somewhat damaged by rebuilding. The chancel has a graceful Dec. arch, and Geometrical windows. In the nave the windows are of the double lancet type, with the spandrils pierced. Two of them have ornamented scoinson arches. There is a very fine recessed Dec. tomb on the exterior S. wall, showing both natural oak leaves and ball-flower. In it has been placed a modern inscription to Sir Francis Sykes, 1804. There is also a small brass to John Clark and wife, 1497. The tower is brick, of the 17th cent. The churchyard has two fine yews and a pathetic monument to two boys who were drowned when bathing. About a mile S.W. of the village is the tomb of a Quaker who refused to be buried in the churchyard. It is still inscribed Nobes' tomb, 1699. When the G.W.R. was built, the line cut through a Roman pavement, which is no longer *in situ.*

Bath Road. (See Introduction, p. 22.)

Baulking (¾ m. N.E. of Uffington station) has a small but interesting church. It is mainly E.E., with a good lancet triplet at the E. end, four side lancets (two N. and two S.), a sill-sedile, and a very beautiful angle-piscina with central pillar and openings N. and W. The wall between the nave and chancel is strange. It only reaches as high as the side wall of the chancel, so that there is a large blank space above it. In the centre is the E.E. chancel arch, with a double squint on the S. and a single one on the N. In the same line are the stairs of the rood-loft. The nave retains two old but plain Trans. doors with original ironwork, but the windows are later—*i.e.* two reticulated windows on the S. and one three-light Perp. window on the N. The octagonal font may be E.E. Note also the Jacobean pulpit, a good wooden roof, and a gilt monument of hard chalk to Robert Grove, 1698. The church is rectangular and has no tower.

Bayworth. (See *Sunningwell.*)

Bear Wood (1½ m. W. of Wokingham) is the seat of the Walter family, who have been for years honourably connected with *The Times.* The present owner, John Walter, Esq., only inherited at the death of his father, A. F. Walter, Esq., in February 1910. It is a large modern house, standing conspicuously on a hill, and very much in view from the whole neighbourhood. It is set in an extensive park, full of fine trees and containing a large artificial lake. The picture gallery contains several very fine pictures, in particular a study of cattle by Paul Potter. A modern church has been built in the N. of the park, and serves the village of Sindlesham, which lies just outside it.

Beaumyss Castle. (See *Beech Hill.*)

Beech Hill (2 m. W. of Mortimer station) is a small village with a modern church. The name is derived from the De la Beche family (see *Aldworth*), who used to have a castle here called *Beaumyss.* Keep along the road through the village until it turns to the R. and descends to the Loddon Valley, with the grounds of Loddon House on the L. A little before the lodge is reached (L.) turn down through a white gate on the R. The site alone remains in a remarkably low position, now so overgrown with shrubs and coarse grass that it would be hard to distinguish but for the moat, a marshy hollow full of rushes and loosestrife. A little S. is *Priory Farm,* built in 1648, on the site of a priory which has entirely disappeared.

Beedon (3 m. N.W. from Hampstead Norris) may possibly be the site of Biedenheaford, where Wulfhere, King of Mercia, defeated the West Saxons. It has an interesting late Trans. church. The details are good E.E. in character, and hardly Norman at all, but there are indications that the chancel was built before the close of the 12th cent. The nave contains the earliest work, with deeply splayed side lancets, and a thick W. window which is clearly Trans. The plain blocked N. door is also Trans., also the S. door, though most of the detail is E.E. The cylindrical font, resting on a moulded base, may be of the same date, but it is sometimes called E.E. The chancel is later in style, but still Trans., though apart from the square abaci the effect is of graceful E.E. The chancel arch is plain. At the E. end is a beautiful lancet triplet, with a band of dog-tooth round the arches. Above is a small circular window. There were originally three lancets on the N. and three on the S. side. The heads of all can be traced, but on the N. side the third lancet has been replaced by a late Dec. window. On the S. side only one lancet remains, E. of which is a late Dec. window, and W. a Dec. low-side window. There is also a Trans. priest's door. The W. bell-cote is supported on a wooden framework. The church is well restored and nicely kept.

Beenham (2 m. N.E. of Woolhampton) has an entirely new church, of which the details are handsome, with the exception of the ugly brick tower.

Benham Park. (See *Stockcross*.)

Besselsleigh (5 m. S.W. of Oxford) is an ancient manor, named after the Besils or Blessels, an energetic family from Provence who became its possessors by marriage in 1350. Sir Peter Besils (d. 1434) we have already met with among the benefactors of Abingdon. He not only gave the stone for building the great bridge. but also left money in his will for repairing it and making fresh roads. The estate presently passed by marriage to the Fettiplaces (see *Appleton, Childrey* and *Little Shefford*), who, in 1634, sold it to William Lenthall, the celebrated Speaker of the Long Parliament, to whose descendants it still belongs. In 1644 an attempt was made by some Royalists to seize and fortify the manor-house, but was frustrated by the prompt action of Major-General Browne, Governor of Abingdon.

The beautiful trees of the park overhang the Oxford and Faringdon road for quite a mile. The old manor-house used to stand not far from the road, a little W. of the church. It has totally disappeared, with the exception of the two old stone gateposts, somewhat inside the enclosing wall, which are conjectured to be the work of Inigo Jones, and a fragment of some buildings close to them, now used as a cowshed. In 1865 a new house was built for the Lenthalls, in a more retired part of the park. The little church is close to the road, and contains many memorials of the Lenthall family, both inside and in the churchyard. Nothing about the church is decidedly Norman. The S. doorway is round-headed, but not convincing; the stone bellcote for two bells, though picturesque, is quite plain, and has no mark of style. The E. and W. windows are very late E.E. (c. 1250-1260)—*i.e.* three foliated lancets with the spandrils pierced. The E. window has also a foliated curtain arch. The N.E. window is reticulated, the other side windows square Perp. There is no chancel arch, only a wooden partition let down from the roof. The S. door has Dec. ironwork, and a wooden porch of Jacobean character. Note also an E.E. piscina, a sill-sedile, a rood stair-turret (N. side) and an old pulpit with sounding-board.

Binfield (3 m. N.W. of Bracknell station) is a large straggling village. The church is in the N. of the parish between the two fine parks of Binfield House and the much larger one of Billingbear, which contains a modernized Elizabethan mansion. Restoration has left very little that is original in the church. The ancient portions are the nave arcades, the S. porch and doorway, the tower, and one, or possibly two, windows in the S. aisle. Most of these are Perp., but some features suggest Dec. The piscina may be Dec. and the font even E.E. But the church, though modernized, contains several interesting objects. There is a Jacobean pulpit, dated 1625, with good sounding-board. Near it is an hourglass-stand of painted ironwork, with the arms of the Farriers' College (three horseshoes) and the legend, " Watch and pray that ye enter not into temptation." Notice also a restored brass to Richard Turner and his wife (1539). It is a palimpsest, showing on the reverse side a mutilated figure and inscription written backwards. The floor is crowded with stone slabs of the 17th cent., a common feature in churches of the neighbourhood. There are also a carved old chest, some remains of an old screen, and a copy of Erasmus' paraphrase of the Gospels, chained near the S. door, which was placed here in 1547 by order of Edward VI.

The chief interest of Binfield lies in its connexion with the poet Pope. His father was a linendraper of Lombard Street, who in or before 1700 removed here to a house of which one room now remains. It was surrounded by 20 acres of ground, and a row of Scotch firs near it is much as it was in Pope's time. Pope was twelve years old in 1700, so that his wonderful effusion called " Solitude " may have been inspired by the Berkshire country. The first part of " Windsor Forest " was written four years later.

BISHAM (about 1 m. S. of Great Marlow in Buckinghamshire) is delightfully situated at one of the most charming points of the Thames Valley. The rich, flat, alluvial plain of the river is broader here than usual, and is bounded on the S. by a steep ridge of the chalk, entirely covered with the magnificent hanging *Quarry Woods*, which are at first some distance from the river, but presently approach it, until, about a mile below Great Marlow, they form its S. bank. In this secluded corner, between the wooded hills and the broad stream of the gleaming river, is set the park of *Bisham Abbey*, with its expanse of smooth lawn reaching to the water's edge and covered with groups of fine trees. Whether the visitor first reaches the scene by river, or by the winding road which descends

BISHAM CHURCH AND ABBEY

among the Quarry Woods, the effect is equally striking.

The manor, at present the seat of Sir Harry Vansittart, was given, in the reign of Stephen, to the Knights Templars, who had a preceptory here. On the suppression of that order the estate was granted by Edward II. to Hugh Despenser. It afterwards came to William Montacute, Earl of Salisbury, who in 1337 built here a priory for Austin Canons, of which the foundation stone was laid by Edward III. (see *Denchworth*). This was surrendered to Henry VIII. in 1536, but the sequel was extraordinary, for Bisham was chosen out of all the monasteries of Engand to be re-established as an abbey. Henry's object seems to have been that prayers might be perpetually offered for his late wife, Jane Seymour, but the desire of the capricious tyrant was as transient as his regret for Jane's death, and the new abbey was forced to surrender its charter in June 1538, six months after it had been conferred.

The priory church had long been the burial-place of the Earls of Salisbury. After four earls of the Montacute family had been buried here the title passed by marriage to the Neville family. The next earl to be interred here was Richard Earl of Salisbury, beheaded at York in 1460; and after him his more celebrated son, the Kingmaker, whose body, together with that of his brother, Lord Montague, had been brought here after the fatal battle of Barnet. The last of the family buried here was Edward Plantagenet, the son of Clarence and Isabel the Kingmaker's daughter, who was executed for trying to escape from the Tower with Perkin Warbeck. Where the dust of these illustrious dead reposes cannot now be said, for their tombs and monuments have entirely vanished.

The manor was granted by Henry VIII. to Anne of Cleves, but the Royal Seal was not attached to the gift, so that Queen Mary disregarded it and in 1552 conferred the manor on Sir Philip Hoby. Another version of the story is that Anne was allowed to exchange estates with Sir Philip. He was a distinguished diplomatist, and an amiable and cultivated man. When he died without issue in 1558 he left Bisham to his half-brother, Sir Thomas Hoby, also a distinguished diplomatist, who in 1565 was sent as ambassador to Paris, where he died the next year.[1] His widow, Elizabeth, Lady Hoby, brought his body back to Bisham, and erected a magnificent monument in the parish church to the two brothers. The epitaph she wrote ends with the lines :

> "Give me, O God, a husband like to Thomas,
>   Or else restore me to my husband Thomas."

She remarried in 1574, her second husband, John Lord Russell, dying in 1584. She survived him twenty-five years and died in 1609 at the age of eighty-one. Her portrait by Holbein, is at the end of the dining-room

[1] The story told by Mr Meade Faulkner that Elizabeth when princess, spent three years at Bisham under the custody of Sir Thomas Hoby, does not seem to be verifiable. Sir Thomas was abroad with his brother Philip for parts of every year between 1547 and 1555, and the record of Princess Elizabeth's residences during her sister's reign seems to leave no room for a prolonged stay at Bisham. Between July 1553 and March 1554 she was principally at Mary's Court; then followed two months in the Tower and six months' confinement at Woodstock. At Christmas 1554 she was recalled to Court, and was in frequent attendance there till October 1555, when she was allowed to retire to Hatfield, where she remained, with an occasional visit to Court, till Mary's death in 1558.

in the abbey, a grim and somewhat formidable person.
Her ghost is fabled to walk in one of the bedrooms,
perpetually washing her hands in Lady Macbeth's
fashion, the crime for which her restless spirit has to
atone being the death of her little son, whom she is
said to have beaten so savagely because he could not
learn to write without making blots that the poor boy
died. A strange confirmation of this story was afforded
in 1840 by the discovery of some children's copy-books
of the 16th cent., one of which was full of blots.
Queen Elizabeth visited Bisham in 1592, and held a
council in what is now the drawing-room.

The existing pile of buildings, the view of which is
very effective from all sides (but which, unfortunately,
are not shown) consist of an Elizabethan mansion,
built by the Hobys on to some remains of the priory,
which date from 1338. These remains are : (1) the
front door and porch ; (2) part of the chapel wall ;
(3) the great hall. The porch is beautiful Dec. work,
which has been most carefully restored. The outer
door is surrounded by several rows of plain mouldings.
The roof has plain quadripartite vaulting, and the
inner doorway three marble pillars on each side. The
door itself is original, of solid oak, with Dec. scrollwork
on it. On the L. are the remains of the chapel wall,
which is far thicker than the later Elizabethan work,
It contains one good two-light window of Geometrical
character, looking strangely early for its date, and two
other arched openings without tracery. The Great Hall
lies R. of the front entrance. It has no distinct 14th-
cent. feature, since its windows have been altered,
and the great E. window blocked by the later buildings.
At the W. end is a large minstrels' gallery. The dark
oak overmantel seems to be Jacobean. On either side
of it is some ancient tapestry of the early 16th cent.,

illustrating the story of Tobit, which formerly belonged
to a bedroom. At the E. end is a long table. said to
belong to the monks, and near it the entrance to the
buttery. Of the Elizabethan buildings three rooms
are noticeable : (1) the panelled dining-room, containing
the family portraits. Besides Lady Hoby's portrait
already referred to, there are portraits of Cromwell,
Henrietta Maria, General Monk, Admiral Van Tromp,
Prince Eugene and others ; (2) above it is the library,
also panelled, and with a fine view ; (3) the drawing-room
has an oriel window with a raised alcove. This window
and others in the room contain old heraldic shields.

The parish church is just outside the park, in a
very beautiful situation close to the river. The ancient
Norman tower (about 1150) is of hard chalk, and,
though the brick battlement is incongruous, has been
little damaged by restoration. All the rest of the
church has been rebuilt, except the Hoby Chapel,
where one window in debased Tudor style has been
left, probably because of the old glass it contains, showing the arms of twelve members of the Hoby family.
The chief interest lies in the remarkable Hoby monuments. The finest is the noble tomb of alabaster
raised by Lady Hoby to the memory of the two brothers,
her husband and brother-in-law, whose statues are
both in complete armour. The inscriptions were
written by Lady Hoby herself, one of the most learned
ladies of the age, in Greek, Latin and English. A
second tomb is that of Lady Hoby herself (d. 1609), who
is kneeling under a canopy, with her husband behind
her, and wears much the same coiffure as in her picture
by Holbein. A third, showing a curious sort of
pyramid with swans at the side, is to Margaret Hoby,
(her first cousin), (d. 1605). In another part of the
church there is a Perp. altar-tomb. There are also

three brasses: (1) Christopher Gray, 1525 (inscription only); (2) Thomas Crockitt, 1516 (one figure); (3) John Brinckhurst, 1581 (three figures).

In 1385 we hear of "idolatrous proceedings" at Bisham. Miracles were supposed to take place at a "holy well," but the bishop denounced them as "diabolical deceits" and ordered the well to be filled up.

A little farther down the river an iron bridge crosses to Great Marlow. In spite of its material and its recent construction, it is light and graceful, and by no means an eyesore. The river-reaches are very beautiful in both directions, especially to the E., where the Quarry Woods border on the stream. Shelley was here for some time in 1817, and loved to spend hours in a boat on the river.

Blackwater River is the principal tributary of the Loddon. It rises near Aldershot, and for most of its course forms the S. boundary of the E. part of the county. It is a dark, sluggish stream, creeping along under its alder bushes, and, flowing through a sandy soil, is not blessed with abundant waters. When however it joins the Loddon in Swallowfield Park it is as large or even larger than that river.

BLEWBURY ($1\frac{1}{2}$ m. S.E. of Upton station) is now quite a small village, with a diminishing population, but in early times it was of considerable importance. It is called a "venerable place" in the charter by which King Edward is stated to have made a grant of land here to Ælfric. It is also slightly connected with the Great Civil War. After the second battle of Newbury Charles retreated, in the night to Oxford via Wallingford. The next day the Parliamentarian cavalry started in pursuit, and, on reaching Blewbury without overtaking Charles, they returned to Newbury, and asked that the foot should join them. Manchester accordingly marched to Blewbury himself, but on arriving there he judged the pursuit hopeless and returned to Newbury. These ineffective measures produced a great deal of criticism. In the 18th cent. we hear of John Wesley making as many as three visits to Blewbury. The village is large and picturesque, lying just under the slope of the bare Downs, but embedded in trees, and containing several good timber-built houses and one or two inns with curious signs. The church is one of the most interesting in the county, and its history is not entirely clear. The key to the difficulty may be given by the two late Trans. arches S. of the chancel, between which on the S. side there remains a flat Norman buttress once external, and therefore part of the original wall which was cut through by the Trans. work. There is a corresponding buttress N. of the chancel, and two at the E. end. If these facts are correct, the original church was early Norman and rectangular, of which there remain the E. and N. walls of the chancel, and also a part of the N. wall of the nave, which is in a line with the chancel wall, but W. of the later arcade, and contains a small original early Norman window.[1] The larger Norman window N. of the chancel and the round window in the E. end gable may also belong to the first church, but this is not absolutely certain. In the Trans. period (about 1170-1180) the church was entirely rebuilt, and given a central tower and transepts. It is not, however, cruciform, since the S. transept does not project beyond the S. aisles. which were built at the same time to both chancel and nave. Whether the N. aisle of nave was also then built is uncertain, for it contains no Trans. features. The existing church is therefore mainly Trans., the principal

[1] Compare the remarkably similar case of Cookham church.

features being as follows : (1) the central crossing, which supports the tower. It rests on four massive piers, and has plain quadripartite vaulting. The tower has disappeared, indeed it may never have been completed, but there is a room above the vaulting, reached by a door high up, and there are five holes in the vaulting, four for the bell-ropes, and a fifth in the centre ; (2) the N. and S. transepts, at the ends of which are the only two decidedly Trans. windows—*i.e.* thick, pointed lancets. There is also a round arch of horseshoe shape, leading from the S. aisle into the S. transept ; (3) the S. arcade of the nave, the capitals of which show foliage very various in pattern ; (4) the chancel, which is vaulted exactly like the crossing, and has a Trans. arcade of two bays, leading into the S. chancel aisle. The style is more E.E. than in the nave and it was probably built last. Late in the Dec. period further changes were made : (1) the N. aisle with its arcade was built or rebuilt, and its windows altered ; (2) the S. aisle of the chance was transformed into a Dec. chantry, all the windows being altered and a piscina inserted ; (3) other Dec. windows were inserted, the E. window and another in the chancel, and one E. of the N. transept. Perp. changes were : (1) the alteration of the windows in the S. aisle ; (2) the N. and S. doors with their porches. The S. has a wooden door with original ironwork, a beautiful timber porch, and the ruins of a stoup. The N. porch has unfortunately been rebuilt with stone in 1882, but retains its old barge-board. In a niche above has been placed a figure of St Catherine ; (3) the W. tower to replace the central one ; (4) the panelled octagonal font. There are many other interesting objects. *In the chancel* there are (1) remains of Perp. screen (to the S.); (2) carved wooden prayer-desks

(Perp.) with some ancient books chained to them; (3) ring (N.) from which the Lenten veil may have hung. Traces of a corresponding S. ring are visible. *In or near the crossing* are: (1) two squints from the transepts: the plain one N. is Trans., the S. one Perp., with foliated tracery on both sides; (2) remains of rood-stairs, entered by a fine Perp. wooden door; (3) a " rood-loft piscina " 12 ft. from the ground, made from the capital of an octagonal Norman pillar (cf. *Lambourn*).

There are several brasses scattered about the church, five of which show effigies: (1) John Balam, vicar, 1496, in chancel; (2) Thomas Latton and wife, 1500, on N. wall of chancel; (3) Sir John Daunce and wife, on a tomb in S. chancel aisle; (4) John Latton and wife, 1548, on floor of chancel (a palimpsest); (5) a modern one to John Macdonald, 1841. There is also an inscription to John Casberde, 1500, and two other inscriptions are mentioned by authorities. In the churchyard there stand a charity school built in 1709 and an almshouse built in 1738.

Lovers of Dickens will be interested to know that a notorious miser, Blewbury Jones, whose life was studied by Mr Boffin, and to whom Bella Wilfer usually referred as " Blackberry Jones " (see " Our Mutual Friend "), was curate of this parish. The living was given in 1781 to the father of John Keble, who after the bad custom of those days, made Morgan Jones curate-in-charge at a stipend of £50. Jones had also about £30 a year of his own, but by spending about £5 a year, and leading a life of sordid penury he is said to have amassed as much as £18,000. If this is credible, the explanation is that he did not hoard in the usual miserly fashion, but invested his money at compound interest.

East of Blewbury is *Blewburton Hill,* a detached chalk hill standing a little in front of the main range. On the top is a magnificent prehistoric camp. On most sides the earthworks have been ploughed up, but on the W. side overlooking Blewbury they are seen to great advantage—a large rampart at the top with four terraces below it.

Blowing Stone. (See *Kingstone Lisle.*)

Boar's Hill. (See *Hinksey.*)

Botley (1 m. W. of Oxford) is a small hamlet of no interest, the first place passed on the W. road out of Oxford, just before leaving the Thames Valley. The river flows in several channels, and has to be crossed many times, whence the road is usually known as the *Seven Bridges Road.* It is worth pointing out that the first two of these bridges are crossed before Oxford itself is left. They are close together in Hythe Bridge Street, which is the real ancient beginning of the road. The first is continuous with the canal bridge, and the second, which may easily escape notice, is just beyond it.

Bourton ($\frac{1}{2}$ m. S.W. of Shrivenham station) is a village built on a small outlier of the Portland Beds, which are otherwise unrepresented in the county. It has a modern church, but a fine ancient village cross, standing on four steps. The lofty water-tower and the almshouses make the village a somewhat striking one.

Boxford is in the Lambourn Valley, about the point where the soil is changing from sand to chalk. It is very prettily situated under the striking bluff of Hour Hill, crowned with a beautiful clump of fir-trees. Somewhat farther N. is Borough Hill, with a prehistoric camp. There have been many Roman remains found in the parish, including a hoard of eight hundred coins. Two roads also are claimed as Roman, but the evidence seems uncertain. The church is entirely poor Perp. and little of it has been left unrestored. The E. window shows some strange corbel heads. The 17th-cent. tower is of brick and flint built chequer-wise, and, being ivy-clad, is picturesque. Inside note a piscina and aumbry, a fine Jacobean pulpit with sounding-board and the date 1618, and a chalk monument with gilt and colour, and interesting Latin inscription to Jacobus Anderton, rector, d. 1672.

Bracknell is a parish formed in 1851 not far from the borders of Windsor Forest. Being in the centre of a good residential neighbourhood, it has grown rapidly. The church is modern.

Bradfield (3 m. N.W. of Theale station) is a pleasant village in the Pang Valley. The church has been entirely rebuilt. The N. arcade is Dec., but everything else seems new. There is a picturesque ivy-clad tower of brick and flint. *St Andrew's College* was founded by the Rev. T. Stevens in 1850, and is now well known as a successful public school. At first it was in low water financially, and passed through bad times, until it came under the energetic rule of Dr Gray. A little east of the school buildings is a chalk pit, which has been hollowed out to form a theatre after the Greek pattern, where Greek plays are performed as far as is possible under ancient conditions. The view from the school over the extensive playing fields and the Pang Valley is delightful.

Bray (1½ m. S. of Maidenhead) is a well-known place on the river Thames between Maidenhead and Windsor. It was supposed by Camden and others to be the Roman station of Bibracte, but that name only exists in the imagination of the compiler of the Itinerary of Richard of Cirencester. All will remember Simon Aleyn, the Vicar who declared that

> " Whatsoever king doth reign
> I'll be the Vicar of Bray, Sir."

But it is not so well known that he lived, not as the song states, in the times of the Revolution of 1688, but in the equally stormy and more perilous times of the Tudor sovereigns, holding preferment under Henry VIII., Edward VI., Mary and Elizabeth successively. The church has a picturesque Perp. tower, a conspicuous object from the river, built over the S. porch, and showing flint work below and chequered work above. The rest of the church is very disappointing, since all interest has been restored away. There is a blocked old arch on the S. side ; also a niche under a pointed arch (apparently a stoup), just within S. porch. At W. end is a tomb with a foliated cross. Another tomb is dated 1622, and there are eight brasses : (1) Sir John Foxley and wives, 1378 ; (2) inscription to William Dyer, 1440 ; (3) Sir William Laken, 1475 ; (4) inscription to Clement Kelke, 1593 ; (5) inscription to William Smith, 1594 ; (6) inscription to Thomas Attlude ; (7) Cicely and Arthur Page, 1610 ; (8) a prie-dieu monument, c. 1610, with brass and the inscription:

> " When Oxford gave thee two degrees in art,
> And love possessed thee, master of my heart,
> Thy colledge fellowship thou lef'st for mine,
> And naught but Death could separate me from thine."

S. of the church is a timber-built house with a passage beneath it. The prettiest building in Bray is *Jesus Hospital*, an almshouse for forty poor persons. In the brick gateway is a statue of the founder with a coat-of-arms, and the inscription, " J. H. Founded in the year 1627 on the sole foundation of William Goddard, Esq." Inside the porch is an old poor-box with the date 1635. The porch leads into a quadrangle, filled by a garden of bright-coloured flowers, with a quaint, leaden pump in the centre. The surrounding buildings are of brick, all but the stone mullioned windows, and show beautiful gables and chimneys. At the W. is the chapel, with four large windows full of late and debased tracery, but not at all bad for the date. The ivy-circled W. window is a prominent feature in Frederick Walker's well-known picture, "The Harbour of Refuge," which is essentially Jesus Hospital, with a few details changed.

Brightwaltham (4 m. N.E. of Great Shefford) is on high ground in the centre of the chalk uplands, surrounded by fine beech woods. The old church was destroyed by Street, who built an uninteresting modern structure. It retains two plain E.E. doorways from the old church, and the ancient Norman font, which is cylindrical, and shows an interlacing arcade. There are also two brasses: (1) John Newman, d. 1517 (the inscription and the effigy of his wife are lost) ; (2) from the tomb of James Braybrooke (d. 1590).

Brightwell (1½ m. N.W. of Wallingford) is a secluded village shaded by trees, lying S. of Brightwell Barrow (371 ft.), a prominent point on the chalk range running E. from Sinodun. The church is mostly Dec., but by no means of one period. The oldest parts are the Trans. S. door (about 1200), the S. arcade, which is probably of the same date, and one small lancet window, now in the passage to the vestry. The N. arcade is certainly Dec., and all the other windows, which however are of different dates. Those in the N. aisle, including the E. window, which has been made interior by throwing out an organ chamber, are late Geometrical. A pair N. and S. of the chancel are late Curvilinear. (The Geometrical E. window is modern.) Finally those in the S. aisle, including the S.W. window of the chancel, are Trans. to Perp. Two of these have very good tracery. The clerestory is Perp., the tower 18th-

Jesus Hospital
Bray

round the edge; (2) brasses to John Yate and wife, 1578; (3) tomb of Sir Edward Yate, 1648; (4) tomb of Sir John Yate, 1658.

The Yates held the manor in the 16th and 17th centuries, and the strange-looking house N. of the church was their ancient mansion. It has been spoilt by bad and pretentious later additions, and is now used only as stables and offices. In 1690 the manor passed from the Yates to the Throckmortons, a Roman Catholic family, who still hold it. Their new *Buckland House*, built in 1757, is in a fine, well-wooded park to the W., but in itself of no merit. Near the E. entrance of the park is a R.C. chapel.

BUCKLEBURY (3 m. N.W. of Midgham station) is a pleasant village in the Upper Valley of the little Pang. The manor, formerly a possession of Reading Abbey, fell at the Dissolution into the hands of John Winchcombe, son of the well-known Jack of Newbury (see *Newbury*). For a century and a half the Winchcombes held the manor. Then the male line failed, and in 1700 the heiress, Frances Winchcombe, married Henry St John, afterwards Lord Bolingbroke, the celebrated Tory minister of Queen Anne. Here, in the intervals of his political duties, he led the life of a "perfect country gentleman," as Swift described him in a letter to Steele written from Bucklebury in 1711. In 1713 Swift again visited Bolingbroke here, in the vain attempt to effect a reconciliation between him and his colleague, Oxford. When in 1715 Bolingbroke fled to France to avoid impeachment, he left his wife behind, whom it appears he never really loved. She lived on for only three years in the old house, and then died. Her ghost, a white lady in a chariot drawn by black horses, is still fabled to haunt the neighbourhood. The old house has entirely disappeared except the kitchen, but the fishpond may still be seen. In the church the best feature is the S. door, which is beautiful and elaborate late Norman (c. 1150). The porch is dated 1603 and has a good barge-board. Inside the church still retains old high pews, a 'three-decker' from which Swift is said to have preached, and a W. wooden gallery. The N. arcade is early Trans. but very plain. The chancel was formerly E.E., but was rebuilt about 1700 by Sir Harry Winchcombe, Bolingbroke's father-in-law. The lancets seem to have been restored again since that time. The E. window is Perp., also one N. of chancel, which contains two diamonds of heraldic glass, and a square painted sundial, dated 1649, with a very lifelike fly painted close to it. The rest of the church—*i.e.* the N. aisle, nave windows and W. tower—is late Perp. Over the blocked N. door there is a curious badge, something like a bird's claw. S. of the tower there are some very curious small carvings. In a row there are : (1) an illegible inscription ; (2) a crucifixion ; (3) a Maltese cross. Below is a rebus of the Winchcombes, a figure combing a wheel.

About a mile S., on the high ground between the Pang and the Kennet, is *Bucklebury Common*, one of the most beautiful scenes in the county. It can be well seen from the Bradfield Road, which crosses it from W. to E. Very effective features are the isolated clumps of pine-trees and the girdle of woods on its sloping sides. E. of Chapel Row the road is bounded for a mile by a double row of fine oak-trees. These are said to have been part of an avenue to Bucklebury House, but they do not lead straight in that direction. This is one of the few points N. of the Kennet, where the Reading Beds are capped by the Bagshot Sands.

Burghfield (2 m. S.E. of Theale station) has a modern church. Under the porch of the W. tower are three old effigies : (1) oaken figure of knight ; (2) mutilated figure of stone knight ; (3) mutilated figure of stone lady.

On the W. wall inside are the brasses of a knight and lady. The font is strange ; it looks like a Dec. bowl on a Norman base.

Buscot (2½ m. S.E. of Lechlade station) lies on the S. bank of the Thames, less than a mile from the point where it begins to border the county. The church and rectory stand apart, and form a picturesque group quite close to the clear willow-fringed river. The church has no aisles. The chancel arch is good Trans., showing zigzag and early foliated capitals. The chancel was originally rude E.E. or possibly even Trans., for the two surviving lancets are very slightly pointed. The other larger windows have had their tracery cut out, but two show interior foliations on the curtain arch. In the chancel note (1) sill-sedile ; (2) two E.E. piscinæ ; (3) Dec. foliated niche ; (4) shouldered aumbry ; (5) two headless brasses, c. 1450 ; (6) two beautiful windows by Sir E. Burne-Jones ; (7) 18th-cent. monuments to the Lowndes family, who then owned Buscot Park. The nave and the W. tower are Perp. The font is original. The picturesque square-built rectory dates mainly from the end of the 17th cent. On the N. side there are portions of an older building. The village lies to the S.E. S. of the Faringdon Road, a little farther on, is the extensive park of Buscot House, built in 1780.

Cæsar's Camp. (See *Easthampstead.*)

Catmore (2½ m. W. of Compton station) is a curious little hamlet lying among the chalk uplands. The church and an old rambling farmhouse are on the hillside by themselves, the rest of the houses being at *Lilley* in the valley below. The structure of the church is entirely Norman. One window is Perp. ; the rest are round-headed, but they have been badly restored.

There are two doors, the N. one plain, the S. with billet moulding and one beak-head above. The porch is restored Norman. There is a plain chancel arch, and a defaced font, of which the top part is certainly Norman. The Jacobean roof has the date 1607 and initials W.E. and J.E. (referring to the Eystons of E. Hendred, who owned the manor). There is a small belfry turret with one bell.

Chaddleworth (3½ m. N.E. of Shefford station) is a village which straggles up a hillside with the church at the top. The church was originally Norman or Trans., but has been so rebuilt that very few ancient parts remain—*i.e.* (1) The N. door is good Norman, with a niche above and stoup inside ; (2) in the N. wall there are two deeply splayed lancets, which seem to be Trans. ; (3) the W. tower is Trans. with an upper Perp. story. The tower arch is Perp., resting on Trans. jambs. The W. window is Perp in a Trans. frame. There is also an old sanctus-bell niche ; (4) the font is plain Norman. In the 18th-cent. two strange pews were thrown out transept-wise. One belonged to the Wroughtons, who still live at *Woolley Park*, which is on the slope of a fine chalk down and surrounded by splendid beech woods. In the sill of one of the windows there is a fragment of an old piscina, brought from Poughley Abbey (*q.v.*) Another fragment of old carving is placed in the porch. In the churchyard there is the stump of a cross and some strange-looking tombs.

Challow, East (station about 2 m. N.W.), has a small church which was greatly damaged by restoration in 1858 and 1884. A few ancient features have survived—*i.e.* the S. arcade, which is early Dec., a handsome stoup of the same date (outside W. door), one Perp. window, and the plain cylindrical font. There are traces of some old glass in one window.

Challow, West, has also a small church. The S. doorway is plain Norman. The door has old ironwork. There is a Perp. wooden porch with a good barge-board. The cylindrical font is also probably Norman. The W. window is a foliated lancet, but all the other ancient windows are Perp. There is a good bell-cote with two bells, a Perp. screen of dark oak, some handsome poppy-heads, and a little old glass in the E. window.

Charlton ($\frac{3}{4}$ m. E. of Wantage) is a hamlet with a small modern church. It contains a manor-house where Charles I. is said to have stayed.

Charney Basset ($3\frac{1}{2}$ m. N.E. of Challow station) is a village on the Ock in a low-lying country where the principal trees are willows. In the centre of the village is a small green, with the shaft of a cross raised on three steps. The church, which is close to the river, is very mixed in style. Of the original Norman there remain the chancel arch, and two doorways with remarkable tympana, showing strange and elaborate carving. On the S. door there is a row of heads with ornamented projecting tongues. The other, which is not *in situ*, but has been set at the E. end of an equally remarkable Perp. squint, shows a man holding by the neck two animals like winged horses.[1] There is one late E.E. window S. of chancel, and a Dec. window S. of nave. The font is E.E. Nearly all other features are Perp., including the other windows, the N. aisle with its arcade, the roof, the screen and the pulpit. Some authorities consider the last two Jacobean. The curious square bell-cote is certainly Jacobean. The low-side window (Perp.) is in an odd position in the N. aisle. The E. window has a little old glass.

[1] Mr C. E. Keyser thinks they are dragons, and that the reference may be to Psalm lxxxvi. v. 20.

Directly N. of the church there is a group of buildings, now a farmhouse, but formerly a grange of Abingdon Abbey. The S. block contains unaltered the original buildings of the later part of the 13th cent. The ground floor was probably used as a cellar, and shows a fireplace with shouldered arch. Above is the solar with a fine timber roof and Perp. fireplace. At the E. end is a small chapel, retaining a piscina and aumbry. The windows of the building are plain, either square openings or lancets.

Chieveley (2 m. W. of Hermitage station) is a large and rather picturesque village with some timber-built houses. In the church the chancel and tower are original; the nave with its N. aisle is new. The chancel is good E.E., with a lancet triplet at E. end and single lancets at the sides. One window is square-headed (late Dec. or E. Perp.) About half way down the chancel is a handsome wooden arch with Perp. tracery at the sides, from which a veil is said to have hung during Lent. Note the curious tomb to Mrs Lucy Fincher, 1687. The font is restored Perp. The tower has three Trans. (or possibly rude E.E.) stories, and a fourth one Dec. The W. door is Perp.

CHILDREY (2½ m. S. of Challow station) is another of the charming villages which lie under the N. slope of the Berkshire Downs. It was for centuries one of the chief homes of the powerful Fettiplace family, who were said to hold land in fifteen counties. In Oxfordshire their principal mansion was at Swinbrook. In Berkshire they held estates at Appleford, Besselsleigh, Childrey, Denchworth and W. Shefford (*q.v.*) But their principal abode was here until the Restoration, when they migrated to Swinbrook. The old manor-house is S. of the church, and is reached by a walk of clipped yews, leading to a Perp. door with a Perp.

window above it. Though much altered it contains an old oak staircase and a room in which Charles I. is said to have slept in April 1644, when marching to Marlborough. In 1526 William Fettiplace founded a chantry and almshouse here, assigning certain lands to Queen's College, Oxford, for their maintenance, in consequence of which its foundation escaped suppression in 1548. The chantry chaplain had also the duty of holding a free school in his house. This was practically an elementary school for the village, and is nearly unique among pre-Reformation foundations. There does not appear to have been a special school building until 1732, when Sir George Fettiplace built the existing schoolroom, which still shows the Fettiplace arms on the wall. The family finally came to an end in 1805, and the manor-house is now held by Mr E. T. W. Dunn. The church claims a high place among the Berkshire churches, not so much for its structure as because of the monuments and other interesting objects is contains. It is cruciform, without aisles, and almost entirely Dec. and Perp. (chiefly the latter). The only earlier features are Trans.—*i.e.* (1) the S. door, which has a round arch and a row of dog-tooth above it ; (2) the blocked N. door ; (3) the font, which is one of the three leaden fonts in the county, and is surrounded by twelve bishops. The chancel was rebuilt c. 1280. The transepts were once of 14th-cent. work, but they have been almost entirely changed to Perp., and the arches leading into them are late Perp. The nave is also Perp. All the windows are old, and very effective. Three in the chancel are Geometrical, one Curvilinear (E. of N. transept), and the rest Perp. There are late clerestory windows in the nave. The tower is also Perp. with a debased upper story and a sanctus-bell niche.

In the *chancel* note (1) sedilia and double piscina (both c. 1280); (2) old screen; (3) poppy-heads and bench-ends; (4) Easter sepulchre—*i.e.* an early Perp. altar-tomb, hollowed at top. In the *N. transept* (St Mary's Chapel): (1) very good 15th-cent. glass in N. window; (2) Dec. tomb with ball-flower under canopy, and cross-legged warrior below; (3) Dec. piscina; (4) squint; (5) steps to rood-loft; (6) encaustic tiles. In the *S. transept* (St Catherine's Chapel): (1) good square-headed piscina with ogee arch; (2) old seat-ends, one with the Fettiplace arms; (3) door in wall leading to blocked arch, where there used to be a small stone pulpit; (4) squint; (5) altar-tomb, with canopy and brasses, c. 1510. There are eleven other old brasses in the church, of which seven are in the chancel—*i.e.* (1) Agnes Finderne, 1441; (2) William Finderne and wife, 1444; (3) William Waldron and wife, 1450; (4) headless priest, c. 1480; (5) another priest, c. 1480; (6) John Kyngeston and wife, 1514; (7) Bryan Roos, 1529; and four in the S. transept—*i.e.* (8) Thomas Walrond and wife, 1480; (9) Jane Walrond, 1500; (10) William Fettiplace and wife, 1513; (11) Elizabeth and Catherine Fettiplace, 1603.

Chilton (1½ m. S.W. of Upton station) is a village in a rather bleak situation on the lower slopes of the Chalk Downs. It contains training-stables. Of the original Trans. church there remain the chancel arch, the S. arcade with central column, showing E.E. details, and the nine-sided font. There is a Dec. image niche on the N. wall. The windows are Dec. and Perp. The N. windows of chancel are ogee-headed lancets and the E. window heavy Trans. to Perp. The tower and S. porch are modern.

CHOLSEY is situated near the point where the Thames

approaches the Berkshire Downs. It is a place of high antiquity. Here in 986 Ethelred the Redeless founded an abbey, in expiation for the murder of his brother, Edward the Martyr, by his mother, Elfrida. But the abbey was soon destroyed, probably by the Danes, who, in 1006, as we learn from the Saxon Chronicle, after burning Wallingford, proceeded by Cholsey to Ashdown (*i.e.* the Downs. See also *Scutchamore Knob*). Its destruction " for its sins " is alluded to in the first charter given by Henry I. to Reading Abbey, which confers on that abbey the Manor of Cholsey. None of the buildings erected here by the Reading monks survive, though the great tithe-barn was only pulled down about a century ago. There are traces of a moat W. of the church, and the road leading to the river is still called the " Papists' Way."

It is possible that the original Saxon church was burnt, together with the abbey, for at the restoration of the chancel in 1878 stones showing the action of fire were discovered. Whether the massive central tower alone resisted the fire, or whether the whole church was rebuilt directly afterwards, we do not know. But in any case the existing cruciform structure is due to the Reading monks, who (about 1130-1140) either transformed the existing church, or built a new church round the old Saxon tower. The only subsequent changes were the lengthening of the chancel about 1260-1270, and the raising of the tower by a story in the 14th cent. The top part of the tower is therefore Dec., but the lower part, which shows primitive masonry and traces of long-and-short work, is claimed as the original Saxon. Some authorities, however, still consider it Norman. It rests on four plain and massive round arches, of which the N. and S. are plain, while the E. and W. have arabesque

Norm. capitals, added by the Reading monks. The nave has a fine Norman S. door. The N. and S. windows are new, the W. window Perp. The transepts show Norman windows, except the N. and S. ones, which are later insertions. On the E. side of the N. transept there is a large blocked Norman arch, formerly leading into an apsidal chapel, of which the foundations have lately been discovered. Probably chancel and S. transept also had E. apses.

The chancel retains one Norman window, but otherwise it has been altered to good late E.E. with lancets at the sides, and an early Geometrical window (restored) at the E. end. On the S. is a good E.E. priest's door. There are three sill-sedilia and a double piscina. There is a blocked squint in W. transept, and a defaced female effigy in S. transept; also brasses to John Barfoot de Chelseye, 1361; John Gate (vicar), 1394 (inscription only); and John Mere (vicar), 1471. There is also the matrix of another brass, to which the inscription has been lately renewed on a modern brass plate: " Pray for the sowles of John Willmot and Agnes 1529." Note also portion of an old stall with poppy-heads.

Churn may be taken as the generic name of the fascinating Down region lying between Blewbury and Upton on the N. and Compton Parva on the S. Towards the E. end of the Berkshire Downs the main summit-ridge, which has been continuous from the Ashbury to the Ilsley Downs, breaks up into an irregular group of lower hills, with an escarpment more advanced to the N. Between these hills and the point where the main ridge sinks down is a broad upland valley, in shape like a flat shallow bowl, from which the grassy Downs swell gradually upwards on all sides. This used to be called Blewbury Plain, but is now widely known as Churn. Its admirable situation for cavalry manœuvres has been recognized, and almost every summer a camp is formed for some weeks on its short turf. The railway between Upton and Compton passes through it, and arrangements are made to stop the train at a platform near the camp. On the W. rise the Ilsley Downs, at the end of the main range, below which may be traced Grimsditch, one of the ancient boundary ditches found in the county. To the N. is *Churn Knob*, crowned by a small but prominent clump of beeches. Here the story runs that Birinus commenced the conversion of Wessex by preaching to King Cynegils. S.E. is *Lowbury Hill* (575 ft.), on which there is a small rectangular camp, certainly once occupied by the Romans, and perhaps originally constructed by them. From both of these hills the views are first rate. Unfortunately, or perhaps fortunately, no regular roads lead to this charming region. There are rough tracks leading up the hill from Upton and Blewbury, where the cyclist will find more pushing than riding. But perhaps the better way is to start from Cholsey or Moulsford, and take the road which ascends the Downs, with the deep and well-wooded *Unhill Bottom* on the L. and *King's Standing Hill* on the R. This name points to a tradition that here was the site of the battle of Ashdown, but this, as we have already seen, is unverifiable (see *Ashdown*). Our road soon becomes a grassy track called the *Fair Mile*, which leads down to Churn, and then merges into the Ridgeway along the Downs. In all these walks there are frequent and delightful views over the Thames Valley, with the Chilterns beyond. The ramble may be extended to Aldworth or Compton.

Clewer (1 m. W. of Eton) is on flat ground S. of the Thames. The name is familiar by reason of the Clewer Sisterhood, whose red-brick buildings are prominent.

Most of the church has been rebuilt, but a few original Norman features remain—*i.e.* (1) the nave arcades, of three arches on either side ; (2) a smaller arch, E. of N. arcade ; (3) arch between S. chapel and S. aisle ; (4) lower part of tower which has two original windows. The side columns of the tower arch are also Norman, but the acutely pointed arch must ·be later. Other original features are the S. door (probably E.E.) and a Dec. window and priest's door in chancel. There is a brass plate (1657), without figures, and a rhyming inscription on another plate to Martin Expence.

COLD ASH (2½ m. N. of Thatcham station, 2½ m. S. of Hermitage station) is a pretty village with a modern church on a hillside sloping up from the Kennet Valley to the glorious *Cold Ash Common*, which is capped by the Bagshot Sands, and is the highest point which that formation reaches in Berkshire (517 ft.). The views are magnificent in every direction. To obtain in perfection the view over the Kennet Valley, which is unsurpassed in Berkshire, it is best to walk a little along the road leading to Bucklebury Common. The broad river valley is bounded on the far side by a densely wooded ridge of sandy common, over which rises the grand *Inkpen Beacon* range, bounding the view. In the centre is the beautifully rounded Beacon Hill, with the wooded Sidown Hill of almost equal height to the R., beyond which the Downs stretch away to Inkpen Beacon itself. From the signpost at the highest point of the common, where heather gives place to the fir woods, there is a fascinating double view, to the E. right down the Valley of the Pang, which turns at a right angle directly below us, and to the W. over the undulating country stretching far out of Berkshire into Wiltshire. If we now continue N., turning R. both now and again on the next opportunity, we reach *Grimsbury Castle*, a fine prehistoric camp, in the centre of a fir and oak forest. At the point where the road cuts through the rampart and ditch, they are very plain to the R. In the S.E. corner of the enclosure is a pool of water never known to fail.

Cole (river) is a stream which flows N. from the Downs to join the Thames near Lechlade. For most of its course it is the boundary between Berkshire and Wiltshire.

Coleshill (4 m. W. of Faringdon) is on a hill sloping to the Cole on the W. boundary. It is a model village with substantial stone-built houses, of which the effect is pleasing. It has the pedestal and shaft of an old village cross. The church is very largely modern. The only ancient parts are: (1) S. arcade (Trans.); (2) N. arcade (E.E.); (3) S. porch with parvise, above trefoil-headed door (Dec.); (4) W. tower (good Perp.), with sound-hole. The only ancient windows are the Dec. lancet in parvise, and the W. window of tower. The S. chapel, rebuilt in 18th cent., replaced a 15th-cent. chantry chapel of which there are some fragments (1) built into the wall; (2) under the tower; (3) in the porch. Note also remains of stoup near S. door, recumbent effigy in S. chapel under foliated canopy, and foliated piscina under E. respond of N. arcade. *Coleshill Park* is large and full of fine trees. The house was built by Inigo Jones, in 1650, and is one of his best works. It is square, and surmounted by a stone parapet, with an effective central lantern.

Combe (6 m. S.E. of Hungerford station), the most S. village in the county, is in an extraordinary situation. It lies S. of the Inkpen Beacon range at its highest part, and sunk deep in a cup-shaped hollow between the three great downs of Walbury Beacon (959 ft.), Combe Hill (936 ft.), and Sheepless Hill (876 ft.). Between the last two a narrow pass leads S. into Hampshire. This village was transferred for civil purposes to Berkshire in 1895, but the little E.E. church is still in the Winchester diocese. The chancel is entirely in this style, showing plain chancel arch, a double foliated lancet at E. end, three side lancets and priest's door. The nave has three Perp. windows and a brick S. door, and porch dated 1652. The wooden belfry is new. The font may be Perp.

Combe Gallows. (See *Inkpen Beacon.*)

Compton Beauchamp (3 m. E. of Shrivenham station) consists of hardly more than the manor-house and adjacent church, which are beautifully set in a wooded hollow right at the foot of the Downs. The manor-house, reached by an avenue of elms, has an 18th-cent. stone front, but 16th-cent. brick at the back. It is surrounded on three sides by a well-kept moat, gay with water-lilies, and the lawns and gardens, enriched with yews and other fine trees, stretch far up the hillside. The cruciform church has some E.E. fragments in chancel—*i.e.* two lancets (one a low-side window), a sedile and a pillar piscina. The other windows in chancel are Dec., including a reticulated E. window with some old glass ; a one-light window high up, which may have lighted the rood-screen. The N. transept has been modernized. The nave shows Perp. features. The tower may also be Perp., but there is little to judge by. Parker thinks the tower arch E.E.

Compton Parva is near the head of the valley among the chalk uplands where the little Pang rises. The church has been rebuilt, with the exception of the tower, which is mainly Perp., but retains an early Geometrical window on the S. side. 1½ m. S. is *Perborough Castle*, an ancient earthwork.

COOKHAM is just S. of the Thames, in the N.E.

VIEW FROM COOKHAM BRIDGE

corner of the county, and is well known for the sur-
passing beauty of the river scenery in the immediate
neighbourhood. This will be seen by most visitors
from the river itself, but the cyclist may gain a fair
idea of it by visiting the bridge and the lock. Looking
down stream from the bridge, we see the broad river
part into three channels, of which the L.-hand one goes
to the weir, and then sweeps round under the woods of
Hedsor; the central stream is the lock-cut, and the
R.-hand one a broad backwater. All the banks are
delightfully wooded and the unrivalled hanging woods
of Cliveden form the background. The lock-cut is
well girdled by trees and is the prettiest on the Thames.
Just below the lock all the branches meet again, and
then follows the finest reach on the river, with Cliveden
Woods on the L. and Formosa Island on the R.

Cookham church has, in common with most riverside
churches, suffered from restoration. It is, however,
spacious and dignified, and has by no means lost all
flavour of antiquity. The original rectangular Norman
church extended as far E. as the massive piers of the
chancel arch, both of which have Norman cores. On the
N.W. a part of the Norman wall remains, with one small
window. Early in the 13th century the E. part of the
N. wall was broken through to form St Catherine's
chapel. This remains unaltered, with four lancet
windows, E.E. door and piscina, and is the best part of
the church. About 1240 the S. wall was also broken
through by a later E.E. arcade of hard chalk to form
the S. aisle, which is lighted by double-lancet windows,
one with the spandril pierced. Next was built St
Clement's chapel on the S.E., in the Geometrical style,
with windows now restored, and separated by an arcade
of two bays from the chancel, which was then E.E.
Later the chancel was altered to Perp., and extended

farther E., and the Lady Chapel was thrown out to the N. of it. The curious Trans.-looking arch N. of chancel is the only difficulty in this account,[1] and it may possibly be not original. Some modern windows inserted in 1860 tend to obscure the church's history. The tower is debased Perp., but, being massive and ivy-grown, is quite picturesque. There are two piscinæ with trefoiled heads, and two large sepulchral niches. The window of the rood-stair is still visible. There are some old niches in the sanctuary. There is a Perp. altar-tomb with brass to Robert Peche and his wife (1510), and mutilated brasses to John Babham and wife (1458), Agnes Mylles (c. 1500), Richard Babham and wife (1527), and Margaret Monkden and two husbands (1503), also a palimpsest brass to R. More (1577) (behind organ), and a desk-kneeler to Arthur Babham, with wife and six children (1651). At the W. end are a monument by Flaxman to Sir Isaac Pocock, and a medallion to Frederick Walker the artist.

Coxwell, Great, is a village on the Lower Greensand, 2 m. S.W. of Faringdon. The manor, together with that of Faringdon, was granted by King John to the Cistercians of Beaulieu Abbey, who had a grange here. The large *tithe-barn*, built in the 14th century, still remains, N. of the village. It is cruciform in shape, and the massive buttresses and solid slate roofing make it very effective. The E. and W. doors are original. Near it is an old Elizabethan farmhouse. The church is small, but of interest. The deep splay of the restored lancets N. of the nave, and the round arch of the S. door, which has been turned into a window, look very

---

[1] The above account partly follows a lecture on the church by Sir George Young. If the Trans. arch is original, the chancel must have been built at an earlier period than Sir George thinks.

BADBURY HILL.

like Trans., but there is no other original feature in that style. The nave also contains two old windows on the S., one Geometrical, with interior foliation, the other Perp. The N. door keeps its original oak with Perp. tracery on it. The chancel is good E.E., with single lancets on the N., and a triplet of grouped and foliated lancets on the E. On the S. is an early Geometrical window, perhaps a little later, and a lancet, prolonged to form a low-side window, now closed with a modern shutter, and with a small stone seat near it. At the E. end are piscina with shelf, two aumbries and two niches. The tower is Perp., but retains E.E. W. window (exactly like E. window). Note (1) sanctus-bell niche; (2) Jacobean pulpit; (3) stairs to rood-loft carried in a bulge and lighted by a small window. There are brasses to William Morys and his wife Johane (c. 1500).

About a mile N. is *Badbury Camp* (over 500 ft.), a prominent rounded hill topped by an ancient earthwork, which has been planted with trees. It is a good view-point, and very prominent from a distance. In several views it appears as a sort of double of Faringdon Clump.

Coxwell, Little (1½ m. S. of Faringdon), has a church originally Norman or Trans., but badly damaged by restoration. When approached from the S. it is very imposing, for there face us a Norman doorway with Perp. stone porch, a Trans. priest's door, an early Dec. window, and three large and handsome Perp. windows. Above is a picturesque E.E. bell-cote with a pierced quatrefoil. But the rest of the church is disappointing. There are no original windows on the other three sides. The chancel arch is Trans. There is a stoup, a plain octagonal font, a Dec. piscina, Dec. roof and Perp. niches at the E. end. In this parish is found the "*sponge gravel*," a curious local variation of the Lower Greensand.

Crockham Heath. (See *First battle of Newbury.*)

Crookham Common with its extension W., *Greenham Common,* forms a delightful sandy plateau in the S. of the county, about 4 m. long, lying between the valleys of the Kennet and its tributary the Enborne. The hillsides which slope to the rivers are densely wooded, but the top is a flat expanse of bare heath from 300 to 400 ft. high. At the E. end there is not a single tree on the summit, but as we proceed W. it is dotted with effective groups of firs. It is traversed from end to end by the road from Aldermaston to Newbury, from which the views are first rate the whole way. Towards the S. the view is bounded by the fine range of Downs stretching to Inkpen Beacon, among which Beacon Hill and its wooded neighbour Sidown Hill show to great advantage. Along this road Essex and his army retreated after the First battle of Newbury. Before they reached Aldermaston Rupert attacked their rear with his cavalry, and caused some confusion, but the infantry lined the hedges and soon forced Rupert to retreat in turn. In 1822 we find William Cobbett journeying along this road " by Crookham, Brimpton and Mortimer." Land which is useless for cultivation has no charm for the democratic farmer. "Nothing," he says, " can well be poorer or more villainously ugly." He is deeply pained to find the " villainous tract " of sand and gravel extends practically from Hounslow Heath to Hungerford.

Crowthorne (1 m. E. of Wellington College station) is a pleasant village in the centre of the Bagshot Sand district, which consists of low hills covered with heathery commons and fir woods. Several pretty villas are springing up in the neighbourhood. The church is modern. 1 m. S. is Wellington College (*q.v.*). About ½ m. E. is Broadmoor Asylum, where criminal

GREENHAM COMMON: NEAR NEWBURY

lunatics are confined. The remarkable Roman road, the Devil's Highway (*q.v.*), passes a very little to the N. (For Cæsar's Camp and the Nine Mile Ride see *Easthampstead*.) The straight road from the railway station to the village is called the Duke's Drive.

CUMNOR (3½ m. S.W. of Oxford) is reached from Oxford by starting on the Seven Bridges Road (see *Botley*), and then ascending a long winding hill. Half-way up, the tall mast used as a station for Marconigraphs is to be seen on the L. At the top we are close to *Cumnor Hurst* (L.)—"the fir-topped Hurst," of Matthew Arnold's "Thyrsis"—crowned by a ring of seven Scotch firs and a single elm, which stands a little outside the ring, but near enough to form one group with the firs. It is on the top of a rounded hill of 520 ft., formed by a patch of Greensand capping the Coral Rag. There is a good panoramic view. Half-a-mile farther we turn R. at a fork, and soon reach the village.

Cumnor Hall wil be always famous in romance as the scene of the tragic death of Amy Robsart, whose life was thought at the time the only barrier to a marriage between her husband, Lord Robert Dudley, and Queen Elizabeth. The manor had belonged to Abingdon Abbey, and at the Dissolution the last abbot was allowed to end his days here in peace. On his death in 1546 the estate was granted to George Owen, Henry VIII.'s physician, from whose son, George Owen, it was in 1560 held on lease by Antony Forster, chief agent and personal friend of Dudley. He was afterwards member for Abingdon, purchased Cumnor Hall, and is described on his monument in the church (see later) as an educated gentleman with refined tastes in music and horticulture. Obviously he was neither the "puritanical churl" of Scott's "Kenilworth," nor the conscience-stricken villain of tradition "who sunk, after the fatal deed, into a man of gloomy and retired habits." On the fatal day, 8th Sept. 1560, there were staying at the hall, besides Amy herself, Mrs Odingsells, widowed sister of Mr Hyde of Denchworth (*q.v.*), and Mrs Owen, wife of the owner. In the morning Amy sent all her servants to Abingdon Fair, but the ladies declined to go. Thus the later statement that Forster had sent away the servants so that Amy might be alone is doubly inaccurate. When the servants returned in the evening, they found her lying at the foot of the hall staircase with her neck broken. It was currently reported at the time, that Dudley had ordered Forster to throw her downstairs, but, apart from the obvious grounds for suspicion, not a particle of reliable evidence was found against either of the accused, nor has any been found since. Dudley's conduct, though his absence from Amy's funeral shows callousness, does not look like that of a guilty man. He writes letters to a kinsman, Sir Thomas Blount, ordering him to go to Cumnor, and make the strictest inquiry, together with John Appleyard, Amy's half-brother. An inquest was held with a jury rather hostile than otherwise to Dudley, who returned a verdict of accidental death. Seven years afterwards Appleyard declared that the jury had been suborned, but when examined by the Privy Council he made an abject retractation of the charge. Nevertheless it is on this point that suspicion naturally fastens. The popular version of the story, as contained in a passage from Ashmole's " Antiquities of Berkshire " (which is quoted by Scott as his authority in the Introduction to " Kenilworth "), is due to a libel on Dudley, called " Leicester's Commonwealth," which was first published in 1584, nearly a generation after the event. In this Sir Richard Verney (or Varney) is named for the first time as joint murderer with Forster, and the miserable ends of both are graphically described, but none of these statements are historically credible. Thus Varney, the arch villain of Scott's romance, has no real connexion with the tragedy at all.

Cumnor Hall was left by Forster at his death to Dudley, now Earl of Leicester. It passed subsequently to the Earls of Abingdon, and was demolished in 1810 by the third Earl, who had already destroyed Rycote. From a sketch which was taken of the house just before, we learn that it was small but handsome, with good late Dec. windows under effective gables, and square doorways. Of these features some were removed to Wytham (q.v.). The house was of course haunted by Amy's ghost, which, as the story runs, had to be " laid " by nine parsons from Oxford. It is interesting to remember that her ghost also walked in Cornbury Park (see " Little Guide to Oxfordshire "). The house was S. of the church but has entirely disappeared.

The church deserves a careful description, as an interesting building within easy reach of Oxford. It was originally Trans., and the chief alterations were made in the Dec. period. The existing walls are Trans., and there are indications of that style in every part of the church, except the S. transeptal chapel. The most striking part is the tower (c. 1170-1180), which has an early corbel table, good lancets, and very beautiful W. door and tower arch. The chancel retains in the style the chancel arch, with nailhead moulding, one small window (N.), two window-frames (S.), and a flat buttress. Outside the S. wall of the nave there is the old Trans. corbel table, below the present clerestory. Also in the N. aisle there are grotesque corbel heads of so rude a character that they can hardly be later than the original Trans. The N. arcade itself, however, is distinctly E.E., and seems to represent the first alteration of the Trans. church. The E. and W. responds are of an earlier character, and possibly may be fragments of the original Trans. arcade. The Dec. alterations are of two dates. Late in the Geometrical period two windows were inserted in the Trans. frames S. of chancel. The transomed window S. of nave is similar in character. The S. transeptal chapel must have been also built at this time, for its S. window has early tracery with intersecting straight lines.[1] The other transept windows belong to the next alteration, about 1350, when the E. window of the church was inserted, and the N. aisle altered for the second time, and given windows with flowing tracery, with S. door and piscina to correspond. The font may be of the same period. Finally, the early Perp. clerestory with wooden roof was set on the existing walls of the nave.

There are many interesting and beautiful objects. First comes the strange and beautiful tomb of Antony Forster, 1572, with a Latin inscription highly commending his virtues and accomplishments. Near it is the alabaster tomb of Sir William Hunter, historian of India, d. 1900. There are two brasses, dated 1577 and 1580. Note also (1) old stalls in chancel with excellent poppy-heads; (2) Jacobean pulpit, with large handsome pew of the same style near it; (3) chained Bible of 1611; (4) Dec. piscina and canopied tomb-recesses in transept; (5) curious statue of Queen Elizabeth which once stood in Cumnor Park; (6) copies of some letters of Amy Robsart; (7) circular wooden staircase to belfry with date 1685; (8) blocked entrance to roodloft. The name of the village inn, "The Bear and Ragged Staff," has an obvious reference to Lord Leicester.

Curridge Common (2 m. S.W. of Hermitage) is one of

[1] *Cf.* similar windows at Ferry Hinksey and at Stanton St John (Oxon.).

Cumnor Church

the smaller commons on the N. of the Kennet Valley,
little inferior to the rest in beauty, with clumps of dark
pine amid the gorse and heather. Right on the common
is a red-brick modern chapel.

Denchworth (2½ m. W. of Wantage Road station) is an
out-of-the-way village in the Vale of the White Horse.
It contains the remains of both a churchyard cross and
a village cross. Near the latter is a pretty timber-built
house. The small cruciform church was badly restored
by Street in 1852. The S. door is restored Norman, the
N. transept arch E.E., and the S. transept arch Dec.
Otherwise the church is Perp. Two of the windows are
good. The font is restored Perp., and there is a low
Perp. tower. Note also a good squint, a sill-sedile, a
ruined stoup, and blocked-up indications of older work
in N. wall. There are four brasses: (1) W. Say, 1493;
(2) Oliver Hyde, 1516; (3) William Hyde and wife,
1562 (this is a palimpsest, the original inscription being
a very interesting one, recording the laying of the foundation stone of Bisham Priory (*q.v.*) by Edward III.,
at the request of the founder, Sir William de
Mountagu); (4) William Hyde, 1567. The Hydes were
formerly lords of the manor, their mansion, somewhat
E. of the church, being now a farmhouse. Here Amy
Robsart was their guest in 1558 and 1559, and was
visited more than once by her husband, Dudley. (See
Cumnor.) The house retains the main Perp. door and
three Perp. windows, all facing W., and another Perp.
door facing E. Two of the windows have ancient hood-
mouldings, the third has blocked tracery. S. of the
house are the remains of the moat and fishponds. The
church once contained a parish library, some books
belonging to which are still at the Vicarage, but which
was destroyed by Street.

Devil's Highway is a remarkable Roman road, leading from London to Silchester (*Calleva Atrebatum*) and mentioned in the Itinerary of Antoninus. It crosses the Thames at *Pontes* (Staines) and thence proceeds in a direction generally W. It enters Berkshire near Bagshot, and forms a track of which the stone causeway used not long ago to be distinctly traceable among the heath and fir plantations, thus giving the road its name. It passes close to Rapley Pond, then by a clump of aged thorns called Wickham Bushes, otherwise " the Town," where traces of a small Romano-British village have been discovered. Here it is joined by a track (possibly Roman) running S. from Cæsar's Camp (see *Easthampstead*), which is about ¾ m. N. It now passes a little N. of Broadmoor Asylum and reaches Crowthorne, where its course becomes less certain. It must run a little N. of the remarkably straight road called the Duke's Drive, which leads from Crowthorne past Wellington College station to Finchampstead Ridges. Near Finchampstead there are some remains of a rectangular camp. From here the road disappears practically, till it crosses the Blackwater close to its junction with the Whitewater, after which it forms the S. boundary of the county, nearly as far as Silchester.

W. of Silchester another Roman road mentioned in the Itinerary of Antoninus runs to *Spinae* (Speen near Newbury). The county boundary trends N. at Silchester for two or three miles, but when it again comes S., the line of the Roman road again coincides with it for awhile. Close to where it re-enters Berkshire is the *Imp Stone*, supposed to be a Roman milestone. There is no inscription to back up this tradition, but the name is old, and may refer to the first letters of a vanished inscription. W. of this point there are few if any traces of the road.

Didcot will be only too well known as a junction

on the G.W.R. which all of the better expresses carefully avoid. The new houses and church which are prominently in view S. of the railway are singularly uninteresting. Strictly speaking, however, these are not Didcot, but Newtown. The real Didcot, which lies hidden a little to the S.W., is of a very different character. Five minutes' walk from the grimy railway station takes us into a rural Arcadia, where the bustle and rumble of the frequently passing trains seem strangely irrelevant. The village is of a peaceful, old-world character, and is embowered in trees. The pretty and interesting church lies opposite to a timber-built house, now used as a schoolroom. It has a singularly beautiful approach, along a smooth sward, with a huge decrepit yew, and an ancient cross with restored head. The pretty wooden porch is modern. The date of the church is somewhat uncertain. The oldest object is the E.E. font. Next comes the S. arcade, which Parker calls E.E., but which seems rather very early Dec. (c. 1270). The new chancel arch rests on old Dec. side columns. The old windows (in S. aisle and N. of chancel) are good late Dec. showing clearly the approach of Perp. There is a singular two-light Dec. window (now internal) over the stairs of the rood-loft, which are nearly perfect. The W. window is Perp. and has some old glass. There are several new windows imitating the old Dec. one, and a new N. aisle. The small shingled tower and spire are supported in an interior wooden framework. The roofs are good, and there are two piscinæ. N. of chancel (inside) there is a grotesque head, from which projects a ring (cf. *Blewbury*). Close to S. wall, but hidden by pews, is a recumbent effigy, possibly of an abbot of Abingdon in the 13th cent.

DONNINGTON (1 m. N. of Newbury) is celebrated for its castle, which belonged to the Abberbury family, and was crenellated in 1385 by Sir Richard Abberbury. In 1415 he sold it to Thomas Chaucer, probably son of the poet, who at once resold it to Sir John Phelipp, who had married his daughter Alice. Sir John died in the same year, and Alice inherited the estate. She afterwards married the unfortunate Duke of Suffolk (see *Ewelme* in " Little Guide to Oxfordshire "). Since the poet died in 1400, this date throws great doubt on the pleasing but unconfirmed local tradition that he himself lived in the castle, and planted three oak-trees in the park. If the tale is true, he could only have been here as the guest of Sir Richard Abberbury. But it is more probable that he has been confused with his son Thomas.[1] The subsequent changes of ownership of the castle are of little interest. During the Great Civil War it was garrisoned by the Royalists and held by Col. Boys. In August and September 1644 it was fiercely attacked, but was relieved by King Charles upon his return from his triumph at Lostwithiel. Directly afterwards followed the Second battle of Newbury, in which the castle was an important point of the Royalist defences. In the night following Charles retreated, after leaving his guns and ammunition in the castle. About ten days later he made a successful sortie, and transferred them all safely to Oxford, before the Roundheads, who lay at Newbury, realized that he was in the neighbourhood. The castle finally capitulated only when the news came of Charles' surrender to the Scots. It was, as usual, demolished. At present the only part standing is the gateway,

[1] Compare the similar confusion between Geoffrey Chaucer and his son Thomas at Woodstock (" Little Guide to Oxfordshire ").

flanked by two round towers. The style is early Perp. but features are few. Note the curious grotesque heads on the upper stories. Of the rest of the castle little remains but the foundations. The ruins are picturesque, and open to all visitors.

The so-called *Donnington Priory* is a modern mansion, built on the site of a small house of Crouched Friars, first referred to in 1404, but of which the founder and the date of foundation are unknown. *Donnington Hospital*, at the foot of the hill near the bridge over the Lambourn, is a very ancient foundation, known to be existing in Edward II.'s reign. It was refounded by Sir Richard Abberbury in 1393, who directed the inmates to attend Mass in the adjoining friars' chapel. In was confiscated in 1545, but restored in 1570 by Charles Howard, Earl of Nottingham, and termed Queen Elizabeth's Hospital. The present buildings are modern but picturesque, and show the royal arms over the door.

Dragon Hill. (See *White Horse Hill.*)

Drayton (2½ m. S. of Abingdon) is in the centre of a flat district. The church has been much restored, but its history can be fairly well made out. The walls of the chancel were until lately the original Norman. On the S. side one sole relic is left, the round-headed priest's door ; but the N. wall, with its Norman windows, was removed in 1872 to build a new organ-chamber. In E.E. times the whole church seems to have been remodelled. The chancel is now entirely E.E., but the only original feature is the lancet triplet at the end. The S. chapel is E.E., as is shown by the piscina and aumbry, and the responds of the arch leading into it. There is also an E.E. piscina in the nave. (There are four piscinæ in the church, of which three are certainly E.E.). In the Perp. period the N. arcade and

H   113

aisle were built, and the tower with its fine arch; also windows were inserted S. of the nave and chapel. There is a Jacobean pulpit, some good seat-ends, and a brass to John Tirrall (1632), who also gave one of the carved pews. A "nearly perfect rood-loft" seems to have finally disappeared, unless the old woodwork now built into the S. porch is a fragment of it. But the gem of the church is the beautiful 15th-cent. alabaster reredos (in S. chapel) with six gilt and coloured panels. It was discovered buried in the churchyard. The village has both a churchyard cross and a village cross.

Duxford is a hamlet and ford on the Upper Thames, about half-way between Tadpole Bridge and New Bridge. (See *Hinton Waldrist*.)

Earley is 1½ m. S.E. of Reading, of which it is now practically a suburb. It is a pleasant place, on fairly high sandy ground, and with a modern church.

East Garston (or more correctly *Esgarston*) is a most delightful village in the Lambourn Valley. It lies deep-sunk, close to the clear, sparkling stream, and consists mainly of a string of thatched cottages interspersed with trees and elder bushes, and with the bare swelling Downs rising up on both sides. The cruciform church is large and fine, but the "complete restorations" of 1875 and 1882 have left very little ancient work. There are two Trans. doorways and an E.E. pillar piscina. Otherwise the church is mainly Dec., with Perp. windows N. of nave. Some of the Dec. windows may be old, especially the curious one E. of the Seymour Chapel. Some fragments of older work have been built into the outside walls. The chancel tower and S. arcade are entirely new. There is a Jacobean pulpit and a ruined stoup.

Eastbury also lies in the Lambourn Valley, between Lambourn and East Garston, and is equally picturesque, since the river runs beside the road, and nearly every cottage has its separate little bridge. The church is modern but the steps and base of the old village cross remain. There is an old red-brick manor-house of the Fitzwarrens, with picturesque gables, clustered chimneys and stone-mullioned windows. Inside is a panelled chamber with beautifully carved mantelpiece. There is also an old octagonal pigeon-house in the village.

Easthampstead (1 m. S. of Bracknell station) has a modern church, containing a brass to Thomas Berwyk, rector (1443). There is an epitaph by Pope to a poet friend of his named Fenton, and four good windows by Sir Edward Burne-Jones. The village stands just N. of the forest region of the Bagshot Sands, which formerly was a part of Windsor Forest, a series of hills forming a plateau from 250 to 400 ft. high, covered with pine woods and heather and very sparsely inhabited. About a mile S. is *Cæsar's Camp*, a prehistoric encampment on high ground. It follows the contours of the hill and consequently takes an odd leaflike shape. Though not a Roman camp, it was certainly occupied by the Romans, and it is said that the road, which leads from the S. entrance to the Devil's Highway (*q.v.*), which is less than a mile S., is also Roman. A little N. of the camp is another remarkable road, called the *Nine Mile Ride*, which traverses the forest in a straight line from E. to W., regardless of ups and downs, and mostly parallel to the Devil's Highway. This is also considered a Roman road by some authorities. It is, however, worth remarking that there are many straight roads in this district which are not Roman. Its course is remarkably lonely, as it hardly passes a single house. The E. part is not very practicable for cyclists, but the W. part is better and gives a good view of the pine forests. There are several other broad and straight grass paths through these forests, many of which curiously radiate in starlike fashion from definite centres. One of these is just S. of Cæsar's Camp. A second, *Upper Star Post* (the highest point on the plateau, 423 ft.), is gained by taking the track leading S.E. from the first point. By going still farther S.E. we soon reach *Lower Star Post* or *Wishmore Cross*, on which as many as ten tracks converge. The view of so many straight avenues, leading away in all directions through the silent pine woods, is most impressive. Before the modern roads were cut these tracks were used as bridle-paths across the Forest District, and Wishmore Cross was a notorious haunt of highwaymen. A gallows used to stand here, the last fragments of which are said to have been carried off as a trophy some time ago by two boys from Wellington College.

Eaton Hastings (3 m. N.W. of Faringdon) is just S. of the Upper Thames. The interesting little church is well placed on a knoll just above the river. It is entirely Norman and E.E., but it is somewhat difficult to state exactly what parts belong to the Trans. period. The N. side of the nave, with door and one window, is pure Norman, also the priest's door (S. of chancel) and the font. The chancel arch is certainly Trans., the blocked S. arcade and the two plain lancets in chancel are probably also in that style, but may be later. The rest of the work is late E.E. (c. 1240-1250)—*i.e.* (1) the chancel, which has a group of three foliated lancets at the E. end, and single foliated lancets N. and S. (note also the sedilia, aumbry and piscina) ; (2) the S. aisle of nave, which has disappeared, but of which the windows and door (all foliated) have been built up in the blocked arcade ; (3) one foliated lancet N. of nave. In the blocked arcade there are also a large foliated arch and two niches. The W. window is late Dec. (restored). The modern village has changed its position and left the church isolated.

Ellensfordmere. (See *Poughley Priory.*)

Enborne (about 3 m. W. of Newbury) has a church of some interest. The nave is Norman and has two good arcades of three bays each. Of these the N. arcade had been blocked, but when the S. aisle was restored the N. aisle was rebuilt and its arcade reopened. The chancel arch rests on Norman imposts, but the arch itself is modern. The font is Norman and also a blocked door in the S. aisle. The chancel is E.E., with a pretty piscina and two single lancets on each side. The E. window is a Perp. insertion, and there is another Perp. window E. of S. aisle. The belfry is supported on an internal wooden frame. Note also (1) two good corbel heads; (2) old frescoes N. of altar; (3) two scratched inscriptions to Nicholas Curatus and Richard Elks (1609). (See also *First battle of Newbury.*)

Enborne River is a tributary of the Kennet on the S. and forms the S. boundary of the county for several miles. It flows in a deep-set and well-wooded valley, which forms the S. slope of Greenham and Crookham commons; after which it turns N.E. to join the Kennet not far from Aldermaston.

ENGLEFIELD (1½ m. N.W. of Theale station) is a place of considerable interest. In 871, just before the battle of Ashdown, the Danes, who had seized and fortified Reading, were attacked here by the Berkshire "fyrd," led by the Ealdorman Ethelwulf, and driven back within the "burh" (see *Reading*). The manor belonged to the Englefield family for several centuries, until in the 16th cent. Sir F. Englefield, a devoted Roman Catholic, who had fled from England at Elizabeth's accession, was condemned for treason and the estate forfeited to the Crown. It was given to Sir Francis Walsingham, Elizabeth's famous minister, who sumptuously entertained her here, building a long gallery to the house from the hillside above it, by which the Queen might mount to the first floor without ascending a step. In the next half-century the estate twice changed owners by marriage, passing on the second occasion to the great Royalist, John Paulet, Marquis of Winchester, who defended Basing House for four years, and after the Restoration lived here till his death in 1675. The Benyon family have now held the manor for more than a century. The house is really an ancient Tudor mansion, but it has been quite modernized, and looks brand-new. Its situation, however, is splendid, on rising ground overlooking a fine deer park with an ornamental lake. The *church* is another melancholy illustration of the mischief often done by well-meaning and liberal lords of the manor. What should have been the finest church in the neighbourhood has been transformed into a tasteless modern building. The only ancient work remaining is in the S. aisle, which shows several E.E. features : (1) the splendid arcade of which the details are E.E., but the fantastic character of the capitals suggests that the date is rather before the end of the 12th cent. ; (2) the lancet triplet at E. end of aisle, which is partly restored, but is old outside and has Purbeck marble columns inside. Between arcade and window is a shelf bracket with good dog-tooth and other work, also a blocked squint, which may be Dec. ; (3) on the S. side the E.E. side columns of one of the windows are still left ; (4) the S. door has an E.E. arch both inside and outside. The W. door also has a head partly old. The Englefield N. chapel was built in 1514, but it has been modernized into an organ-chamber. To it have been relegated a Trans. pillar piscina, the oldest feature in the church, and some remains of the Perp. screen of dark oak. There are several good monuments. In the S. aisle is an effigy of a warrior (c. 1300) and a wooden effigy of a lady. In the chancel is a good Perp. altar-tomb in grey marble, from which the brasses have been torn. There are several monuments to the Englefield family, a member of which was buried here as lately as 1822. The handsome monument to the famous Marquis of Winchester has a sixteen-line inscription by Dryden. Among the Benyon monuments is a curious sculpture depicting the sudden death of Mrs Mary Benyon in 1777.

Ermine Street. (See *Speen.*)

FARINGDON is an important market town on a branch line of the G.W.R. It lies near the western extremity of the Coral Rag plateau. To the S. of Faringdon the Coral Rag gives place to the Lower Greensand, which however does not extend N. to the town itself, but one of its outliers caps a prominent little hill just to the E. This is crowned by the Faringdon clump, locally known as the " Folly," a group of dark firs, which is one of the most conspicuous landmarks in the Vale of the White Horse, and from which there is a fine view over the flat Valley of the Upper Thames.

The town is of high antiquity, and there is a tradition that in Saxon times it was the site of a king's palace. Alfred the Great himself is locally believed to have lived here, and it was the deathplace of his son, Edward the Elder, in 924. In Stephen's reign an " adulterine " castle was built here by Robert of Gloucester, but was soon utterly destroyed by Stephen himself. In 1203 John gave the manor to Beaulieu Abbey in Hants. No traces of the monks' habitation here are now to be found except in the neighbouring village of Great Coxwell (*q.v.*), where they had a grange. We hear of Henry III., with his queen and Prince Edward, being entertained at Faringdon by the Abbot of Beaulieu. In 1400 the town was slightly connected with the rebellion of the Earls of Kent, Salisbury and Huntingdon against Henry IV. Failing to surprise the King at Windsor, the earls marched westward and passed through Faringdon to Cirencester, where they were defeated by the citizens. The rest of the local history is closely connected with the two notable families of the Untons and the Pyes. The Untons lived at Wadley House (S. of the Oxford Road, 1 m. E. of Faringdon), where Queen Elizabeth was entertained in 1574 by Sir Edward Unton. The most remarkable member of the family was his second son, Sir Henry Unton, who was knighted by the Earl of Leicester for gallantry at Zutphen. He was after-wards sent as ambassador to France and became very intimate with Henry IV. When the young Duke of Guise spoke of Queen Elizabeth "impudently, lightly and over boldly," Sir Henry sent him a famous challenge, of which, however, nothing came. After his premature death in France his widow, Dorothy, kept the estate and entertained King James at Wadley in 1603. The Pyes lived at Faringdon House (just N. of the church), which Sir Robert Pye bought from the heiress in 1622. His son, also Sir Robert Pye, married Hampden's sister, and took an active part in the Great Civil War on the side of the Parliament. In 1644 Faringdon House itself was seized and garrisoned for the King. In April 1645 it was attacked by Cromwell in the course of his cavalry raid round Oxford. He attempted to over-awe the garrison " by sheer audacity," but the tactics which had just proved so successful at Bletchingdon

House (see " Little Guide to Oxfordshire ") failed here, and after two days he was forced to retreat. Next year Sir Robert Pye was placed in command of the troops who were ordered to attack his own home, and the garrison surrendered to him in July 1646. It is incorrect to say that the house at this time belonged to him, for his father did not die until 1662. The estate remained with the family till the 19th cent. In 1790 Henry James Pye, great-great-grandson of Sir Robert the Parliamentarian, was appointed poet laureate. He was called by Sir Walter Scott " eminently respectable in all but his poetry, which was contemptible." He seems to have been the most hopelessly unpoetical of the wonderful succession of poets laureate in the 18th cent. His first ode to George III. was so crowded with allusions to " feathered songsters " that it provoked the epigram :

" When the pie was opened
The birds began to sing.
Wasn't that a dainty dish
To set before the King ? "

In Byron's " Vision of Judgment " occur the lines :

" The monarch, mute till then, exclaimed, ' What, what !
Pye come again ! No more, no more of that ! ' "

One of his poems, " Faringdon Hill," celebrated the beauties of his own home. Admiral Sir Thomas Pye was uncle to the laureate. He was a man of poor ability, but excessive vanity. His nickname was " Nosey," and he is said to have believed that every woman he met fell in love with him.

The town has few ancient memorials. The castle has disappeared. The Salutation Inn is pointed out by tradition as the site of Alfred's palace. Wadley House is approached by a fine avenue, and retains some ancient woodwork. Faringdon House, which has beautiful grounds, was rebuilt in 1780, after a fire, by Pye the laureate, who is also said to have planted Faringdon Clump, though this does not seem to be absolutely certain. In the market-place is a picturesque old town hall, supported on stone columns. The fine cruciform church, however, well maintains the dignity of the town, though its spire was destroyed during the Civil War. It is almost entirely late Trans. and E.E. The oldest feature is the plain Norman N. door. Its porch has now been turned into a baptistery, containing the octagonal font (late Dec.). The nave, with aisles and S. porch, central tower and transepts, are all of one date (c. 1200). The style is essentially E.E., but retains a few Norm. details—*i.e.* some round arches and square abaci. The chancel is pure E.E., but perhaps not much later in date. In the nave note the magnificent Trans. arcades, with round arches, E.E.-looking columns, sunken quatrefoils in the spandrils, and round-headed clerestory windows. The round-headed S. door has good E.E. ironwork. The S. aisle retains its round-headed windows, but in the N. aisle and the W. wall late Perp. windows have been inserted, also a Perp. W. door. The central tower rests on four splendid piers with square abaci. The arches are pointed and have sunken quatrefoils above. The tower itself is of a massive simplicity, with lancets only on the S. and W. sides. It is essentially E.E., but of the same date as the rest. (*i.e.* 1200). The N. transept has a pretty inserted Dec. window with interior foliation. The S. transept was destroyed in the Civil War, but was rebuilt in 1853 in the original style. The chancel is entirely lighted by lancets, one of which forms a low-side window with original grating and shutter. There is a large E.E. piscina, beautiful sedilia (c. 1260-1280), in style Trans. to Dec. but retaining the dog-tooth ornament, and three aumbries. The woodwork with poppy-heads is modern. On the wall are six effigies, but they seem to belong to three brasses only—*i.e.* (1) Thomas Faringdon, wife and daughter (c. 1450); (2) John Parker and wife (1485); (3) John Sadler, vicar (1505).

The *Unton Chapel* is the aisle of the N. transept. It contains several good 16th-cent. monuments—*i.e.* to (1) Sir Alexander Unton and his two wives, with brasses (d. 1547); (2) Sir Thomas Unton (d. 1553); (3) Sir Edward Unton (d. 1583), who married a daughter of the Protector Somerset; (4) Sir Henry Unton, the ambassador (d. 1596). His monument was erected by his wife, Dorothy, a very pleasing effigy of whom was kneeling at his feet, but it has been banished to the *Pye Chapel*, now the organ-chamber, N. of the chancel, which is debased in style and contains several ugly monuments, among them that of Admiral Pye (" Nosey ").

Farnborough (6 m. W. of Compton station) is a small village, lying high on the chalk uplands, not far S. of the Ridgeway. The small rectangular church was originally Norman. In the last restoration a Norman door and two small Norman windows were reopened in the thick N. wall, and an E.E. pillar piscina was replaced. The other windows are insertions of little interest. An original Perp. window has a little old glass. The tower is Perp.; the chancel arch and font new. (See also Introduction, p. 12).

Fawley (4½ m. N. of Great Shefford station, 6½ m. S. of Wantage Road station) is a village with a modern church lying a little W. of the Wantage and Hungerford road. Half-a-mile S. is *South Fawley*, where there is an old Elizabethan house, formerly the seat of the

Moores, but now used as a farm. If a turn be taken W. of the Wantage and Hungerford road, the house is the first on the L. It is reached by some old elms, forming part of an ancient avenue. The house was built a little after 1600. It has good gables, an embattled parapet, square windows with stone mullions, and picturesque chimneys. On the E. is a fine Renaissance porch. S. of the house are traceable the bowling-green, a raised terrace and the fishponds. The well is very deep and worked by a huge wheel. Inside the house there is a splendid dark oak staircase, a long panelled room, said to have been used by the Moores as a chapel, a panelled bedroom, and another bedroom, where there is a window-pane on which is scratched, " D——r Molly Moore, ch——ng Nelly Moore, Pr——y Anastasia Moore." These young ladies were daughters of Sir Richard Moore (d. 1737), and all died unmarried.

Fernham is a hamlet 2 m. S. of Faringdon, with a modern church, W. of which is an old-looking farm-house, forming a quaint pile of buildings.

Finchampstead (2 m. W. of Wellington College station) is in a wild and pretty part of the county. The road from the station, bordered by giant Wellingtonias, leads uphill to *Finchampstead Ridges*. Here it turns and runs along the top of a beautiful common of heath and bracken, which to the S. slopes downwards over hanging woods to the valley of the Blackwater, allowing far views over Hampshire and Surrey. To the N. are thick pine woods. Presently the road turns L. and descends to the village. The church stands by itself, finely placed on a little hill to the N.W., which some antiquaries believe the site of an old camp. The church walls, including the circular E. apse, appear in the main the original Norman, but there are no existing features, only slight traces of the original windows. There are, however, a very fine early Norman font, and a Norman or Trans. pillar piscina with aumbry. The other ancient features (arches and windows) are late Dec. or early Perp. A door in the aisle is dated 1590. The carved pulpit may contain fragments of the old screen. The brick tower is dated 1720. There are brass plates to Elizabeth Hynde, 1580, and a black marble tomb to Richard Palmer, 1670. Note the fine yews.

Foxcombe Hill. (See *Hinksey.*)

Frilford (3½ m. W. of Abingdon) is situated on the Oxford and Wantage road, which suggests by its straightness that it was originally a Roman road. The ground-plan of a small Roman villa was discovered here in 1884. Also midway between Frilford and Garford are several Romano-British graves. The road passes through Frilford Common, a charming open expanse, with a fine view of the Berkshire Downs, seen over the woods to the S. of it.

Frilsham (2½ m. E. of Hermitage station) is a village in the Upper Valley of the Pang. There seems to have been a Roman villa here also, and a Roman altar was discovered here in 1780. The church is very plain Norman, with N. and S. doors and two small windows in that style. The other windows are Perp. There is a Norman font, some late poppy-heads in the nave, and a modern brick tower.

Frogmore. (See *Windsor.*)

FYFIELD (5 m. W. of Abingdon) has a very interesting church which was burnt down on 26th Oct. 1893. The woodwork perished, but the stone was comparatively little damaged, and a very careful restoration has made the church much the same in appearance as it was before the fire. The oldest parts are the three doors in the nave, two of which are very late Trans. (c. 1200), and the third, the S. door, somewhat later (E.E.). These were retained when the church was rebuilt in the 14th cent. by Sir John Golafre, lord of the manor, who died 1363. In the next century another Sir John Golafre, who died 1442, grandson of the former, built or rebuilt the N. aisle of the nave in Perp. style, intending it for his chantry. The ugly octagonal W. tower is modern. The finest parts of the church are Dec., and due to the elder Sir John Golafre. The nave has no signs of the original style, except the Dec. corbels of the vaulting shafts, but the S. transept has a string-course with ball-flower running round it (like the chancel) and a Dec. window. Note the quaint tomb of George Dale, Fellow of Oriel and Principal of St Mary's Hall, Oxford (d. 1625). The chancel is very good Dec. (c. 1325). A cornice band with ball-flower runs high up on both sides. The windows had to be restored considerably after the fire, but may be seen to be old on the outside. There is much beautiful work— i.e. (1) the sedilia under ogee canopies ; (2) the elaborate and beautiful piscina (both these are late Dec., but the next two features are later, and may be called Trans. to Perp.) ; (3) stone reredos (or rather the cornice of the reredos), with a tabernacle in the centre ; (4) stone credence table (on N. side), supported by a carved pillar[1] ; (5) splendid Tudor tomb (N. side) under rich canopy, ornamented with foliage. It is said to belong to Lady Catherine Gordon, the " White Rose of Scotland," who married Perkin Warbeck, and three other husbands, the last being Christopher Ashfield of Fyfield, where she died in 1527. The windows have good outside corbels, two representing Edward II. and Isabella. There is also a priest's door. The N. aisle has good Prep. arcade and windows (restored). Two

[1] Lately removed to the nave.

bays form the Golafre Chantry, containing the magnificent tomb of Sir John Golafre the younger (d. 1442), with an armed effigy above and shrouded skeleton below. Note the piscina and blocked stairs to rood-loft. Sir John also founded a hospital here, and was a benefactor to the bridge at Abingdon (*q.v.*). The chancel and chantry screens perished in the fire, but have been replaced by good modern work. The font has a Dec. base.

N.W. of the church is the old manor-house, originally built about 1325 by the elder John Golafre, who married the daughter of John de Fyfield. The entrance hall and the solar, with open timber roof, are partly the original Dec. work, and the doorway still shows a row of ball-flower. The hall may have included the adjacent dining-room. It has a flat roof with timber rafters, and several archways with Dec. mouldings leading out of it. Above the porch is the Lady's Bower, a tiny chamber lighted by a pretty little oaken Dec. window. The only other Dec. window, also oaken, has been set in the gable of the solar. At the far end of the solar there are indications of a vanished minstrels' gallery. Below in the kitchen may be noticed the massive rafters which form the solar floor, and there is a good plain Dec. door in the larder. Another room opening from the solar has a fireplace with the date 1664. This is out of place, for it belongs to the E. part of the house, which was rebuilt in the 17th cent., and shows windows with straight mullions. In the topmost story of this part the timber of the gables intrudes into the rooms with a very quaint effect. The house was well restored by James Parker, the Oxford antiquary, who lived here some years. Half-a-mile E., in the fork of the roads leading to Abingdon and Oxford, is a large but now decrepit tree, usually known as the Tubney

Elm. It is probable that this was the tree referred to by Matthew Arnold in the lines:

> "Maidens, who from the distant hamlets come
>   To dance around the Fyfield Elm in May."

Tubney Church, a little distance farther on the Oxford Road, was built in 1848. Two or three large elms are growing near it. The extensive Tubney Woods spread out to the N. of the hamlet.

Garford (4½ m. W. of Abingdon) is a small village in the flat valley of the Ock. The little E.E. church was mainly rebuilt in 1878. The E. and W. windows are lancets, and the S. door has E.E. mouldings and iron-work. There is one other old window (Perp.) S. of nave. Note the old hourglass-stand, a sort of iron cage.

Garston. (See *East Garston.*)

Ginge. (See *West Hendred.*)

Goosey (about 1 m. N. of Challow station) may be named from its large grassy common, round which the cottages are scattered at intervals. One shows two clipt yews. The little rectangular church has no arch and is mostly restored E.E. There is one Norman win-dow (S. of nave), in which has been placed a fragment of old glass. All the lancets are restored. The bowl-shaped piscina, the stoup and the door-key are all E.E. There is a good Dec. roof, but resting on E.E. corbel heads. The chancel windows are debased Perp. The bell-cote is supported on an interior wooden frame. There is an old octagonal font.

Greenham (near Newbury) has a new church. (For Greenham Common see *Crookham Common.*)

Grimsbury Castle. (See *Cold Ash.*)

Hagborne is the name of two villages under the E. part of the Berkshire Downs, where the Upper Greensand extends into a wide plateau. This corner of the county, though not in general prolific in trees, is devoted to fruit-growing, which gives it a pleasant and somewhat distinctive appearance.

HAGBORNE, EAST (2 m. S. of Didcot station), is one of the prettiest villages in the county. It is full of quaint and delightful old houses, many half timbered, others with tiled fronts. The brick is often set zigzag fashion, and the gables and thatched roofs are charming. The prettiest bit is to the W. of the village, where several of the best of the old houses stand round the tall uninjured village cross, raised on its pedestal of six steps, with the church in the background. There are the stumps of two other ancient crosses, one in the centre of the village, and another just beyond the hamlet of Coscote, W. of the village. In Coscote itself is one of the best of the old houses, with good barge-boards over the gables, and fronted with ornamental tiles. The strikingly handsome church presents some architectural difficulties. The oldest portions are apparently some grotesque and rude corbel heads on which the chancel arch rests. There are three in a cluster on the S. side, and one large one on the N. Another of these heads is on the E. respond of the S. nave arcade. All are decidedly Norman in character. If we compare them with the similar figures at E. Hendred, we shall reach the conclusion that the chancel arch and S. arcade to which they belong, and which show mainly E.E. features, really date from c. 1200, when the style had not entirely freed itself from Trans. details.[1] The N. arcade, which has octagonal pillars, though similar in character,

[1] Arcades of this date occur in the neighbouring churches of Ardington, Harwell and E. Hendred. It is supposed that a sudden influx of prosperity into the district caused several churches to be rebuilt about the same time.

seems pure E.E., and therefore somewhat later in date. The tower arch is also E.E. Both arcades run nearly the whole length of the church, only the E. bay of the chancel standing clear of them. In this bay, and parallel with the arches, are the only two lancets in the church, apparently of the same date as the arcades. The long side aisles which flank the arcades overlap the chancel, so as to form side chapels. These aisles have been altered, so that the outside of the church is entirely Dec. and Perp. The N. aisle, with door (showing good ironwork) and windows, is late Dec. The E. bay has been railed off by a fragment of an old Perp. rood-screen and used as a vestry. It is lighted by two windows with some good Dec. glass. Note especially the Purification, in which the Child is holding a basket with *three* pigeons. The monuments in the aisle to John York and his wife (brasses dated 1403 and 1413), who claim to have founded the aisle, must refer to the S. aisle, and have been removed. There are two other brasses, dated 1445 and 1627. The S. aisle is now entirely Perp., with all its windows, S. door, and an exterior cornice, showing grotesque figures. There is a squint leading from this aisle. Other Perp. alterations are : (1) the large E. window ; (2) the clerestory on both sides ; (3) the flat panelled roof which has several interesting carvings ; (4) the font, near which is a small chrismatory niche ; (5) the wooden pulpit ; (6) the two good wooden porches ; (7) the splendid W. tower, which has a good stair-turret, and a niche for the sanctus-bell at the top, a very unusual place. Note also the three piscinæ and the rood-stairs.

Hagborne, West, contains no church, but has some picturesque cottages.

Hampstead Marshall (2½ m. S.E. of Kintbury station)

East Hagbourne

is a village the manor of which has been held by many celebrated persons. The name is derived from Gilbert the Marshal, who held that office in Henry I.'s Court. Of his descendants the most famous was William the Marshal, Earl of Pembroke, who governed in Henry III.'s minority. As his five sons died without issue, his daughter brought the estate and office into the family of the Bigods, Earls of Norfolk. One of these was Roger Bigod, who quarrelled fiercely with Edward I., on which the King for a time took away the manor. On his death the office of marshal was separated from the manor, which passed to various owners. At last in the 17th cent. it was bought by Sir William Craven (see *Ashdown*), who built here a magnificent house, not, however, as is sometimes stated, for his mistress, the Queen of Bohemia, for she died in 1662, before the house was begun. It was entirely burnt down in 1718, and only its site can be traced. A relic of it exists in eight pairs of gate-pillars, three of which are set up on high ground in the park. The other five pairs are in the walls of the great garden. The central drive of the park is open to vehicles and foot passengers, but not to cyclists. The little church is in a corner of the park, and not very interesting. It consists largely of brick and flint with a brick tower, and was rebuilt in the time of James I., and restored in 1893. The N. aisle is early Perp., with an arcade and two good windows. On the S. there are a plain Norman door and two late Perp. windows. The fittings, including the pulpit (dated 1622), are Jacobean.

Hampstead Norris is a village named after the Norreys, who were large landowners in the neighbourhood. It is well situated in the upper valley of the Pang, close to its source. The rectangular church retains two Norman doors (N. and S.), but is otherwise mainly E.E., and lighted principally by lancets, of which those in the chancel are good and unrestored. The N. porch and W. tower are Perp. On the N.E. of tower the figure VIII. is let in in bronze. There is also an opening for the sanctus-bell. There is a modern vestry and organ-chamber. Also the chancel arch and font are modern. The rood-loft stairs are vaulted and lighted by a tiny Perp. window. Facing it on the S. side is a larger Perp. window, which lighted the rood-loft. Note also (1) trefoil-headed piscina (E.E.), double aumbry, and sill-sedilia; (2) E.E. stoup; (3) Jacobean roof with date 1635; (4) square piscina in nave; (5) fragment of carving framed on S. wall.

Hanney, East (1½ m. N. of Wantage Road station), is an uninteresting village in the flat part of the Vale of the White Horse, on the road between Oxford and Wantage.

Hanney, West, is 1 m. to the W., and contains a fine cruciform church. Of this it is somewhat difficult to give a connected account, for it is very mixed in style, and since the last restoration the chancel, S. transept, S. arcade, clerestory, W. window, and N. porch must be considered new. The only ancient parts are: (1) The N. door, which is pure but late Norman, with twisted side columns and arabesque capitals. The Norman windows in the N. wall of nave seem new. (2) The tower, which is Trans., and over the N. transept. The Trans. arch leading to transept is now blocked by an ugly hoarding, and entrance is by a W. door, E.E. in character. The windows are lancets, with the exception of a pretty inserted Dec. window. The top story is late and debased Perp. (3) The font, which is also Trans., with vertical bands of rose-moulding on the bowl; (4) the chancel arch (good E.E.); (5) the S. aisle, which is good late Dec., and best seen from outside. It shows a door, three windows and a cornice in the style. Note also a blocked squint, Perp. screen, Jacobean pulpit, and rood-loft staircase. There are six good brasses on the chancel floor: (1) a priest of 14th cent., but the date is defective; (2) Humphry Cheyne, 1537; (3) John Ayshcombe, 1591; (4) Christopher Lytcott, 1599; (5) Francis Wellesborne, 1602; (6) Oliver Ayshcombe, 1611. Note tablet to Elizabeth Bowles, who died 1715, aged one hundred and twenty-four. Also altar-tomb to John Ayshcombe, 1655.

Near the church are a red-brick 18th-cent. house and a pleasant old gabled house called the Priory. Of an old manor-house of the Yates, N. of the church, there are but few traces.

HARWELL (2 m. S.E. of Steventon station) is a pretty village embedded in trees, many of them fruit trees, which contrast effectively with the bare chalk slopes immediately to the S. The interesting cruciform church presents some difficulties. The nave arcades, and the transepts, which are lighted by deeply-splayed lancets, were built about 1200, and represent the somewhat undeveloped E.E., which has not yet wholly shaken off Trans. features. The graceful W. tower is later E.E. (c. 1250). Note the foliated arch in the second story, and the plate tracery in the top story. The nave doors and the font are plain E.E., but the windows have been altered to Dec. (now restored). The chancel is entirely later Dec., though the windows do not seem all of the same date, the low-side windows being earlier than the rest. The fine five-light E. window has peculiar tracery. The side windows have a little old glass. There is also a good priest's door (Dec.). Both the roof and the chancel arch are Dec., the latter springing from two large grotesque figures, of which there are three other examples in the chancel. The double sedilia is also Dec., but the pretty double piscina is E.E., the only trace of this style in the chancel. The interesting old screen, which has a squint, shows Dec. shafts with Perp. upper part. Note also foliated cross on floor. There are few traces of the Perp. style. There is a brass in N. transept to John Jennery and wife, 1599.

Hatford (about 3 m. E. of Faringdon and 3 m. N. of Challow station) has an ugly new church, the old church, which has some beautiful features, having been allowed to tumble into ruins. It was originally Norman, of which there remain S. door (good), chancel arch, another plain door and a window. It was largely altered about the time that E.E. was passing into the Geometrical style. Four windows in all belong to this period. Note also the two low-side windows, the trefoiled piscina, a Dec. sepulchral recess with male effigy, and a large Perp. "pulpit" window. There are three brass plates, dated 1614, 1629 and 1637. In this church Sir Edward Unton (see *Faringdon*) married the daughter of Protector Somerset.

HENDRED, EAST (2½ m. S. of Steventon), is a very interesting village, and one of the prettiest that lie under the Downs. In the Middle Ages it was famous for its cloth industry, and an important annual fair was held on the Golden Mile, a green road stretching to the summit of the Downs at Scutchamore Knob (*q.v.*). Its former prosperity is shown by the large number of timber-built houses, many thatched and others gabled, which are scattered up and down among the thick-growing trees. At the very entrance of the village, between two converging roads, stands a small ancient chapel, sometimes called *Champ's Chapel*. This was built by the Carthusian monks of Shene in Surrey, who were formerly owners of Hendred Manor. It

is now boarded up and surrounded by a railing, but
there is little which cannot be seen from the outside.
The chapel is Perp., and shows a door and three windows
in the style. Inside are the rood-screen, two image-
brackets and an aumbry. On the N. are two cottages,
of which the timber-built one with a barge-board
seems to have been the residence of the monks. Proceeding S. down the street we pass an Elizabethan
farmhouse, and several other old-looking houses.
Presently on the L., at the bottom of the hill, is the
manor-house, belonging to Mr J. J. Eyston, whose
ancestors acquired the manor by marriage in 1450.
The family was connected by marriage with that of
Sir Thomas More, of which there is a large picture
in the house. They are also Roman Catholics, and the
chapel attached to the house is one of the very few in
England in which Roman services have been continu-
ously held. It was plundered and outraged by the
soldiers of William of Orange when they passed by this
way. They are stated to have dressed up a " mawkin "
in the chapel vestments, and burnt it on a bonfire at
Oxford. The front of the house is old, though restored,
and shows the monogram of the Jesuits under one of
the gables. The chapel was E.E., and retains two
lancet windows, cut in the thickness of the wall ;
otherwise it is restored or modern. One of the lancets
has some old glass with the initials of Hugh Faringdon,
Abbot of Reading. In the vestry are two altar-slabs
from Poughley (*q.v.*), one with a recumbent effigy.
A little farther we reach the parish *church*. The
earliest part, the arcades, though light and graceful,
date from about 1200, so that the E.E. style has not
entirely shaken off Trans. features. Note the rudimentary character of the foliage " stalk," and the
early grotesque heads just above the capitals, indeed, in

one instance, among the foliage. Nearly all the windows are now restored Dec., some of which seem to have been original. The nave roof also contains some old Dec. work. The aisles had a curious peculiarity, being wider at the E. end than the W. In the S. aisle a Perp. pillar was placed in the centre at the E. end. At the late restoration the whole S. aisle was widened, and the old pillar, with two new ones similar to it, now forms a second S. aisle. The effect is very curious, as the three tall columns support the roof without capitals or arches. At the E. end of the aisle is the *Eyston Chapel* (c. 1500), with three old Perp. windows, showing a little old glass. It is separated from the chancel by a Perp. arcade of two bays, and from the S. aisle by a fragment of the Perp. rood-screen and rood-loft. Part of the old screen is also said to have been used for the choir stalls. The W. tower, with window and tower arch, is also good late Perp. The bells are good, and the clock dates from 1528, one of the oldest in England still doing its work. Above the new screen is a curious piece of Perp. carving. There is an old Dec. piscina, a handsome Jacobean pulpit with sounding-board and carved head of Charles I. The reading desk is pre-Reformation and curious. Besides the Eyston monuments there are brasses—*i.e.* John Eyston, 1589, and Henry Eldysley, cloth merchant, 1439. This inscription and another, dated 1479, but apparently lost, testify to the importance of the cloth industry here in the 15th cent.

Hendred, West (about ¾ m. W.), is a smaller but pretty village. The church is in a delightful situation, with a stream murmuring past it, and a bold chalk bluff rising just behind. Also the churchyard contains a fine yew-tree and the stump of a cross. The church is interesting and unrestored ; nearly all late Dec. with

Ferry-Hinksey

some Perp. alterations. The chancel is uniform late Dec., with reticulated windows, chancel arch, piscina, low-side window and corner buttresses. The nave has two late Dec. arcades, but the windows are mainly early Perp. The N. door is plain (blocked). The S. door is also plain, but has a good Perp. porch, with stone rib in the roof. In the S. aisle there is a piscina and two brackets. The W. tower is Perp., but retains late Dec. W. window. There is much good woodwork— *i.e.* (1) font cover, 1630 ; (2) reading desk (these were perhaps patched up out of an old screen) ; (3) Jacobean pulpit ; (4) old panels boarded up for vestry ; (5) old benches ; (6) old pews, one of which has a good Dec. end. There is also a good deal of old tiling, and a little old glass.

About a mile S. is the pretty hamlet of *Ginge*, lying round the wooded hollow from which the W. Hendred stream flows, close under the main chain of the Downs. The principal farm has some Elizabethan parts, but is much restored.

Hermitage has a new church, and a station on the Didcot and Newbury line. (For the beautiful scenery near it see *Cold Ash*.)

Hinksey. The two Hinkseys lie at the foot of the Cumnor Hills, each about 1 m. from the nearest part of Oxford. *North Hinksey* is reached by a pleasant footpath starting from the Seven Bridges Road, which crosses one backwater of the Thames by a pretty wooden bridge and another by a ferry. This was the scene of Ruskin's attempt to utilize the muscle of Oxford in roadmaking instead of cricket and football. But the road experimented on is just as muddy as it was before. The little *church* was originally Norman, of which there remain the beautiful S. doorway, two small windows, a flat buttress and a blocked arch on the N., and the original low-side window on S., now blocked. Above it is a later low-side window (a plain lancet), and a third low-side window to the N. is Perp. The chancel arch is modern Norman. The plain W. tower is Trans. and has a cap resembling those found in Sussex churches. There is a pretty Geometrical window under a triangular arch, three Perp. windows and a debased one. Inside are two plain aumbries, a piscina, and two monuments to the Finmore family. One begins, " Reader, look to thy feet! honest and loyal men are sleeping under them ! " The view of the church from the gate is highly picturesque, with the broken cross and yew-tree in the foreground. In a field on the hill above is the well-house built over the spring which once supplied Oxford with water. It was from near here that Turner drew his celebrated view of Oxford.

Hinksey, South, is reached by a fieldpath starting with a causeway across the waterworks, which afterwards crosses the railway by the so-called " Jacob's Ladder " or " Elephant's Back." Then comes the pathway from which the Scholar Gipsy turned once to watch

" The line of festal light in Christ Church hall,"

a view now hidden by the growth of the ugly suburb of Grandpont. The *church* has few marks of style. There are two lancets and one Perp. window. The font is E.E., the tower Perp., and the chancel 18th cent. There is also a double piscina (Dec.). In the N.W. corner of the village there are some oldish-looking houses.

The two Hinkseys are the gateway of the " warm green-muffled Cumnor hills," which, with the curve of the Thames which encircles them, between Bablock-hythe and Sandford, form the country beloved of

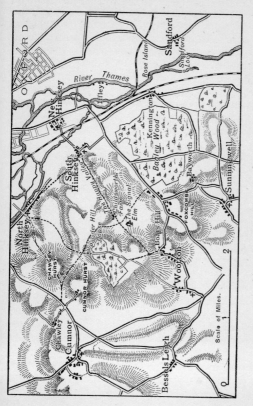

MATTHEW ARNOLD'S COUNTRY

Matthew Arnold, and referred to at length in "Thyrsis" and "The Scholar Gipsy." All will remember the line :

> "In the two Hinkseys nothing keeps the same."

North Hinksey is the starting point of two fine walks, one through beautiful trees to an upland path leading to Chawley Hurst and Cumnor Hurst (see *Cumnor*), the other to Powder Hill Copse, "the high wood" of "Thyrsis." At South Hinksey starts the more celebrated path leading to the "signal elm." This first passes the Happy Valley, an odd **V**-shaped hollow, and then reaches Childsworth Farm. A curious isolated tree on the ridge beyond is usually taken for the tree Arnold meant. But it is an oak, not an elm ; it does not crown the far ridge, nor look on Ilsley Downs, and, so far from being difficult to find, it is prominently in view from the path by the Happy Valley. The limits of space forbid the adequate discussion of this question here, but it may be stated that, in spite of these grave objections, no more probable identification of the tree has yet been made. The main pathway leads to *Boar's Hill*, the topmost ridge, capped by the Lower Greensand. From here the view was a splendid panorama of the country bordered to the E. by the Chilterns and to the S. by the Berkshire Downs. But so many new houses are being continually built on the hill that the view becomes more and more difficult to get every year. The place is now crowded with well-built villas, and has become almost a suburb of Oxford. The side facing Abingdon is sometimes called *Foxcombe Hill*.

Hinton Waldrist (6 m. N.E. of Faringdon) is an out-of-the-way village on the Coral Rag plateau, and half-a-mile S. of the ferry over the Thames at *Duxford*. The church is E.E. and Dec., but restoration has made most of it uninteresting. The fine Dec. tower has good unrestored windows, and there is an old stoup, and an E.E. priest's door with roll-moulding. Nearly everything else has been made new.

Hodcott. (See *West Ilsley.*)

Hungerford is an important town on the Kennet, just S. of the Bath Road. It was originally a royal manor, but the manorial rights, including important fishing privileges, were given to the inhabitants by John of Gaunt, Duke of Lancaster. In the town hall there is kept a horn, said to have been presented to the town by the Duke to confirm his gift. Charles I. was here in November 1644, and on 6th December 1688 William of Orange marched into the town, where he lodged at " The Bear," and two days later received here James II.'s three commissioners, of whom Halifax was the spokesman. There is little to see in the town. The path to the church is pleasantly fringed with lime-trees, but the building is modern. It contains a defaced cross-legged effigy, said to be of Sir Robert de Hungerford, 1340. On the E. wall above is the Norman-French inscription, which is arranged to follow the course of a quatrefoil inside a circle.

HURLEY (4 m. N.E. of Henley) is one of the most interesting villages on the banks of the Thames. From the Henley and Maidenhead road a by-road leads riverwards, first passing among the pretty timber-built cottages, among which the Bell Inn, with its dark oak, is prominent, a hostelry dating from the 15th cent. Presently the road divides, the R.-hand branch going to the lock, the L.-hand to the church and other old buildings. In Saxon times a church stood here, in which by tradition was buried Edith, sister of Edward the Confessor. Soon after the Conquest, church and manor were given by Geoffrey de Mandeville to found a Benedictine Monastery, as a cell of Westminster. The ancient church was incorporated with the new buildings, and the whole dedicated by St Osmund, Bishop of Sarum, in 1086. The ancient buildings which still remain form a quadrangle called Paradise, of which the church is the S. side. It was long believed that the style of this building was early Norman, and that it was entirely rebuilt in 1086. But later authorities consider that the extreme simplicity of most of the work points to a pre-Conquest origin, and that nothing was done to it in 1086 except to lengthen it at the W. end. Its shape is a long rectangle without aisles, and with no break in the roof-line. On either side is a row of plain small, round-headed windows. On the N. wall the distinction between the Saxon and Norman windows is quite clear. At the E. end there are two of the Saxon windows with a round window above. At the W. end there are a good Norman door and window, both showing zigzag. At a restoration in 1852 the N. windows were reopened, but the S. windows were made to look new, and the W. door and window damaged. The modern Norman S. door may have been added at the same time. The only additions to the original work are the priest's door, and window near it (late Dec.), and the good Perp. font. Within the altar rails is a large 17th-cent. tomb to a member of the Lovelace family. On the floor are : (1) a floreated cross ; (2) a brass plate with Latin inscription to one of the D'Oyleys ; (3) stone with mutilated fragments of brass and inscriptions such as " Jesu Mercy," " Lady, help " ; (4) two 18th-cent. brasses.

The remains of the monastery lie N. of the church. To the S. of the quadrangle are six of the church windows, and a plain blocked door not far from the junction of the Saxon and the Norman work. On the E. and W.

side the buildings are new, but show some old masonry. On the N. are the ruins of the refectory. The lower part of the S. side is Norman, with two round arches (one blocked) resting on imposts. The upper part is Dec. and shows four foliated openings. On the N. side are the arches of three fine Dec. windows, of which the tracery has disappeared. More W. is a blocked Elizabethan window. The inscriptions are comparatively modern, but the statements on them are true. On the W. side of the road there are two old barns and a circular dovecot, which also were part of the monastery buildings.

At the Dissolution the estate was conferred on the Lovelace family, who built a magnificent house, *Lady Place*, on the site. In 1688 the head of the family was Richard Lord Lovelace, a red-hot supporter of the Prince of Orange, whose friends used to meet here in " a subterraneous vault, in which the bones of ancient monks had sometimes been found. In this dark chamber some zealous and daring opponents of the Government had held many midnight conferences during that anxious time when England was impatiently expecting the Protestant wind " (Macaulay's History, ii. c. 9). The whole passage is worth reading. The house was destroyed in 1837, but the site of the vaults is still to be traced in the midst of the beautiful garden which surrounds the ruin, dainty with turf and grand with fine cedars. The river itself adds less to the picture than usual, for at this point it has not that park-like beauty so conspicuous above at Henley and below at Bisham. About the lock it is broken into three or four channels, which flow through rather ragged meadows. The lock part, however, is pretty, and the river has a quiet charm.

Hurst (2 m. S. of Twyford station) is a pleasant

village shaded by fine trees, and not far E. of the Loddon.
The church contains several interesting objects, but
restoration has spoilt its structure. The oldest part
is the N. aisle, which has a good Trans. arcade, three
deeply recessed lancets (now restored but apparently
original), and a N. door of the same date with E.E.
features. The tower is brick of the 17th cent. The rest
of the church is modernized. There is a good wooden
roof, a Jacobean pulpit, and an Elizabethan screen with
royal arms and Prince of Wales' feather. The hourglass
and stand are highly curious, showing a painted scroll,
with date 1636, and inscription :

> " As this glasse runneth
> So man's life passethe."

There are several monuments, of which the most
interesting are : (1) marble tomb of Lady Margaret
Savile (d. 1631); (2) altar-tomb with brasses of Richard
Ward, wife and fourteen children (1579) ; (3) large tomb
of Richard Harrison and his wife (1684) ; (4) strange
tomb of Henry Baker (1651), whose recumbent effigy
has a child at its head and a skeleton at its feet ;
(5) altar-tomb to Richard Bigg (1677).

Archbishop Laud, as we learn from his diary, preached
more than once in Hurst church, when he was the guest
of Sir Francis Windebank, Secretary of State, at his
family mansion of Haines Hill. He also stayed at
Hurst Place, which has now disappeared. The only
relics of it are two vases at the entrance to *Bill Hill*
(about 1 m. S., see Map). E. of the church is Hurst
House, a pleasant mansion of brick and stone, said to
be originally Tudor. Just S. is a picturesque almshouse founded by William Baker (d. 1685). Also note
a fine bowling green at the Castle Inn. Near the

entrance gate to it is a fine yew, and there is another one in the churchyard.

Icknield Way or *Ickleton Street* is the ancient name for the *Ridgeway* (*q.v.*). The name is also sometimes applied to the Port Way (*q.v.*), which is considered by some authorities as a branch of the same road.

Ilsley, East (2½ m. N.W. of Compton), lies effectively in a cup-shaped hollow of the bare chalk Downs, which swell up from it on all sides. Its position has made it the chief sheep market for the extensive sheep-grazing country of the Downs. At the principal fair, held in August, the little town is simply packed with sheep. The passing visitor cannot fail to notice the large number both of sheep pens and of public-houses. Another specialty of this Down country is training-stables. Just at the N. foot of the Ilsley Downs, at the point where the roads diverge for East and West Ilsley, there may be noticed on the ordnance map the strange name, *Kate's Gore*. This marks the site of a mansion and training-stables, now vanished, once belonging to the Duke of Cumberland (George II.'s brother), at which the celebrated horse, " Eclipse," was born. (See *Ascot*.) The church has a Trans. S. arcade. The S. aisle generally is plain E.E. with three lancets and triangular piscina. There is an inserted Perp. window; also an early Geometrical one, perhaps of the same date as chancel, which is late E.E. (about 1240-1250). The one unfoliated window has dog-tooth moulding on the outside. The aumbry also shows dog-tooth. Over the lancet at E. end is a circular window enclosing a quatrefoil. The tower is late Dec. N. aisle and chancel arch are modern. Note also (1) restored Norman font with nine sides; (2) Jacobean pulpit; (3) old glass in chancel windows; (4) rood-stairs blocked; (5) brass to wife of William Hildeslea (d. 1606). This family were lords of the manor and their name is the old way of spelling Ilsley.

Ilsley, West, is 1½ m. W. up the valley, and is still more closely penned by the Downs than East Ilsley. The church is without interest. Near Hodcott Farm the Pang sometimes rises in very wet seasons. Usually it rises between Compton and Hampstead Norris.

Impstone. (See *Devil's Highway*.)

Inkpen (3 m. S.W. of Kintbury) has a church which was very sumptuously restored in 1896, with handsome new rood-screen and reredos. The curious red-tiled belfry is supported on oak beams. The only ancient parts remaining are: (1) three foliated lancets (E.E.) on N. side; (2) two plain doors, which may be E.E.; (3) large Perp. window at W. end, with a little old glass. There is also a plain octagonal basin to the font and a mutilated cross-legged effigy.

INKPEN BEACON is the summit of a very fine chalk range, which mostly forms the N. boundary of Hampshire, but at this point crosses into Berkshire for a mile or two, during which it rises into the highest point reached by any chalk hill in the British Isles. The range is in essence a continuation of the N. Downs of Surrey, but there is a break for several miles W. of the Hog's Back, during which the chalk hills are low. Afterwards they rise into the present fine range, which is one of the chief ornaments of the Kennet Valley. Inkpen Beacon itself is an impressive down, with a broad flat top, on which it is somewhat difficult to find the highest point. It was long supposed that the down was over 1000 ft. high, but the latest ordnance survey gives the height as 954 ft. Moreover, the hill to the E., on which *Walbury Camp* stands, is slightly higher—*i.e.* 959 ft.—and is therefore the actual highest point in Berkshire. The camp is a very fine example of the pre-

BERKSHIRE

historic earthwork, larger even than Letcombe Castle.
Between these two points is Walbury Hill, a third
summit over the 900 ft., on which *Combe Gallows*
stand, a gaunt and suggestive wooden framework,
which, according to a condition in the lease, must be
kept in repair by the tenants of Eastwich Farm. The
view from these heights over the Kennet Valley seems
to show a succession of rich woodlands stretching E.,
in contrast with which the chalk slopes which bound
the view to the N. look bare. Looking S. the situation
of Combe, deep-set in its circular hollow, is charming,
but the Hampshire landscape beyond reveals only
ridge after ridge of bare chalk hills.

Kennet River. The Kennet is the largest and most
charming of the tributaries of the Thames. It enters
the county at Hungerford and joins the Thames at
Reading. Since it rises in the chalk uplands of Wiltshire its waters are transparently clear, so that the
trout may be plainly seen swimming about in them.
The banks are thickly clothed with poplars, willows and
other trees. The bounding sandhills slope upwards
on both sides to form a definite valley, between heights
which are covered, now with extensive commons and
fir woods, now with beautiful parks. Finally the Inkpen Beacon range rises up to the S., forming a fine
background to all views. Near Reading the river
reaches a more open country and becomes canal-like
in appearance.

Kennington (2½ m. S. of Oxford) has a modern pseudo-
Norman church, rebuilt in 1828, of which the outside is
rather well done. Near the village the Thames divides
to form Rose Island, which, with its picturesque hotel,
is well known to boaters. Bagley Wood (*q.v.*) is close
on the W.

King's Standing Hill. (See *Churn*.)

MILL ON THE KENNET

Kingston Bagpuize (6 m. W. of Abingdon) is a straggling village with a modern church on the Oxford and Faringdon road.

Kingston Lisle (2½ m. S.E. of Uffington station) is a pretty and trim village, though not of as high interest as some others which nestle under the Downs. The little church was originally Norman, in which style there only remain a plain N. door with Dec. ironwork, a restored window and the cylindrical font. The chancel shows mostly late Dec. work—*i.e.* a reticulated E. window with a foliated niche on either side, two other windows, foliated piscina, and sill-sedile. The chancel arch is new ; nave windows late and bad. The square wooden belfry has a small shingled spire. There is some good modern woodwork. The manor-house, though 18th cent., is imposing, with a good central lantern. In front is a lawn with clipt yews, which falls into a splendid wooded ravine. The park is famed for its trees. S.W. is a very fine avenue of elms, which crosses the Port Way and goes some distance up the Downs. On the road leading S. from the Port Way, and standing in front of some cottages, is the *Blowing Stone*, described at length in the first chapter of " Tom Brown." It is a Sarsen stone of irregular shape, and perforated with some holes. By blowing into the top hole one can produce " a grewsome sound between a moan and a roar." Local tradition of course connects it with King Alfred, and says it was used as a summons to gather his army, but this is merely an idle tale.

Kintbury is in the Kennet Valley half way between Newbury and Hungerford. The cruciform church was much damaged in a " restoration " about 1850, in which it lost all its original windows. Only one is possibly original, the Dec. window N. of N. transept, which may have been once the E. window of chancel. In 1880

Bodley and Garner restored the church in the true sense, but the mischief had been already done. Doors, arches and tower, however, still retain original work. The S. and W. doors are pure Norman, the former showing zigzag and billet. Of the three central arches the chancel arch is Norman; also that leading into the S. transept (if original, for the transept is now of brick), but that leading into the N. transept is Trans. The tower has a Trans. arch, and is altogether either Trans. or rude E.E., but with a Perp. battlement. The priest's door may be original. The church also contains two squints, Trans. piscina and strange aumbry, a Scheemaker monument and a brass dated 1624 to John Gunter. E. of church is an ancient cemetery discovered by Mr Walter Money.

LAMBOURN is a very interesting town lying in the heart of the Chalk Downs which swell upwards from it on all sides, but at such moderate gradients that the place does not seem to be as closely pent with hills as one would suppose. Formerly it was very inaccessible, but now it is connected with Newbury by a light railway. Its connexion with history is slight. A charter of Canute is extant defining the rights of the minister of Lambourn concerning tithe, and is one of the earliest documents on the subject. Lambourn was a possession of King Alfred, who bequeathed it to his widow, Ealdswith, and was once visited by Charles I. Its present prosperity is due to the training-stables, for which the smooth turf of the Downs is admirably adapted. In the centre of the town stands the large and fine cruciform church, one of the best in the county, but partly damaged by restoration. Originally it was Trans., and shows in the nave two fine arcades in that style, solid and impressive. The four arches of the central crossing are slightly more developed Trans

Other Trans. features are the arches between the nave aisles and the transepts, the fine W. door, with a circular window in the gable above, and a lancet window E. of the N. transept. There is a curious rood-loft piscina, as at Blewbury, left high up on the wall. Unfortunately the restorations of 1850 and 1861 have introduced a good deal of bad pseudo-Norman work—*i.e.* the clerestory, some W. windows, the pulpit, the font and a gallery near the central arches leading to the tower. The rest of the work is all Dec. and Perp., and is mostly concerned with the three chapels which flank the chancel, two on the S. and one on the N. side. To the S. of the chancel is a five-light Dec. window with a sill-sedile. Near it is a very beautiful Dec. piscina, and farther W. an arch leading to *St Mary's Chapel*, which is entirely Dec., with an interesting E. window, and another remarkable arch leading into the S. transept, showing a moulding ornamented with a pattern of heads and running dogs, mixed with four-leaved flowers and a small ball-flower ornament. On the floor are brasses to John Estbury (d. 1372) and Thomas Estbury (d. 1400), and also to Roger Garrard and wife (1631). Farther S. is the *Holy Trinity Chapel*, which is fine late Perp. and contains in the centre the altar-tomb of John Estbury (d. 1508), with brass. About this tomb the old men of the almshouse he founded say a service every day, with a special intercessory prayer, to be seen in a glazed frame. On the N. of the chancel is the *Essex Chapel*, entered from the N. transept by a Dec. arch but otherwise entirely Perp. It contains the alabaster tomb of Sir Thomas and Margaret Essex, 1558, a discarded 17th-cent. font and some old glass dated 1532. There is a third Dec. window (flamboyant) S. of the S. transept. The great W. window is Trans. to Perp.

There are several other Perp. windows—*i.e.* the great E. window, the side windows of the nave aisles, and three in the transepts. The S. porch is Perp. and has a parvise, lighted by a window opening into the nave. The tower is Trans. with a Perp. upper story. Besides the monuments in the chapels there are in the chancel a tomb to Thomas Garrard and wife (1583) and a double brass to another Thomas Garrard and wife (1619). In the nave there is a black letter inscription to Thomas Garrard, and a strange medallion to Charles I.

Between the church and the Red Lion Inn is a village cross with original steps and shaft and restored head. Near are the almshouses of John Estbury, which have been completely rebuilt. N. among trees is Lambourn Place, looking very Elizabethan, but showing clearly the date 1843. It is on the site of an old mansion of the Essex family. 2 m. N. are the *Seven Barrows*. In reality the number is much larger, but a group of seven which lie close together gave the name to the whole. They are in an unusual situation, in a hollow among the Downs, instead of crowning the topmost ridge. The road runs between them and the racecourse, and then beside a beech copse to the top of the Downs. The point at which it intersects the Ridgeway (772 ft.) has a commanding view N. This seems to be the point from which Jude the Obscure, in Hardy's tale, after climbing the hill from Marygreen (Lambourn) gazed longingly northward towards distant Christminster (Oxford).

Lambourn River. The Lambourn, the principal tributary to the Kennet on the L. bank, rises only just above the town of Lambourn, in a series of deep, transparent pools surrounded by trees, from which it issues in full volume, the clearest and brightest of chalk streams. These pools appear to act as a reservoir, rendering the flow of the stream equable, so that in dry summers the Lambourn has often more water in it than other streams in the neighbourhood.[1] This little stream is a most charming companion to the traveller by the valley road between Lambourn and Newbury. Its valley is bounded by swelling chalk slopes, until near Newbury, when sandhills take their places, and it is also full of delightful villages. Perhaps the prettiest river views are got from the bridges just above and below Welford.

Leckhampstead (about 2½ m. N.E. of Welford) has a new red-brick church, and is of no interest.

Letcombe is the name of two pretty villages which lie close to the Downs, somewhat N. of Wantage.

Letcombe Regis (4½ m. S.W. of Wantage Road station) is interspersed with beautiful trees which contrast finely with the bare chalk slopes. The church has a good Trans. tower with Perp. upper story, also a Trans. cylindrical font. The chancel has a few traces of Dec.—*i.e.* in the restored S. door and the piers of the chancel arch. Otherwise the rest is Perp. On the N. side the windows are original, and there is an old door with mutilated stoup. The E. window is old Perp. and has some good glass—*i.e.* a Resurrection in the centre and several shields. There is a headless brass to Alice Eltbury, and a tomb to Alexander Fettiplace, 1709.

Letcombe Bassett is 1 m. S. The road is beside the little chalk stream, running in a wooded dingle. Just

---

[1] For instance in the summer of 1905 I found the Lambourn with plenty of water, when the Pang was half dried up. There is a tradition that the Lambourn is fuller of water in the summer than in the winter, an interesting phenomenon if true, and one requiring explanation.

at the village the stream leaves a steep-sided wooded ravine, which is utilized for watercress beds. The houses are above on the far side, the church being highest of all. Of the original Norman chancel there remain: (1) two plain windows, of which the S. one now lights the vestry; (2) a blocked door (N.) with plain tympanum and the emblems of the Four Evangelists carved on the capitals, two on each; (3) the chancel arch, which has arabesque work on the imposts. Late in the E.E. period (about 1260-1270) the chancel was lengthened, and the double lancets and early Geometrical windows inserted. The font and the N. door (with niche for stoup inside) are of the same date; also the tower, which has been repaired with brick on its W. side. There is an inserted late Dec. window S. of nave, and a Perp. one N. of nave. The S. arcade and aisle were added in 1862. Note also E.E. foliated niches on either side of chancel arch. Above is the exit of the rood-stairs which were carried in a bulge outside.

On the down immediately E. of the village is *Letcombe Castle*, a very fine prehistoric camp, with a tall and well-preserved rampart. To the W. is a remarkably deep combe in the Downs, usually called the *Punch Bowl*.

Lilley. (See *Catmore*.)

Littleworth (2 m. N.E. of Faringdon) is a hamlet with a modern church.

Lockinge, East (3 m. S.E. of Wantage Road station by private road), is the seat of Lady Wantage. The house is modern, but it is set in a beautifully timbered park, among the outliers of the chalk downs, here very picturesque. Behind the house is a wooded knoll over which a flag usually flies. The church is in the park close to the house. It has been much enlarged, and the chancel and nave, its only original parts, now form the N. aisle of the new chancel and nave, an additional aisle having been built on the S. side. The old nave has good Norman N. door (with Dec. ironwork), a Perp. window, and Norman font. The old chancel has several Dec. features—*i.e.* chancel arch with a foliated recess on each side, E. window and two side windows, which are very late in the style, and have their panelling prolonged outside, suggestive of low-side windows. S. of chancel are piscina, aumbry, sedile and squint, all E.E. The tower is debased. One stone bears the date 1564. There is a Jacobean pulpit and an E.E. chest.

Lockinge, West, is separated from East Lockinge by the park. The two together really only form one village. On the Downs to the S. is a tall white cross set up by Lady Wantage in memory of her husband, Lord Wantage (d. 1901).

Loddon River. "The Loddon slow, with verdant alders crowned " is an apt description of this quiet stream. In fact this line of Pope's is worth more than the whole elaborate legend of Lodona which precedes it. (See "Windsor Forest.") It rises close to Basingstoke and flows N. It is joined by the Blackwater in Swallowfield Park, and finally joins the Thames just opposite Shiplake. Its course in Berkshire lies chiefly among flat meadows. It is in some parts a good boating river, especially on both sides of the bridge where it is crossed by the Reading and Wokingham road, and its banks, fringed with willow, poplar and alder, invite comparison with the Cherwell.

Longcot (3 m. W. of Uffington station) is a small village, with a small rectangular church. Of E.E. work there remain the walls of chancel, with one lancet (N.) and the trefoil-headed N. door. The E. window and another are Dec. and there are several Perp. windows, of which two are large and two others low-side windows. The tower is dated 1722. There are two piscinæ, two aumbries, a Jacobean pulpit, and some of the rood-loft stairs. A brass records the refitting of the church in honour of the Rev. John Hughes (vicar 1853-1895). He was the brother of the author of "Tom Brown," who used often to visit him here. (See also *Uffington*.)

LONGWORTH (6½ to 7 m. W. of Abingdon and E. of Faringdon) is a pleasant, out-of-the-way village on the top of the Coral Rag Plateau. The church is interesting and picturesque. The date of the arcades is the one difficulty. The N. arcade, which is ruder and earlier than the S., has sometimes been considered Trans., but probably both arcades are E.E. The S. porch and the font are also E.E. The S. aisle was altered late in the Geometrical period. It contains four good windows, each with a quatrefoil in the head, and a trefoil-headed piscina. The chancel arch and that leading into the N. chapel are Dec. The rest of the work is Perp.—*i.e.* (1) all the other windows, which are not churchwarden ; (2) the clerestory on the S. (that to the N. is churchwarden); (3) the W. tower, which is inside the church, with three fine arches facing into church, and a flight of stone steps to the belfry ; (4) the battlements of the S. aisle and porch. The N. aisle has only one Perp. window, and is of little interest. The chancel has two Perp. windows, a Perp. piscina, a quaint Jacobean screen, and a good modern reredos. There are three brasses : (1) John Henley, rector (1422) ; (2) Richard and Johane Yate (1500); (3) Elynor Godolphin (1566). The church looks well from the S., with its good Geometrical and Perp. windows, and effective battlement. There is a sundial dated 1621. From the churchyard there is a very fine view N. over the Thames Valley, with *Harrow-down Hill* in front, a curious detached and wooded hill. Longworth was the birthplace of Dr Fell (see *Sunningwell*) and R. D. Blackmore, the novelist.

Lyford (3½ to 4 m. N. of Wantage Road station, but reached by circuitous routes) is the out-of-the-way village on the Ock where the Jesuit Edmund Campion was arrested on 16th July 1581. He was in safe hiding at Stonor, but was induced to visit Mr Yates at Lyford. On the fatal Sunday he celebrated mass before about fifty persons. Directly afterwards Elliott, a renegade spy who had been present, brought a body of constables to the house. Campion hid in the priest's hole, but was found next morning. He was finally executed at Tyburn in December. The moated grange in which Mr Yates lived still exists, but retains hardly an ancient feature. There is another moated house, near the church, now a farm, but once an Elizabethan mansion and still showing some mullioned windows and a stack of old chimneys. Also another ruined timber-built house, and a number of almshouses, founded in 1611, which have been rebuilt, but still look quaint and interesting. The church is entirely E.E., but for a Perp. clerestory in nave, but it has been a good bit modernized. Most windows are lancets, and there are two low-side windows. Both doors are plain. There is a modernized bell-cote, supported on an interior wooden framework. Font and piscina with shelf are also E.E. There is an aumbry with a shouldered arch. Note also the Jacobean pulpit, the nave roof, the old wooden screen and a blocked squint.

MAIDENHEAD looks so modern that it might have been called into being by the holiday river traffic, to which it so largely ministers. But really it is quite an ancient town. The fanciful notion that it owed its name to one of St Ursula's eleven thousand virgins, whose head was sent here as a holy relic, is unconvincing. In fact, whatever the first part of the name may mean, the last syllable is *hythe*—*i.e.* wharf. Up to about 1250 the place was called South Elington. Then the new wharf on the river brought an increased population and a new name. A chapel was desired, and finally erected irregularly in 1270. The bishop refused a licence, and it was not till 1324 that it was definitely constituted as a chapel of Cookham parish. In the reign of Edward VI. this chapel was suppressed, a grievous wrong. Thus the rise of the town, as well as its present prosperity, are due to the river, but in mediæval times its importance, like that of Henley, was rather due to the road. Here the Great Bath Road crosses the Thames by a bridge which at first was wooden and for the maintenance of which a guild was incorporated in 1352 (cf. *Abingdon*). During the rebellion of the three Earls against Henry IV. in 1400 the bridge was successfully held by the Earl of Kent against the advancing forces of Henry. His object was to protect the retreat of his friends, whom he joined by a withdrawal in the night. (See also *Faringdon* and *Sonning*.) We have a full account of a curious service in which Richard Ludlow was admitted to the "hermitage of the bridge of Maidenhead" in 1423. In July 1647 a meeting was permitted here at the "Old Greyhound" between the captive Charles I. and his children. In 1688 Maidenhead Bridge was held for James II. by an Irish regiment. In the night the inhabitants beat a Dutch march, on which the Irish took to their heels. The ornamental stone bridge now existing was built in 1772. A little S. is the fine span of Brunel's railway bridge. There are no antiquities in the town, which is chiefly visited by pleasure-seekers eager to pass through

Boulter's Lock to the beautiful reach of the Thames lying under Cliveden Woods.

Maidenhead Thicket used in old times to have a bad reputation for highwaymen.

Marcham (3 m. W. of Abingdon) is a village in the Ock Valley. The church has not had justice done to it hitherto. The large nave, built in 1837, is singularly ugly, and the position of the altar as awkward as possible. But yet there are many remains of old work. (1) The fragment of the old chancel, and a N. chapel of nearly the same size, are E.E. and separated by a good arch. The windows have been restored, but those at the E. end are worth notice. One is a triple lancet, with original Purbeck columns, the other Dec. (2) The W. tower is also E.E. Inside it is vaulted, and a good E.E. arch leads into it. The belfry staircase is good, with three rectangular slits and a gable at top with small quatrefoil. (3) The S. porch is E.E. with a Dec. niche above the outer door. The inner door, square-headed with cinq-foliated doorway, is good early Perp. (4) Some of the pews show old linen-work.

Marlstone (1½ m. S.E. of Hermitage station) has a rebuilt little church, but with an old Norman door (N.), plain but good. S. is the sundial, dated 1607, with motto, "Life as this shade doth fly and fade." The church is surrounded by tall elms, and lies among parks where fine cattle graze.

Marsh Lock (about 1 m. S.E. of Henley) is in a beautiful spot in the Thames Valley. The delightful road from Wargrave to Henley keeps on the R. of the river valley the whole time, with fine woods on the R., and at last descends to the river close to the lock itself, near which are an old mill and picturesque wooden bridges. Above on the R. stretch the beautiful hanging woods of *Park Place*, one of the most striking groups of foliage in the Thames Valley. The grounds contain a so-called "*Cromlech*," formed of a group of ancient stones removed here from Jersey in 1785, a reprehensible practice which fortunately has not been largely followed (see, however, *Virginia Water*).

Midgham has a new church. Midgham House is in a fine park overlooking the Kennet Valley.

Milton (1½ m. N.E. of Steventon) is reached from Steventon by a pleasant pathway, which for part of the way is beside the winding mill-stream of the Ginge brook. The church is rebuilt all but (1) the tower, which has a Dec. W. window and Perp. upper story; (2) the S. porch, which is partly old, and shows an internal stone-rib, and small Perp. side windows.

Monkey Island, in the Thames, is often the goal of boating parties from Windsor and Eton.

MORETON, NORTH (3 m. N.W. of Cholsey), is a pleasant village, lying in a cup-shaped hollow in the plateau which stretches from the Chalk Downs towards the Dorchester clumps. From the plateau there is a fine view of chalk hills in three directions. The church is beautiful and interesting, but has been partly spoiled by the bad modern painting in the chancel. The only trace of Norman in the building is an elaborately carved corbel in the Stapleton Chapel. The plain cylindrical font is also probably Norman. About 1260-1270 the church was almost entirely rebuilt. The chancel, with chancel arch and early Dec. side windows, is entirely in this style. The E. window, in spite of its straight mullions, is excellent Geometrical work, perhaps a little later than the rest. The nave arcade is of the same date as the chancel, though the work is not so characteristic of the period as that of the arches leading S. and W. into the S. chapel. of which the W. arch shows beautiful stiff-stalk foliage. About 1295-

THE THAMES NEAR PARK PLACE

1300 [1] the chapel was rebuilt by Sir Miles Stapleton as the Stapleton Chantry, which now forms the principal glory of the church. It was at the same time enlarged by an extension to the E., so that one of the original chancel windows now opens into it. The style of the five fine windows in the chancel is late Geometrical, and suggests the date c. 1300. The E. window is full of beautiful old glass, the subjects of which are stated in a note hung up in the church. There is a remarkable piscina, ornamented with ball-flower, and having an angle pillar. Two small brackets also show the ball-flower. On the floor there is a tombstone with a floreated cross. Outside notice the corbels, the buttresses, and the cornice with grotesque animals. In the Curvilinear period the external features of the nave were altered, so that it now shows four late Dec. windows and two Dec. doors. There is a good foliated piscina, some old glass and the remains of the rood-loft stairs. The W. tower, with door and window, is good Perp., the window W. of the nave aisle is debased Perp. There are two brasses, to Thomas Mayne (1479) and James Leaver (1629). Outside the W. wall lie some fragments of a stone screen and canopy-work. They seem to belong to an old Perp. tomb, which is variously related to have come from either S. Moreton or Cholsey. The vicarage has a fine stack of old brick chimneys. It is entered from the road by a Perp. garden gate, near which is a timber-built barn, showing herringbone-work in brick.

Moreton, South (2 m. N.W. of Cholsey), lies just N. of

[1] The date is fixed by an inquiry held in March 1299 to consider the legality of Sir Miles Stapleton's gift of a field at North Moreton, for the endowment of two chaplains to celebrate Mass daily in the chapel here. A meadow of 17 acres near the church is still tithe-free and called the Chantry field.

the little Hacker brook, which is here dammed up to turn a mill and is of respectable size. The church is of strange shape, divided by the central arcade into two almost equal parts, so that the S. aisle is as large as the nave and chancel. An old Saxon door has been discovered, blocked up in the masonry at the W. end. The two W. bays of the arcade are Trans., also the S. wall, which has one original lancet ; but the two E. bays are E.E. In the centre there used to be a small round-headed doorway, but a modern arch has been cut to make the arcade continuous. The S. doorway and the foliated lancet near it are also E.E. The other windows are Dec. and Perp., some rebuilt. The ancient ones are the good Dec. W. window, two square-headed late Dec. windows and one Perp. (all three S.). The church has suffered from a bad restoration in 1840-1850, which spoilt many of the windows. The N. door is Dec. Notice also (1) double E.E. piscina ; (2) S.E. buttress, bearing a plain shield in a cinq-foliated recess (Perp.). W. of the church are some traces of an ancient earthwork.

Mortimer is really *Stratfield Mortimer*. It is quite a large place if it be taken to include the crowd of houses on Mortimer Common, at the top of the hill 1½ m. W. of the station. The parish church was wholly rebuilt in 1866. This led to the discovery under the tower of the stone cover of a *Saxon tomb*, broken in two. The date must be about 1020, some two hundred and fifty years earlier than any other tombstone in Berkshire. The inscription is marginal and runs :

" + VIII KL. OCTB. FVIT POSITVS AEGELPARDVS FILVS KYPPINGVS IN ISTO LOCO. BEATVS SIT OMO QVI ORAT PRO ANIMA EIVS. + TOKI ME SCRIPSIT."

The tomb is probably that of Ædelward, historian

and Ealdorman of Hampshire mentioned in the Saxon Chronicle, A.D. 994. Toki was a powerful courtier of King Canute. In Domesday Book it says that a Cheping (Kypping) held two Stratfield manors in the reign of Edward the Confessor. The inscription is supposed to mean " Ædelward, son of Kypping."

Close by are two brasses to Richard Trevet and his wife, 1441. In the organ-chamber is a window in which a quantity of interesting old glass has been pieced together. In the centre is a portrait of William of Wykeham, with his motto, " Manners maketh man." He is known to have been a tenant of the Earl of Mortimer. A shield above may commemorate the marriage of Anne, heiress of Mortimer, with Richard, Earl of Cambridge and grandfather of Edward IV. Note also a portrait of the Tiburtine Sibyl and the badge of a bee.

The great beauty of Mortimer is the fir woods, which stretch W. of it mile on mile. *Silchester* is within easy reach, but just over the Hampshire border.

Moulsford is a pleasant riverside village. The little church has been entirely rebuilt (in E.E. and Dec. styles). It has a picturesque wooden tower and an ivy-grown wooden porch.

Newbridge (6 m. N.W. of Abingdon) is, in spite of its name, one of the oldest bridges on the Thames (dating from the 13th cent.), and crosses it just at the junction of the Windrush with the broader stream. The bridge has five pointed arches and triangular buttresses facing upstream. The position was of importance in the Civil War. In 1644 the bridge was held for the King and attacked by Waller, who forced a passage on 2nd June, the immediate result of which was Charles' night retreat from Oxford on 3rd June. In 1649 the mutinous Levellers tried to cross here, but were repulsed, and finally crossed the Thames higher up.

NEWBURY is the largest and most important town in the Kennet Valley. The name may have been given to distinguish it from its older neighbour, Speen (*q.v.*), which claims a Roman origin. At the Conquest the manor fell to Arnulf de Hesding, who built the church. The castle was built about 1140 by one of the Earls of Perche and was soon held for the Empress Matilda by John the Marshal (see *Hampstead Marshall*). Consequently in 1152 it was taken by Stephen after a three months' siege, and utterly razed. King John was a visitor to the town, and gave a charter to St Bartholomew's Hospital (see later). In 1302 the town sent two members to Edward I.'s Parliament, but discontinued the privilege after 1337. In the Wars of the Roses the town was held for the Yorkists, but was attacked and taken by a Lancastrian army in 1460, on which all Yorkist partisans were mercilessly executed. In the Middle Ages the cloth industry flourished here greatly. The central figure was the celebrated " Jack of Newbury," by name John Smallwood, afterwards altered to Wynchcombe, an industrious apprentice who married his master's widow, and became not only a rich master-clothier, but also the leading citizen of the town. His great exploit was leading in person a body of one hundred and fifty of his " lads " to fight the Scots at Flodden (1513). He also successfully carried through the clothiers' petition, which obtained for their industry something like free trade with foreign countries. When Henry VIII. visited Newbury he was Jack's guest, and offered to knight him, which honour Jack refused (see also *Bucklebury*). In Mary's reign three martyrs were burnt at Newbury, the chief being Julius Palmer, Fellow of Magdalen and Master of Reading Grammar School. In 1620 Dr Twiss, the Puritan divine, was made vicar here, and the house in which

NEWBURY AND ITS NEIGHBOURHOOD

he administered the Sacrament to Lord Falkland on the day of his death is still pointed out. In the Civil War occurred the two famous battles for which Newbury is chiefly known to history (see later). In the 18th cent. John Wesley preached here several times. The town is still prosperous and has lately started races.

Newbury is only moderately rich in antiquities. The church was entirely rebuilt in the 16th cent. by Jack of Newbury himself, whose monogram, J.S., is on the roof. It was finished in 1532 by his son, the date being on a corbel over the tower arch. It is accordingly rich Tudor, very handsome and effective, but needing little description. Note the clustered columns, from which arise the lofty arches which support the handsome timber roof; also the uniformity of the windows. The low parclose screen shows good panelling. The Jacobean pulpit is dated 1607. The brasses and inscriptions are under the tower. The chief is to John Smallwood, otherwise Wynchcombe (*i.e.* Jack himself), with his wife and children, 1519. Other brass plates are dated 1596, 1635 and 1641. On the W. wall is an illuminated history of the church with dates, very well worth consulting.

Of *St Bartholomew's Hospital* the foundation is unknown. In 1215 King John gave it a charter by which the Hospital was to have the profits of a two days' annual fair to be held on St Bartholomew's and the following day. The oldest part of the existing buildings is the chapel, in which Jack of Newbury was married. It still shows three late Perp. windows and an old timber roof. It was desecrated and turned into a school in the reign of Edward VI. For some of the other buildings an inscription on a chimney gives the date 1696. There is little of interest in the buildings facing the main street, but down a side street will be found a picturesque old brick front. In

Northbrook Street may still be seen *Jack of Newbury's house*. About half-way down the street is the Jack Hotel, with a signboard showing the hero himself. The next house N. is Jack's house. The street front is modern, but facing a little lane at the side may be seen fine old half timber-work, with a wooden oriel window, gable and barge-board. A little E. of the market-place stands the *Old Cloth Hall*. When no longer used by the guild it fell into disrepair, but it has lately been restored and turned into a museum. The outside shows beautifully picturesque old woodwork, dating from Jacobean times. Note especially the carved heads on the brackets supporting the projecting upper story. In the market-place itself are the town hall and the Corn Exchange, both comparatively modern, and just S. has lately been placed a successful statue of Queen Victoria.

The site of the *First battle of Newbury* (20th Sept. 1643) is in the Kennet Valley S. of the river, and S.W. of the town. If we take the most westerly of three roads leading S. from Newbury, and ascend the hill, we come to a point from which we can overlook the battle-field to the W. Here (1 m. from Newbury), just where another road crosses the one we are on, is the monument to the illustrious Royalists slain in the battle. Lord Falkland alone is mentioned by name, but the monument also honours his fellow-victims, the Earls of Carnarvon and Sunderland, the former being referred to by the symbol ♋ and a crown, the latter by S and a crown. The inscription quotes Thucydides, Livy and Burke. It was at the unveiling of this monument that Matthew Arnold uttered the panegyric on Falkland which stands first in " Mixed Essays."

The battle resulted from an attempt of Charles to intercept the London trained bands, which, after raising the siege of Gloucester, were retreating to London under the command of Essex. When, on the evening of 19th September, Essex, marching S. of the Kennet from Hungerford, reached Enborne, he found the enemy in position at Newbury Wash directly in front of him, and barring the London road. It must be observed that this does not mean the Bath road, which was N. of the Kennet, but the Aldermaston road over Crookham Common. Essex took up his position for the night at *Crockham Heath*, on the ground lying between the village of Enborne and the Enborne stream. In the morning he was compelled to attack. On the Royalist right wing the Life Guards under Biron had made the mistake of guarding the Kintbury road on the lower ground. This allowed the enemy to seize some higher ground which commanded them, and it was during a desperate charge to drive them away from it that Falkland was killed. The cavalry fight on this wing gave little decided result. On the left wing Rupert, after three headlong charges, drove away the cavalry opposed to him. He then attacked some of the London trained bands, but made no impression on them. In the centre the Parliamentary infantry, advancing slowly and steadily by lanes and hedges, gradually gained a footing on the Wash, where the Royalists were posted, and, after several hours' hard fighting, forced them a little back. But when night fell the Royalists were not defeated and still lay in front of the London road. As, however, they had suffered heavily, and ammunition was failing, Charles retreated into Newbury during the night, leaving the London road open.

The chief human interest of the battle centres round Falkland. Clarendon's account of his death will be familiar to all, but the well-known details must not be omitted. For many weeks he had been deeply despondent, and had been heard to ejaculate, " Peace, peace,"

But on the morning of the fight his cheerfulness returned. " I am weary of the times," he is reported to have said, " and foresee much misery to my country, but I believe I shall be out of it ere night." In so beautiful a character these words surely indicate rather some foreshadowing of the end, than the reckless despair, scarce distinguishable from suicide, to which they have been sometimes attributed. He put on clean linen and received the Sacrament before riding to his post. When the fatal charge, already described, was made, his way lay through a dangerous gap in the hedge, swept by the enemy's fire. As he boldly spurred his horse through it he was struck down and at once killed.

The *second battle* took place somewhat N. of Newbury (27th October 1644). The committee of both kingdoms had decided that a combined attempt must be made to crush Charles on his return from the W. after the victory of Lostwithiel. Accordingly a large force under Essex and Manchester, with Waller, Skippon and Cromwell as captains, was sent westwards to intercept the King. At first the intention was to prevent him from relieving Donnington Castle, on which he was known to be moving. But the force advanced so slowly that when, after passing Thatcham and Bucklebury Common, they encamped on Clay Hill (somewhat E. of the Newbury and Hermitage road) they found Charles had already relieved Donnington, and drawn up his army in a strong position between the Lambourn and the Kennet, with Shaw House and Donnington Castle as part of his defences, and Prince Maurice on Speen Hill guarding his rear. On this position the Parliamentary leaders planned a combined attack. A flanking column under Balfour and Skippon, with Waller and Cromwell, marched to the N. of the King's army by Hermitage, Chieveley, Winterbourne and Wick-

ham Heath, and about three o'clock attacked his rear
at Speen. Prince Maurice was promptly driven down
Speen Hill with the loss of his guns. The Guards
were next attacked, but the Royalist troops rallied to
their assistance, and the defence was maintained till
nightfall. Meanwhile Manchester had, in the morning,
covered the flanking march by a sham attack, which had
been pushed too far and resulted in some loss. But
instead of carrying out the plan agreed upon and attack-
ing Shaw House as soon as the attack on Maurice began,
he unaccountably delayed until there was only half-an-
hour of daylight left. The attack on Shaw House,
when at last he delivered it, was completely repulsed,
and the combined movement failed. Next morning
Charles was discovered to have skilfully evacuated his
position during the night, leaving his guns and ammunition at Donnington Castle. No attempt at effective
pursuit was made until it was too late, and the sole
advantage of the battle to the Roundheads was that
Newbury itself was left in their hands. (For further
details see *Donnington* and *Shaw*.)

Newbury is in the main the " Whitbury " of Kingsley's " Two Years Ago," but the details seem purposely
confused. The Whit must be the Kennet.

Speenhamland, through which the Great Bath Road
passes, is now merely the N. part of Newbury. Of
old it was famous for its hostelries, of which the two
most famous, the " Pelican " and the " Bear," will no
longer be found there. At present the leading hotels
are the " Chequers " and the " Bruce Arms."

Nine Mile Ride. (See *Easthampstead*.)

Oare is a small hamlet of no importance about ½ m.
N. of Hermitage.

Ockwells (2 m. W. of Bray) is a timber-built old mansion,
probably dating from the 15th cent. It is a picturesque

old pile, lying in a secluded part of the county. The windows have wooden frames. It has been lately restored, so that the modern brick looks new. Inside is an old hall, panelled, and with a good deal of old glass. The manor belonged first to the Norreys family and afterwards to the Fettiplaces.

Padworth (about 1½ m. S.E. of Aldermaston station) is a little village among the pine forests which clothe the hills S. of the Kennet Valley. The little church is pure Norman, the only addition, apart from modern " restoration," being the late Perp. windows in the nave. The chancel arch and the N. and S. doors show fine arabesque work of about 1150. The W. window may be original, also the quaint piscina, and possibly the aumbry, which has a modern door. The E. end is a vaulted apse, but badly restored and filled with modern windows. Just S. of the chancel arch there are traces of frescoes. The belfry is supported on a wooden framework. Note also defaced tombstone on floor of nave, and magnificent yew-tree.

Pang. The Pang river is a clear chalk stream, which runs through a pretty and well-defined valley. It rises S. of Compton and first flows S., but being unable to reach the Kennet, because of the barrier of Bucklebury Common, it turns first E., then N., and finally joins the Thames at Pangbourne, after a re-markably circuitous course. In wet weather its source is occasionally farther up the valley, near W. Ilsley. In dry summers it usually has less water than its sister-stream, the Lambourn.

Pangbourne is a pretty riverside village, where the Pang runs into the Thames. It has of late years been a good deal spoilt by overbuilding. Rather more than ½ m. S. the Oxford and Reading road descends to the riverside just at the point where there is a view up a fine reach of the Thames backed by Hart Wood on the far side. It then runs to Pangbourne, with the river on the L. and a chalk bluff on the R. This fine road has been somewhat spoilt lately by the erection of villas on the chalk slopes. In Pangbourne itself the lock and lasher are very charming, and farther E. the wooden bridge leading to Whitchurch. The church has been rebuilt, except the 17th-cent. brick tower. Inside is a Jacobean pulpit, and a fine monument to Sir John Davis and his two wives (1625). Outside there is the large cedar-tree. Bere Court, once a residence of the Abbots of Reading, is now modern.

Park Place. (See *Marsh Lock*.)

Peasemore (4½ m. N.W. of Hermitage) is a tree-shaded village with a rebuilt church, containing a brass plate to Thomas Stampe, 1636, another with a coat-of-arms, and a memorial of William Coward, 1769, a sort of local " Man of Ross " on a small scale.

Perborough Castle. (See *Compton*.)

Port Way is a remarkable ancient road running along the foot of the Berkshire Downs, and more or less parallel to the Ridgeway (*q.v.*). It runs from Streatley through Wantage to Ashbury, and manages *en route* just to miss nearly all the thick-sown villages, which perhaps may be taken as evidence of its antiquity. It seems doubtful, however, whether it is as old as the Ridgeway.

Poughley Priory (about 2 m. N. of Welford station) was founded on the site of an old hermitage by Ralph de Chaddleworth about 1160. It was dedicated to St Margaret, and assigned to Austin Canons. It was one of the foundations suppressed by Wolsey in 1524 to build Christchurch in Oxford. The site is now occupied by a farmhouse, and there is very little to be seen. To reach it from Welford station take the road up the valley for ½ m., and just where the road crosses the Lambourn take a rough track leading N. This reaches the farm in about 1½ m. When near the farm woods lie at no great distance on both sides. The ruins of the kitchen, dormitories and attics are unimportant. There are some blackened beams, an old wooden staircase, a large chimney and one square corbel with some carving. But on the E. side is an old wall of flint and stone intermixed, with a blocked two-light window (foliated lancet), and near it the squatting figure of a monk. Above it is the date 1613 and the initials M I R I. In the deep hollow E. is the site of the fishponds. (See also *East Hendred*.)

Purley (1½ m. N.W. of Tilehurst station) is a village separated from the Thames by the dense woods of Purley Park, which border one of the most striking reaches of the river. The little church is in a strangely isolated situation in the centre of the woods, with the river just showing at the end of a vista through the trees. It has been rebuilt, but retains a few Norman features—*i.e.* the chancel arch (now placed at entrance to organ-chamber) and the font ; also a restored Trans. door (N.). There are two old windows, one a lancet, the other late Perp. The tower is brick of the 17th cent., and shows the Bolingbroke arms on the S. side. At Purley Hall Warren Hastings lived, when waiting for his trial.

Pusey (4 m. N. of Challow, 4½ m. E. of Faringdon) has a small church rebuilt in the " Georgian " style. Outside the S. transept there is a brass plate to Richard Pusey, 1655. There are also two monuments to the Dunch family, one by Scheemaker to Jane Pusey, 1742, and a quaint epitaph to a child, William White, 1655. The manor is said to have been originally con-

ferred on the Pusey family by Canute, to be held by
tenure of a horn, called cornage. A horn is still kept
at Pusey House, but its date is much disputed. It is
said to have been produced in court in 1681 and its
authenticity acknowledged. The original Puseys have
long been extinct, the present family having taken the
name when they acquired the property by marriage.
The present house was built only in 1753. The Pusey
woods are fine.

Cherbury Camp, a fine prehistoric earthwork, is 1 m.
E. There are three complete lines of entrenchment,
the inner being the highest, divided by three trenches.
It is remarkable to find so fine an earthwork lying in
absolutely flat country.

Radcot Bridge (2½ m. N. of Faringdon) is an ancient
bridge (13th cent.) with three pointed arches ribbed
beneath, and in the centre a pedestal said to have
formerly supported a figure of the Virgin. The main
stream of traffic now passes by a new cut, avoiding the
old bridge. Here in 1387 Robert Vere, Duke of
Ireland, minister of Richard II., was surrounded by
the forces of the Lords Appellant. He was defeated
and saved his life by swimming down the stream, and
escaping across Berkshire.

Radley is a small village containing St Peter's
College, one of the best known of the smaller public
schools, whose motto is " sicut columbæ." Its
buildings stand on the site of the old manor-house,
which belonged first to the Stonehouse, and then to
the Bowyer, family, but was leased by the latter to
the trustees of the school. The college was opened
by its founder, Dr Sewell, on 9th June 1847. The
old manor-house, a red-brick mansion of the date of
Queen Anne, now forms part of the extensive pile of
buildings, which contain many treasures, such as old

chairs, pictures and carpets, which Dr Sewell bought
for his foundation. The whole stands high on a wide
plateau, surrounded by magnificent old trees, and the
park forms extensive and beautiful playing-grounds.
At first the success of the school was doubtful, and some
of Dr Sewell's treasures had to be sold. In 1860 its
debts amounted to £40,000, the responsibility for which
was assumed by Mr J. C. Hubbard (afterwards Lord
Addington). Fortunately, the tide soon turned, and
raised the school to the high position it now holds, so
that Mr Hubbard recovered all his money. The chapel
contains much beautiful woodcarving and stained
glass, also a famous and very valuable Thibet carpet.
The village church is entirely Perp., except for the
restored early Dec. windows in the S. transept, which
may not be original. Some of the Perp. windows contain
old glass. The S. arcade is wooden, but rests on stone
bases. The chancel has an exterior cornice and pin-
nacles at the end. It may be later than the rest, and
there is a tradition it was rebuilt in 1635 by Elizabeth
Stonehouse. The windows, however, as restored,
are of the same pattern as those in the nave. The
excellent new woodwork was the gift of the late Sir
George Bowyer, lord of the manor. The Norman font
was found in the village, and replaced in the church
about 1840. There is a large monument to William
Stonehouse (d. 1631). The low tower is good Perp.

READING, at the junction of the Kennet with the
Thames, is the county town of Berkshire, where the
assizes are held, and is by far the first in importance
both in size and manufactures. From 1295 to 1885
it sent two members to Parliament, and it still sends
one. It has a long and remarkable history. The Saxon
town, described as *villa regia*, was in the winter
of 870 seized and fortified by the Danes. In the

READING

spring Ethelred and Alfred attacked them, but were defeated in a battle in which Ethelwulf (see *Englefield*) was killed, and chased over the Loddon, thus leaving Berkshire open to attack. A little later came the battle of Ashdown. The Danes were again plundering and burning at Reading in 1006, during the second period of invasion. A Norman castle was built here, and held for King Stephen, but no trace remains except the name Castle Street. Berkshire was now considered a royal county, and visits of kings to Reading grow frequent. Thus Henry II. witnessed here the famous duel in an island in the Thames between Robert of Montfort and Henry of Essex, accused of throwing away the King's standard in the battle of Coleshill. This is the fight told at length by Carlyle, in which the figure of St Edmund appeared "minatory, on the rim of the horizon." [1] In 1185 Henry II. was here again, when he gave an audience to the patriarch Heraclius, who tried to induce him to lead the third crusade. John held a council here about ecclesiastical troubles. In 1219 Henry III. was here, to be near William the Marshal, who lay dying at Caversham. Several other kings and queens have visited the town, including Elizabeth, who was here several times. Many parliaments have been held here, and in 1625, when the plague was raging in London, the law courts were transferred hither. During the Civil War, Reading was first held for the King. In 1643 it was attacked by Essex, who, after a sharp siege and the failure of the King's attempt to relieve it, forced it to surrender. After the first battle of Newbury Essex in his retreat abandoned Reading, which again received a Royalist garrison. In 1644, however, it was aban-

[1] "Past and Present," Book II. c. 14.

doned, when Essex again advanced, and this time remained in Parliamentary hands. During the invasion of the Prince of Orange in 1688 Reading was one of the few places which saw serious fighting. Six hundred Irish, who were holding the town for James, were attacked by less than half that number of William's troops, who drove them through the town into the market-place, and then, aided by the vigorous co-operation of the citizens, thoroughly routed them.

The most illustrious citizen of Reading is Archbishop Laud, who was born here in 1593, the son of a clothier, and educated at the Grammar School. In 1638 he procured a charter for the town from Charles I., and in 1640 endowed it with £200 a year, to be spent mainly in apprenticing poor boys and portioning poor girls. Sir Thomas White, founder of St John's College, Oxford, was also born at Reading ; and, in later times, Judge Talfourd. Bunyan was often at Reading, disguised as a carter, with a long whip, to avoid arrest.

Perhaps, however, the most interesting part of Reading history centres round its former abbey. It appears that there had previously been an abbey in Saxon times, which had probably been destroyed by the Danes in 1006. The great Abbey was founded in 1121 by Henry I., who was afterwards buried before the high altar. The great church was not finished until 1164, and was consecrated by Becket, in the presence of Henry II. Of the interesting events which have taken place within the Abbey walls a mere summary must suffice. Its colossal wealth and dignity enabled it to play the host to a long roll of kings and queens. Many illustrious dead were laid in the church subsequent to its royal founder, among them the Empress

Matilda—whose epitaph as preserved by Camden was:

> " Magna ortu, majorque viro, sed maxima partu,
> Hic jacet Henrici filia, sponsa, parens."

—also William, eldest son of Henry II., and two children of Richard King of the Romans. The most important marriage solemnized in the church was that between John of Gaunt and Blanche, heiress of Lancaster (1359). In the great hall councils of the Church and parliaments of the State have frequently been held, some of great historical importance, such as the occasion when Richard II. declared himself of age (1389), or that on which Edward IV. declared Elizabeth Woodville his wife (1464). In 1538 Hugh Faringdon, the last abbot, was accused of high treason, flung into the Tower, and, after a mockery of a trial, hanged in front of his own gateway. When even Froude admits that " Cromwell acted as prosecutor, judge and jury," it seems superfluous to inquire what charges were brought against him. Indeed we have notes in Cromwell's own handwriting, arranging for both trial and execution. The Abbey and its enormous revenues, amounting to over £1900 a year (perhaps twenty times that value in our present money), fell into the hands of the robber king, who turned the buildings into a palace. This was visited by most of his successors, the last royal occupant being Charles I. in 1625. After this the buildings became ruinous, and seem to have been drawn upon freely for repairing the parish churches and other purposes.

Besides the fame of the Abbey, Reading owed its prosperity in the Middle Ages to its cloth industry, which has now disappeared. Its place, however, has been taken by other famous industries, which have

made the town the busiest in the county. As a local
poet sings, Reading is

> " 'Mongst other things so widely known
>   For biscuits, seeds and sauce."

Reading sauce has been made by Messrs Cocks for
nearly a century, and Messrs Huntley & Palmer's
biscuit manufactories, and Messrs Sutton & Sons'
seed nurseries are very prominent features of the town.
Reading is also a great market for corn and an important
railway centre. The consequence is that its population
has grown in the course of the 19th cent. from 9000
to 72,000, and the area covered by houses has expanded
in proportion. The central streets are broad and
handsome, with good shops and public buildings, and
some of the suburbs are pleasant, but the continually-
growing wilderness of small red-brick houses has quite
destroyed the picturesqueness of the town as a whole.

Of its remarkable history Reading shows but few
traces. The ruins of the Abbey are now very fragmentary. Passing E. of St Lawrence's Church, we
first have on the S. the inner gateway, which led from
the faubourg or outer court (still called the Forbury)
to an inner court reserved for the monks. Of the
four outer gateways not a trace is left. The tower
was rebuilt in 1861 by Sir Gilbert Scott, who may,
more suo, have considerably altered the original work,
especially as the tower had fallen in the preceding year.
As it stands, the lower parts seem to be Trans. in style,
with Dec. windows in the upper story. These light
a hall in which the Abbot Faringdon was himself tried
for his life. The site of the Forbury (N. of road) is
now occupied by public gardens, which are connected
with the ruins at the S.E. corner by a tunnel under

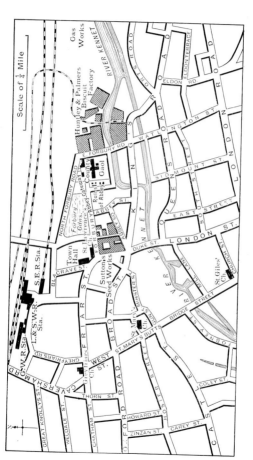

CENTRAL PART OF READING

the road, partly built of carved stones from the ruins
themselves. The ruins are massive fragments of flint
and cement, from which every carved stone has been
removed, so that there are no indications of style. Yet
they still appear so huge and majestic that it is hard to
realize that they are a comparatively small part of the
original Abbey buildings, which must have been
colossal. Of the late Norman Abbey church the nave and
chancel have disappeared, but some ivy-covered fragments of the transepts remain—*i.e.* the E. walls of the
apsidal chapel in both transepts, and in the S. transept
the W. and S. walls as well. To the S. are, in order,
first a vestry, then the chapter-house, then some traces
of the long dorter (or monks' dormitory), and finally the
rere-dorter, stretching nearly to the river Kennet.
Directly W. of all these buildings ran the cloisters.
The chapter-house is impressive in its ruins, though its
apsidal E. end has disappeared. On the W., leading
into the cloisters, were a door and five round-headed
windows, of which only the frames remain. The
dorter was raised on vaulted cellars, but little remains
except the W. wall adjoining the cloister.

The parish churches are not a very interesting
group. *St Lawrence's* has been so much restored and
rebuilt that it is now difficult to distinguish how much
of the work is original. We know that the tower and
the nave arcade were altered in 1434, and the chantry
chapel also has good Perp. windows. The S. wall
seems late Trans. (c. 1200), with a door and window
both round-headed, and the chancel arcade is E.E., but
all this work now looks quite new. In spite of this the
church is handsome and dignified, both inside and out.
There is a good font, and some bench-ends, both Perp.,
and a piece of old carving near the pulpit. The W.
window commemorates the principal benefactors of the

town—*i.e.* Laud, Sir Thomas White, and three kings, Henry I., Henry VII. (see later), and Charles I. There are several monuments—to John Blagrave, the mathematician, 1611 ; a *prie-dieu* to Martha Hamley, 1636, another to Lydall, and brasses to (1) John and Joan Kent, 1415 ; (2) John Andrew, 1428 ; (3) E. Butler and wife, 1584 ; (4) W. Barton, 1538, a palimpsest, the reverse being effigy of Sir John Popham, 1463. *Greyfriars' Church*, at the corner of Caversham Road, contains the finest old work in the town. It was rebuilt in 1863 to incorporate fragments of an old monastic church, erected on ground given by the Abbey to the friars in 1285. The land originally given in 1233 had been close to the river, and proved unsuitable, as being liable to floods. The ancient parts are the two magnificent Dec. arcades, the chancel arch, and the restored W. window, which is of a fine reticulated pattern, and has a little old glass. At present the church has no chancel. There are a few old tiles. Near here were discovered in 1906 the remains of St Edmond's Chapel, founded in 1284, but afterwards turned into a barn. Some carved stones from it have been deposited in the room above the Abbey Gateway. *St Mary's*, at the end of Minster Street, was rebuilt in 1551 with materials from the ruins of the Abbey. It has also partly been rebuilt in modern times, with the result that its architecture is very queer and confused. Thus on the N. side there is an early Norman door. The S. arcade is rude E.E., and was evidently brought wholesale from the Abbey. The N. arcades and the whole of the chancel are modern E.E., and have been assimilated to the earlier work. Yet in the chancel there strangely occurs a Dec. Easter sepulchre, which must be original. The windows are all restored. The tower is late Perp., of a chessboard pattern. There is a font, dated 1616, an alms-box with strange inscription, dated 1627, and a wooden gallery and screen also of the 17th cent. There is a *prie-dieu* tomb to W. Kendrick and his wife (1635), and brass plates to W. Baron (1416) and John Boorne (1558). *St Giles'*, which was much damaged in the Civil War, was made almost entirely a new church in 1873. Some old carved stones have been blocked up in an arch under the tower. There are two restored piscinæ, and a defaced brass to John Bowyer, 1521. The other churches are entirely modern.

Near to St Lawrence's Church is the site of the ancient *Grammar School*, now removed to the London road. The traditional story is that St John's Hospital had been suppressed by the Abbot of Reading, and the funds appropriated by the Abbey. When Henry VII. heard this, he directed the Abbot to apply the money to some pious use, on which the Abbot founded the Grammar School. This story, however, is controverted by a writer in the "Victoria History of Berkshire," who asserts that the school existed before the Abbey, and was given to the Abbey in 1190. The question appears a difficult one. At the school Julius Palmer, the Newbury martyr, was master, and Laud was educated. He afterwards interfered to secure the appointment of a capable headmaster. Near St Lawrence's Church is also the *Town Hall*, which contains the *Museum*. This is of the highest interest, for here are deposited all the interesting and beautiful objects which have been excavated at Silchester. (For details see under *Silchester*.) The visitor should purchase the two excellent penny guides, one to the Silchester Collection, the other to the General Museum. In the latter may be noted a few objects of great local interest, such as the pewter chalice found at Reading in the grave of a Saxon priest, the Greek two-handled cup that was dredged out of the Thames, the Roman funeral urn of marble which had been used for a flower-pot at Earley, and the scanty relics of the Abbey.

Fuller tells a good story about Henry VIII. and the Abbot of Reading, which is too long to quote, and yet can hardly be omitted. It relates how Henry cured the " weak and squeezie stomach " of the Abbot by the heroic remedy of imprisonment upon bread and water.

Remenham ($1\frac{1}{2}$ m. N. of Henley station) is a little riverside village lying opposite to the beautifully broad and straight reach on which Henley regatta is held. Regatta Island, with its gleaming temple, is not very far down the stream, and the wooded Chilterns rise beyond. The church has been entirely rebuilt, save for one late Dec. window on N. side. Its apsidal termination shows it was originally Norman. There are brasses to Thomas Maryet (1591) and John Newman, rector (1622).

RIDGEWAY (THE) is an ancient roadway running along the top of the Berkshire Downs, and otherwise called Icknield or Ickleton Street. It is considered to be pre-Roman, though it is probable that the Romans used it. The track is a broad one, and is mostly bordered by a low green bank on either side. It is, as a rule, covered with grass, but it is far from smooth, being full of ruts and other inequalities, so that, although it is delightful to walk on, the cyclist will find it very tiresome. As the Downs are mostly cultivated up to the summit (with the exception of the higher and steeper ones, such as White Horse Hill), the Ridgeway supplies a path by which the range may be traversed from end to end. The view is almost entirely N., over the Vale of the White Horse and the Thames Valley, but it is finer on the W. part of the range than in the E.

part, since in the latter case the bare lower chalk slopes are too prominent in the foreground. The top is usually bare, but it is occasionally broken by clumps of beeches, known locally as follies. As nearly all the points of interest on the Downs are described separately, a brief summary will suffice here. The road is described from W. to E. Starting from the Downs above Ashbury, we soon have *Wayland Smith's Cave* on our L. Then the track climbs behind *White Horse Hill*, with *Uffington Castle* above it on the L. A long descent follows, then another up and down, and presently another ascent to the high point where the Ridgeway is crossed by the *Lambourn and Wantage road*. Then another descent with the *Punch Bowl* L., and a slighter rise to *Letcombe Castle* (also L.). In another half-mile we reach the Wantage and Hungerford road, close to the Red House. Here the track divides, reuniting in ½ m., after passing the White House. In another ½ m., at a fork, take the L. branch, and also at another fork, just beyond the *monument to Lord Wantage* (see *Lockinge*). Next the Ridgeway Reservoir, formed in 1898, is passed L., and we reach the large clump of trees which marks *Scutchamore Knob*. Then come the flat Ilsley Downs, and presently the Oxford to Newbury road is struck. Soon afterwards the track descends to the *Churn Basin*, ascending again by the *Fair Mile*, leaving *Lowbury Camp* on the R. From here a descent can be made to the Thames at Moulsford or Streatley. (All names in italics are separately described.) The whole route on the Downs is about 20 m.

Ruscombe (less than 1 m. N.E. of Twyford) has a church with a very plain E.E. (or possibly Trans.) chancel, built of flint, and lighted by small lancet windows in frames of hard chalk. The nave and tower are curious 17th-cent. brick. On the vane is the inscription C. R. 1639. There is a Jacobean pulpit.

Sandhurst is a largish straggling village equidistant from Wellington College and Blackwater stations, in the S.E. corner of the county. The church has been rebuilt, but retains an old beam in the roof with an inscription stating it was set up in the twenty-third year of Charles I. (*i.e.* 1647). There is a brass to Richard Geale, wife and nine children (1608), and a tomb to Wm. Chislett (1671). The *Royal Military College* is in the E. of the parish, close to the county boundary, and 1½ m. from the church. The buildings, erected in 1812, are low and plain, yet have a certain dignity. The extensive grounds are charming, being well wooded and containing two beautiful lakes, just N. of which (in Surrey) is the Royal Staff College.

Sandleford Priory (1½ m. S. of Newbury) is now a modern-looking mansion lying among grounds which are full of cedars and other fine trees, and slope to the banks of the Enborne stream. The Priory was founded for Austin Canons between 1193 and 1202, by Geoffrey, fourth Count of Perche. In 1320 Edward II. stayed a night here. About 1480 the revenues were given to Windsor Chapel, a statement having been made that the monks had wholly left the Priory. In 1775 the property was left to Mrs Elizabeth Montagu, who in 1781 built the present house from Wyatt's plans, converting the ancient chapel into a dining-room. Mrs Montague was for fifty years the leading hostess in the intellectual society of London, and to her assemblies were first applied the name " blue-stocking." Of this two explanations have been suggested, one that it was due to the unconventionality of Benjamin Stilling-fleet, who used to come to the assemblies in blue worsted instead of silk stockings ; the other, that the

ROYAL MILITARY COLLEGE, SANDHURST

ladies at these parties wore blue stockings as a distinction. Mrs Montagu's parties were in London, but we hear of friends visiting her at Sandleford.

Scutchamore Knob is a remarkable barrow on the ridge of the Downs, 2½ m. S. of East Hendred (*q.v.*). It stands in the centre of a fine clump of beeches, and a large hole has been dug on its N. side. The name is a corruption of *Cwichelm's hleaw* (or hill), which has also been altered to Schoochamfly. Cwichelm was a chieftain or prince in authority under the King of Wessex, and he may well have defended the line of the Downs against the advance of the Mercians, as his son Cuthred did, somewhat later. In 871, the Danes, after leaving Reading, are said in the Saxon Chronicle to have "turned along Ashdown to Cwichelm's hleaw," just before the battle of Ashdown. In 1006 the Danes, after burning Wallingford and Cholsey, turned again to Cwichelm's hleaw, and stayed there out of bravado, because it had often been said that if they came to Cwichelm's hleaw they would never go to the sea.

Shaw (1 m. N.E. of Newbury) is a village with a new church.

SHAW HOUSE, the most interesting Elizabethan mansion in the county, was built by Thomas Dolman, a Newbury clothier who had grown rich and retired. His fellow-citizens seem to have been envious of his good fortune, and angry at his ceasing to employ labour, and vented their spleen in the following lines:

> "Lord have mercy upon us, miserable sinners,
>   Thomas Dolman has built a new house
>   And has turned away all his spinners."

Dolman's retort was to carve over the main door "μηδεὶς φθονερὸς εἰσίτω" and on the portico the couplet:

> "Edentulus vescentium dentibus invidet,
>   Et oculos caprearum talpa contemnit."

In the Civil War another Thomas Dolman owned the house, and was a zealous King's man. During the second battle of Newbury (*q.v.*) the house was fortified as part of the Royalist lines, and bore the brunt of Manchester's attack. The attack early in the day was only meant as a feint, but some of the Puritans went further than they intended, and were repulsed from the house with considerable loss. Late in the afternoon a serious attack was made, and the garden on the E. side of the house was the scene of a severe struggle, but the defence was maintained till night stopped the fighting. After the battle the Dolmans took for motto :

> " King and law
> Shouts Dolman of Shaw."

Thomas Dolman was made a knight by Charles II., and in 1663 entertained that monarch, with his queen and the Duke of York, at Shaw House. Queen Anne also slept here in 1703. The house is of good red brick, in which the stone-mullioned windows are set, and has several excellent gables and old chimney stacks. The chief front (S.) shows the characterstic " E "-formation, but more striking are the N. side, which has an effective colonnade between its projecting wings, and the E. side, which has two fine bay windows at both ends. Just inside the upper bay window at the S.E. corner (now belonging to the drawing-room) is a bullet-hole with a Latin inscription stating that when Charles I. was dressing on the morning of the battle a shot was fired at him through the window, which narrowly missed him. The interior is panelled throughout in oak, and used to contain several interesting relics of the battle, most of which were sold by auction in 1905. In the garden the ramparts which formed the original defences still exist on all sides but the N., and, shaded by well-

grown yew-trees, make delightful walks. On the S.
side there is a break in the ramparts, in which are set
four old cannons, said to have been captured in the
battle.

Shefford is the name of two villages close together in
the Lambourn Valley.

East or *Little Shefford* is a place of high antiquity.
In 1890 an Anglo-Saxon cemetery was discovered here,
and many important finds were sent to the British
Museum. Mr Walter Money believes that it was here
and not at Shifford-on-Thames that King Alfred is
reported to have discoursed proverbial wisdom in 890.
A third theory is that of Prof. Skeat, who concludes
from the reading of one of the three MSS. of the
" Proverbs " that Seaford in Sussex is meant. The
question is of no historical importance, for the work in
question only dates from the end of the 12th cent.
In the Middle Ages the ubiquitous Fettiplaces were lords
of the manor here, and their splendid 15th-cent. manor-
house only finally disappeared in 1870. The old
church, near the Lambourn stream, is disused, but still
kept in fair repair. It contains a Trans. window and a
small rood-stairs window; but both are blocked.
Otherwise the windows are late and poor Perp. There
is a Norman font and a plain piscina. There are two
splendid Fettiplace monuments : (1) an alabaster altar-
tomb to Sir Thomas Fettiplace (c. 1450) and his wife
Beatrix, a noble Portuguese lady who may have been
related to the royal family of Portugal, though her
identification seems very uncertain; (2) canopied
Purbeck marble tomb to John and Dorothy Fettiplace
(1524), with brasses and shield. At the W. end is a
coffin-slab with three crosses discovered in 1887. Under-
neath was an oak coffin with the skeleton of an ecclesias-
tic holding a pewter paten and chalice. On higher

ground (S.) is a new church, one window of which contains some 15th-cent. glass taken from the old church. It represents the Annunciation. The Virgin is seated, and a very small Gabriel is speaking to her out of the cloud.

West or *Great Shefford* is about 1 m. higher up the valley. The interesting church is probably entirely Trans., though there is the usual doubt whether the earlier parts may not be pure Norman and the later E.E. There are four later inserted windows. The chancel is lighted by deeply splayed lancets, with an inserted Dec. window (S.), and a Perp. window E. The lancets which were removed to insert the latter may be traced outside. The nave has two lancets N. and two Perp. windows S. The S. door is certainly Trans. and the plain N. door may be so also. Two stories of the tower, including the arch and W. window, are also Trans., and are round, a very rare formation. The upper octagonal story is Perp. The cylindrical font may be pure Norman. Note plain piscina and pewter paten. The farm near the church has been built on the ruins of the old manor-house. It shows some old brickwork and a panelled chamber where Charles I. slept a night in November 1644. Little else remains, the great hall having been divided into smaller rooms.

Shellingford (3 m. S.E. of Faringdon) has a church of some interest. The chancel arch and three doors are Norman. The chancel arch with its arabesque work, and the N. door with its beak-heads, point to a date of about 1140-1150. The other two doors have Trans. features, the S. door showing both zigzag and dog-tooth mouldings. The tower and spire are E.E., and also the walls of the chancel. The chancel windows are mostly Dec., but there is one large Perp. window (N.) with panelled soffit arch. The nave has one late Dec. window, the others are Perp.

There is a Dec. octagonal font, a good wooden roof to the nave, an Elizabethan pulpit, and low-side window (N. of nave). Two windows have some old glass. S. of the church is the so-called *Shellingford Castle*, a long and low Perp. building, once the offices of the manor-house. It has now been turned into a row of cottages. The windows are square and plain two-light Perp., and there is a fine Perp. chimney with a sundial on it. The manor-house is not extant, but traces of the fishponds and garden are to be found.

Shinfield (3½ m. S. of Reading) has a restored church of little interest. There is a plain Norman N. door, and some fair Dec. and Perp. windows. Two of the monuments are of the *prie-dieu* type (dated 1607 and 1627). The 17th-cent. red-brick tower is picturesque, and there are three good lime-trees. *Three Mile Cross*, a hamlet 1 m. W., is the scene of Miss Mitford's "Our Village."

Shippon is a hamlet 1 m. N.W. of Abingdon. In it is a quaint ivy-clad house, with a curious little Perp. window close to the door. It is said to have been a cell of Abingdon Monastery, and used as an infirmary. The church is new.

SHOTTESBROOK (3¾ m. E. of Twyford and about 4½ m. W. of Maidenhead) is an out-of-the-way manor containing the most interesting church in E. Berkshire (key at gardener's, S. of church). It is one of the three instances of collegiate churches in the county. In 1337 the parish church was made collegiate by Sir William Trussell, who founded a college with warden, five other chaplains and two clerks. This lasted until its suppression in 1548 under Edward VI. Towards the end of the reign of Edward III. (apparently about 1370) both church and college buildings perished by fire. After this disaster the present church was built. It is therefore certainly very late Dec., and most of the

Curvilinear windows show by the stiffening of their mullions that the Perp. period is close at hand. The church is cruciform with a central tower on which is set a gracefully ribbed spire. There is also a good staircase turret. The central crossing is plain, only the chancel arch being moulded. At the four corners are corbel-heads. All the windows are good Curvilinear, especially the five-light E. window. Outside are good corner-buttresses. The S. porch is beautiful ; also the blocked N. porch. In chancel note three fine sedilia, piscina with bracket, double aumbry and blocked Dec. door. In each transept is a piscina. The octagonal font is beautiful Dec. ; there are considerable remains of old glass. There are several monuments. In the chancel is an alabaster " coffin " monument to William Throckmorton, the last warden of the college before its suppression in 1535. In the N. transept are the tombs of the founder and his wife, with canopies divided by a niche. The fine tabernacle work has been partly damaged by restoration. Here also (under the pews) are brasses to (1) Lady Margaret Pennebrygg, 1401 ; (2) Richard Gyll, " sergeant of the bakehouse" to Henry VII. and Henry VIII. (1511) ; (3) two figures of a priest and a franklin under the same canopy (in nave), c. 1380 ; (4) Thomas Noke, his three wives and children. In the reign of William III. the manor was held by Mr Francis Cherry, a stout Jacobite and friend to the non-juring clergy. He is said once, when hunting with King William, to have ridden his horse into a dangerous part of the Thames, in the hope that the " usurper " might follow and be drowned.

Shrivenham is a pleasing village with wide streets and well-kept cottages. The grounds of the manor-house are extensive and well timbered, and contain a pretty lake. The church has a fine central tower (Perp.), resting on four arches, each with several orders of plain mouldings, which are carried to the ground without capitals. The rest of the church is debased 17th-cent. work, with round arches resting on columns broader at the base than at the top, and square-headed windows filled with a sort of late Perp. tracery. The church, however, is dignified and well proportioned, has excellent woodwork throughout, and is admirably kept. In the E. window are three coats-of-arms, dated 1505, 1607 and 1790. The marble font appears to be Trans., and must belong to an earlier church. There are monuments to (1) John Wildman, the Anabaptist (1693), and John his son (1710), who, according to the inscriptions, seem to have spent most of their lives in prison ; (2) John Shute, afterwards first Lord Barrington, adopted son of the younger John Wildman ; (3) Admiral Barrington of the White (1800), with an inscription by Hannah More, and an old flag which he captured (now in chancel).

A little N. is the hamlet of Watchfield, with a modern church.

SILCHESTER (2½ m. S.W. of Mortimer station) is the site of the Romano-British town *Calleva Atrebatum*. For a full account the reader must be referred to Dr Cox in the " Little Guide to Hampshire," since, owing to the eccentricity of the boundary-line, the place is wholly in that county. If the boundary had continued along the Devil's Highway (*q.v.*) it would have bisected the old town, leaving the N. half in Berkshire. As, however, some account of the remarkable Silchester finds, now deposited in Reading Museum, is required of a guide-book writer, it seems advisable to prefix to it a very short description of the site where they were found. On the top of the Silchester plateau is an almost complete circle of Roman wall 1½ m. round. Inside are now cultivated fields, but buried beneath them are the foundations of the ancient city. These have been systematically examined during the last twenty years, so that now a plan of the town has been drawn up, and a medley of objects discovered illustrative of its life. The only foundations which have been left permanently uncovered are those of the *forum*, with the *basilica* W. of it in the centre of the town, two or three smaller buildings N.W. of the forum, and also a circular temple more S. In all other cases after the site has been explored the earth has been filled in again. Just outside the wall on the E. is an earthen amphitheatre. For detailed information we turn to *Reading Museum*. On the staircase are splendid examples of the mosaic floors discovered. Of the two rooms devoted to the antiquities the smaller is called the architectural room. Of the basilica or town hall a fine Corinthian capital remains. Of the great gateway of the forum there are some Doric capitals and one of the large bases. Of the three temples and the baths little is known except the plans. But the great find was made in 1892—*i.e.* the foundations of a *small Christian church*, of which a model is here shown, together with a drawing of the beautiful mosaics on the chancel floor. Of the six gates there is a model of the W. gate only. The private houses are of two types, referred to as the corridor type and the courtyard type. In many cases of both types the Roman method of warming the winter rooms can be well observed. The beautiful specimens of wall-painting are also noticeable. The larger room devoted to the collection contains cases fitted with an endless succession of interesting objects, of which only a few can be mentioned. The most interesting of all will not be found, but only a photograph and a model of it. This is the head of one of the Roman Eagles, a most rare

THE THAMES AND WITTENHAM CLUMPS

W

treasure. The traces of the dyeing and silver-refining industries deserve careful examination; also the glass, whether used for windows or for bottles. One piece of glass has Christian symbols, a fish and a palm-branch. It is interesting to note that the principle of the safety-pin was known to the Romans. There are several inscriptions, one of the best being that of a workman who, having finished a pipe, wrote on it, *Fecit tubum Clementinus.* Space prohibits further illustration, but hours of interest may be spent in examining the collection.

Sinodun is the easternmost of two remarkable hills, which are usually known, from the clumps of beeches on their tops, as the *Dorchester* or *Wittenham Clumps.* The W. hill, sometimes called Harp Hill, is about 400 ft. high, and Sinodun is a very little lower. The two clumps, with the range running E. from them, on which Brightwell Barrow (371 ft.) is the highest point, form a detached outlier of the chalk, and from their remarkable shape and isolated position are conspicuous objects in the Thames Valley. The Thames itself runs just N. of them and their N. sides are well wooded. The way up them is by the road leading from Little Wittenham. At the top of Sinodun there is a remarkably fine ancient earthwork, consisting of a perfect double vallum with a trench between. The views of the Thames from both hills are very beautiful.

Sindlesham. (See *Bearwood.*)

SONNING (3½ m. N.E. of Reading) is one of the prettiest riverside villages. As we row down through the flat meadows which lie N.E. of Reading the beautiful hanging woods of *Holme Park* come nearly down to the river on the right. Below the charming lock and weir are Sonning bridges, stated to be among the oldest on the Thames. The river divides into three or four branches, and on the island in the centre is a mill with cool, plashing waters. The principal bridge is of brick, with eleven arches, but it has been repaired so often that it does not look old. On the Oxfordshire side, crossing a backwater, there is now a bridge of white painted iron, which does not harmonize with the scene. In 1902 this was erected in place of a picturesque old wooden bridge. Energetic protests were made at the time by lovers of the river, but æsthetic considerations were not allowed to prevail over utilitarian. Otherwise the village has nothing to offend the eye. It is of high antiquity. During the century and a half (909-1058) that Berkshire was part of the diocese of Ramsbury (Wilts), the bishops were occasionally called bishops of Sonning,[1] and there is no doubt that there was an episcopal residence here from early times. When the diocese was united to that of Salisbury, the bishops still held a palace here up till the reign of Elizabeth. After Richard II. had been deposed his child-wife fled here for protection to the Bishop of Salisbury of the time, and here she was visited by the three conspiring Earls (see *Faringdon* and *Windsor*) who " gladdened her with lies." The site of the palace is a rounded mound in the park, which may be well seen from a path leading from the church to the towpath. The church is much restored, and full of elaborate modern ornament. There are a few ancient features. Thus the nave arcades are E.E., though the Dec. clerestory above them is new. The E. window is reticulated, but all the other windows are new or restored. There is an elaborate Dec. arch with fine carving between the chancel and N. aisle, though it has been partly altered. The tower, with W. door and window, is Perp. There is an old

[1] On the meaning of the title see Dr Cox's article in the " Victoria County History," vol. ii.

SONNING BRIDGE

oak screen, partly repaired, a large monument to Sir Thomas Rich (1667), and as many as nine old brasses. With the N.W. buttress of the N. aisle there is incorporated a Saxon coffin-lid. The rectory has a panelled drawing-room, and a large garden with a fine cedar.

Sotwell (1½ m. N.W. of Wallingford) has a rebuilt church, retaining two Perp. windows (N.). There are some indications in the masonry of an older Norman church, including some carved stones, the heads of two small round-headed windows (blocked) in the chancel, and a round-headed niche. There is also a blocked shouldered arch.

Southcote House is an old 15th-cent. mansion 2 m. S.W. of Reading and ½ m. S. of the Bath road. It is of red brick, with stone dressings, and still retains parts of the original building, including a detached watchtower. It is surrounded by a moat, and approached by a bridge, which has replaced the ancient drawbridge. Over this the ghost of a lady on a white horse is said to ride every night at twelve o'clock. The mansion was purchased in 1588 by John Blagrave, the "mathematician," now buried in St Lawrence's Church, Reading. In 1643 Essex held a council of war here.

SPARSHOLT (2½ m. S. of Challow station) is another of the charming villages which nestle under the Downs. The church is extremely interesting. There are some indications of an original Trans. church—*i.e.* (1) two string-courses in the nave, one external, the other internal; (2) N. and S. doors; (3) the lower and middle stories of the tower. The upper one, which is Geometrical, looks restored. There is also an old cylindrical font, which is at least Trans., if not older. The church was completely rebuilt late in the Dec. period (c. 1330). It was cruciform, but the N. transept has been destroyed, the original Dec. window being built up in the wall. This has a small fragment of old glass, a beautiful woman's head. All the windows have reticulated patterns, except the E. window, which is modern Dec. There are no arcades, only two plain arches. In the nave there is a wooden Dec. roof, and two windows with a little old glass; also two inserted late Perp. windows in the clerestory, one of which has a quantity of old glass. The chancel shows much rich Dec. work with elaborate canopies—*i.e.* (1) sedilia and piscina; (2) Easter sepulchre (N.); (3) sepulchral recess (S.), under which is a panelled tomb, with the effigy of a knight. Note also the small door to the vestry (N.) (which is old, but has modern windows) and the external cornice with gargoyles. In the S. transept notice (1) Dec. screen; (2) long narrow squint (splayed) (there was a corresponding one on the other side, now blocked); (3) piscina with wooden shelf; (4) three wooden effigies, one of a knight on a modern tomb, two of females, which have been placed under canopied tomb-recesses. All are good Dec. There are nine brasses in the church, of which four have effigies. The oldest is that of William de Herleston, rector (1353), a very early and interesting brass, more fragmentary now than in Ashmole's time, who records it in his "Antiquities of Berkshire." From the words "*hanc cancellam,*" which he quotes, it has been inferred that Herleston was the rebuilder of the chancel. He certainly belonged to the Achard family, at that time lords of the manor, for the Achard arms are above his effigy. Mr C. E. Keyser believes that he was son of the Achard whose canopied tomb is in the chancel, and at whose cost and in whose memory presumably it was rebuilt; and also that he was brother of Sir Robert Achard, who is said to have rebuilt the S. transept in 1327. The other brasses with effigies are (2) a mutilated head and shoulders; (3) a lady with two children; (4) a layman in robes (both about 1500). The other five brasses are 17th-cent. plates.

Speen (about 1 m. N.W. of Newbury) is with hardly any doubt the *Spinae* mentioned twice in the Itinerary of Antoninus. It is at the point where the Roman road coming W. from Silchester (see *Devil's Highway*) bifurcates, one branch, sometimes called *Ermine Street*, going by Wickham Common and the ridge between the Kennet and the Lambourn on to *Corinium* and *Glevum*, the other to *Cunetio* and *Aquae Solis* (Bath), and keeping more or less on the lines of the present Bath road. Probably Spinae was not a Roman town, but only a posting-station, though there is some evidence that a settlement grew up round it. Later on, when Newbury grew in importance, Speen became little more than a suburb of the larger town. The church was rebuilt in 1860 and the tower in 1871. Nothing old remains except (1) the E.E. Purbeck columns in the nave, which have new bases and capitals; (2) a Dec. window with flowing tracery on N. side. The two Castillion monuments (1598 and 1603) are good. In the churchyard are two fine limes. Near the church is " Ye ancient Ladye well," restored in 1902, when an arch was built over it. (For the part taken by Speen Hill in the second battle of Newbury, see under *Newbury*.)

Speenhamland. (See *Newbury*.)

STANFORD DINGLEY (about 3½ m. N. of Midgham station, or 3½ m. N.W. of Aldermaston station) is a pretty village in the Pang Valley. The church, though small, has some remarkable features. There are two Trans. arcades, one of two bays, the other of three. The E. bay in both is very plain, and might be pure Norman, but the other bays are distinctive Trans. work.

The piers are large and handsome for so small a church. The pointed chancel arch is also Trans., and there is one Trans. window, the lancet E. of N. aisle. In the S. aisle there are two strange features (apparently E.E.). (1) The E. window of the aisle is a quatrefoil set in circular frame, widely splayed inside. (2) The S. door is trefoiled, with a rose ornament introduced at the points of the trefoil, and with a pointed arch above.[1] The door itself has E.E. ironwork and an old lock. The wooden tower has a slate cap, and is supported on an interior wooden framework (probably Perp.). A blocked door and the W. window are also early Perp. All other windows are restored or modern, and the chancel is brick of the 18th cent. The font is plain cylindrical Norman, and perhaps the earliest feature in the church. There are several excellent remains of wall-painting and brasses to Margaret Dyneley (1444) and John Lyford (1610). The churchyard is surrounded by chestnuts.

STANFORD-IN-THE-VALE (2 m. N.W. of Challow station) is a large village in the Upper Ock Valley. The fine church is mostly E.E. and Dec., but presents some architectural puzzles. The only Norman feature is the door in S. porch. The porch itself is Perp. with corner vaulting-shafts, which supported a roof no longer existing. The E.E. features are late, and suggest that the church was rebuilt about 1240. They comprise (1) the W. window in N. aisle, a foliated lancet triplet; (2) the N. door and porch, which has a gable higher than the present N. aisle roof; (3) the tower, which has three E.E. stories and a top Perp. story. Probably of the same date are the N. arcade and the blocked trefoil-headed clerestory above it, but it is possible that these

---

[1] Mr C. E. Keyser considers this door late 12th cent.

are Dec., for the piers are of the puzzling variety which shows no capitals, and whose date it is always difficult to fix. The chancel arch is of the same date. The existing clerestory is debased. A second great alteration of the church was made in the Dec. period. The chancel is entirely Dec., with five good windows. Three are of the ordinary flowing type, but two show something like Kentish tracery, which suggests that the date of the whole may be 1310-1320. This again is an uncertain point. The windows contain some old glass, and there is a strikingly beautiful and unique piscina, with tabernacle work above it, used as a reliquary. There is a double aumbry on N. side and a priest's door. The interior bulge containing the rood-stairs is lighted by two small windows. A remarkable squint starts by a passage behind it and is carried on a pillar past the vestry door. The windows of the vestry and N. aisle are of the square-headed type, which is probably very late Dec. There are three Dec. windows also S. of the nave, including a low-side window, which are rarely found in the nave. Besides the Perp. features already mentioned there is a large window with old glass above the S. porch. The pulpit and the wooden font are Elizabethan. There is a brass to Roger Campdene (1398), with large half-figure, and a monument to Capt. Francis Knollys (1640).

STEVENTON is a large and picturesque village just where the flat country begins to rise up towards the lower slopes of the Downs. Here there was formerly a small alien priory belonging to Bec, and holding the manor. The Abbey sold the property late in Edward III.'s reign. The village is traversed by the Abingdon and Newbury road, close to which is the spacious village green. Cutting this road at right angles is the main village street, along the whole of which runs a remarkable raised flood-path, bordered by trees on either side. In the W. part of this street there are about six remarkable timber-built houses. One shows a gable with oriel window and the date 1657. The two best of these houses are quite to the W. beyond the railway crossing. The furthermost of these has a good barge-board, and two windows with wooden mullions. Farther W. is the interesting church, of which the shape is somewhat peculiar. There is a large S. aisle, which overlaps the chancel, but does not reach entirely to the E. end, and over the W. bay of this aisle is built the tower. The S. arcade is of four bays, and of very composite structure. The two W. bays (*i.e.* the one under the tower and the next one to it) are Dec. The third bay, with one of the columns, is late Trans. (c. 1180), which is strange, since there is no other trace of that style in the church. The column has good E.E.-looking mouldings. The E. bay, opening from the chancel, is under a wide low arch which appears to be Perp. The bulk of the church is late Dec., there being only one earlier Dec. window (restored) N. of chancel. The most striking Dec. work is in the tower, with the S. door beneath it, and the two arches supporting it, which show ball-flower, oak leaves, and rose mouldings. The N. door is also Dec., and all the windows in the nave and S. aisle. There are only three Perp. windows— the W. window, and two in the chancel—*i.e.* the E. window, and the S. window (in that part not overlapped by the S. aisle). The round-headed W. door seems to be debased Perp. The font is Perp. (restored). There are two piscinæ, one Dec., the other Perp. The wood and iron work of the S. door are Perp. The sedilia are square-headed (mutilated), and there is also a mutilated niche S. of E. window. The woodwork is good.

Stevenson

There is a Jacobean pulpit, a piece of an old Perp. screen (in S. aisle), several old pews, and a coved roof of good oak. There are two brasses, one with two figures but no inscription, the other to Edward Wiseman and wife (1584). Also tomb of Edmund Wiseman (1689). The old cross is restored and there are fine yews.

Stockcross (2 m. W. of Newbury) has a modern church. S. of the Bath road is *Benham Park*, which has a pair of gate-pillars taken from Hampstead Marshall (*q.v.*).

Stratfield Mortimer. (See *Mortimer*.)

STREATLEY is a village on the S. bank of the Thames, opposite to Goring, and ¾ m. from Goring station. In the ordnance map it is marked as the site of a Roman ford over the Thames, but there is no evidence of any Roman road or settlement, beyond the fact that several Roman coins have been found here. The village has several picturesque houses, and is at one of the most beautiful parts of the Thames, just before it enters the chalk gorge by Goring Gap, between the Berkshire Downs R. and the Chilterns L. The river views have been much praised, especially those at the wooden bridge leading to Goring and at the mill. Indeed it may be that they have been over-praised, for G. D. Leslie [1] quotes the following lines from a brother artist, apropos of some beautiful spots too frequently painted :—

> " Every soul is sick of Knowle,
>   At Haddon Hall one grumbles ;
>   Of Streatley Mill we've had our fill,
>   And murmur at the Mumbles."

Beautiful river views are also got from the hill-slopes, especially from *Streatley Hill*, a bold chalk bluff which rises steeply and directly behind the village. The church

[1] See " Our River."

has been rebuilt except part of the tower, which is late Perp. There are brasses to Eliza Prout (1440) and Thomas Burinton (1603). The church-lover should cross the bridge to Goring church. (See " Little Guide to Oxfordshire.")

Sulham (2 m. S. of Pangbourne) has a modern church.

Sulhampstead Abbots (about 3 m. S. of Theale) is a village among the fir woods. The church is largely, but not entirely, restored. There is a good Trans. N. arcade. The chancel is E.E., partly new, but the small side lancets are original. The doors and windows of the nave and aisle are Perp. (most of them restored). There is a good cylindrical Norman font, a round-headed piscina (restored), and a belfry supported on wooden framework, also a fine yew-tree.

Sulhampstead Bannister (about 2½ m. S. of Theale) is also among the woods. Its strange little church, built in 1800, is hardly Gothic at all. It has a quaint wooden belfry tower.

Sunningdale is a newly formed parish with a modern church. It is in the beautiful country of the Bagshot Sands, just S. of Windsor Forest, and many country houses and villas are springing up in the neighbourhood.

Sunninghill (1½ m. E. of Ascot) is an older village in the same district and equally now devoted to villadom. The church has been rebuilt, but in the churchyard there is a fine yew-tree. The *Wells Hotel* has two chalybeate springs, once famous. In this parish there was once a house of Benedictine nuns called Bromhall, within the limits of Windsor Forest. It was suppressed in 1522, and not a trace of it now exists.

Sunningwell (3 m. N. of Abingdon) is a village very prettily situated at the foot of Foxcombe Hill, with a

THE THAMES AND STREATLEY HILL.

pleasant path leading down the hill to it. It has been connected with some famous men. A story is told that Roger Bacon used the tower for astronomical observations. Dr Jewel was rector here, but had to flee in the time of Queen Mary. Another rector was Dr Fell, Dean of Christchurch, who died in 1649 from the shock of hearing of the execution of Charles I. The cruciform church has a Dec. E. window of an uninteresting type, but is otherwise entirely late Perp. (restored). The heptagonal porch at the W. end was built by Dr Jewel in 1550-1552, and is a not unsuccessful blend of the Gothic and Classical styles. The church contains some fine poppy-heads, fragments of an old screen, and repaired Elizabethan pulpit. Inside the altar-rails are monuments to Dr Fell and others of his family. There is a fine yew-tree.

SUTTON COURTENAY (2½ m. S. of Abingdon) is a most delightful riverside village. It is little known to the ordinary boating man, who, as he passes by the straight cut to Culham Lock, may be inclined, contemptuously and inaccurately, to describe it as lying on a " backwater." In reality its peculiar secluded charm is largely due to its position on the main stream, yet apart from the river traffic. The great river is dammed up on its left bank for several hundred yards to provide water power for a paper mill, which, now ruined and deserted, is the one eyesore in the village. A pleasant path runs along the dam, crossing the series of lashers by which the water tumbles over into the broad and deep Sutton Pool, one of the least-known haunts of peace on the Thames. Both river and village are shaded by abundant willows and " immemorial elms." The central part is the pleasant green, round which stand the church and three remarkable old houses. They are not shown, and even the enthusiastic antiquary may feel himself here an intruder upon the spirit of old-world quietness. The existence of these three old houses in the same village is a matter requiring some explanation. In 687 the manor was given by Ini, King of Wessex, to Abingdon Abbey. When subsequently Cynulf, King of Mercia, gave back Andersey to the monks, he received in exchange for it Sutton Manor (see *Abingdon*). Sutton thus first became a royal manor, which it continued to be for many centuries. But the monks did not lose all connexion with it, for Ethelred the Redeless gave the Abbot a piece of land in the parish (sometimes called the rectorial manor), and William II. gave back the church to the Abbey. Hence in Henry III.'s reign there occurred a violent dispute, for Henry had allowed the Pope to appoint a young Italian to the rectory, although the Abbot had just appointed his brother. When the Italian was inducted, resistance was made by the friends of the Abbey, and a fight occurred in the church itself. Subsequently the Abbot was persuaded to submit to the Pope. Meanwhile Henry II. had given the royal manor to Reginald Courtenay, who has given his name to the village. The existing building called the Court House is part of the first manor-house, and from its ecclesiastical character may be safely pronounced to have been the chapel. About 1350 the Abbot built, on the land which had been granted to the Abbey, a country house, either as an occasional residence, or as a home of rest for infirm monks. This, from its ecclesiastical character, was subsequently called the Abbey. In course of time the owners of the manor grew tired of their old home, and built the present manor-house, not far from the first one. This was probably done in the Tudor period. The complicated changes of ownership after

The Hall: Sutton Courtenay Manor

the Courtenays lost the manor, it would be tedious to recount.

The *Court House*, also called the Manor Farm, has lately been made part of a modern house which has been built on to it. It is a rectangular building with an open timber roof, and is of beautiful very late Trans. work (c. 1200). The principal doorway is round-headed, with rows of dog-tooth and nail-head, and side columns with E.E.-looking foliage. Opposite to it is a plainer doorway, with two round arches at different heights. It was lighted by deeply splayed lancets, of which three have been reopened and two more can be traced. At the E. end there is an inserted Perp. window, of which the tracery has disappeared. The large fireplace is a Tudor addition.

The *manor-house* is approached by two gateways, the inner of which has two fine pillars. The front shows six gables with barge-boards, a wall covered with rough-cast, latticed windows with wooden frames, and a front door with old ironwork. The house has no architectural work in stone, but the interior wood-work is thoroughly delightful. The owner, Captain Lindsay, is, moreover, a connoisseur, who has enriched his home with art treasures drawn from many quarters. There is a magnificent staircase of old oak, and a smaller one, leading to the drawing-room. Most of the rooms, including three of the bedrooms, are panelled with oak, and the fireplaces are excellent throughout. The remarkable chimney-piece in the drawing-room comes from an old house at Steventon. Three bed-rooms have old carved wooden beds. The two principal rooms are the hall, which has a flat half-timbered roof supported on oak columns, and the " banqueting-hall," which has an open timber roof, and a minstrels' gallery with a carved front. At the back of the house is a picturesque courtyard, showing 17th-cent. features. At the side is a very fine yew walk, formed by three ancient giants, whose branches curve downwards to the ground.

The *Abbey* is approached by a gateway, and an avenue of old elms. The back parts of the house are now modern, but the front, which faces W., retains some original late Dec. windows, and looks very ecclesiastical, though modern alterations have partly spoilt it. In the centre is the great hall, with a lofty old oaken roof. The top part of the windows was originally under dormer gables, but these have been destroyed and the windows cut square. On either side is a gabled wing. In the N. wing was the solar, a large room lighted by two good Dec. windows, and with an open timber roof, now hidden by a modern ceiling beneath it. The patterns of the windows should be compared with those in Cumnor Hall (see *Wytham*), which was built by the Abingdon monks at the same time (c. 1350-1370).

The *church* is also interesting, but its architecture is very mixed, and authorities differ about many of the details. As to the style of the tower, for instance, opinions are very various. It seems however fairly certain that the lower story is plain Norman, the middle Trans. and the upper Dec. But there appears to be no more plain Norman in the church, though there are several Trans. features—*i.e.* the columns of the chancel arch and the E. arch of the S. arcade (see later). The lancets N. of the chancel also may be Trans., though it is possible that they are E.E. but inserted in Trans. frames. The font also is probably Trans., though its ornaments are elaborate for that style, and some authorities consider it E.E. or even Dec. In the Dec. period several changes were made, in particular both the nave arcades were rebuilt. The great puzzle of the church is the E. bay of the S. arcade, where the Dec. columns are more elaborate than the rest, and there is a solitary ball-flower over one of them. But set upon these columns there is a Trans. arch, pointed, and showing zigzag and embattled mouldings. There seems no adequate explanation of its extraordinary position. Can it, for instance, be a fragment of the earlier arcade left unaltered ?[1] There are five Dec. windows in all, two early and one late in style in the nave, a late window S. of chancel, and the E. window (restored). The clerestory on the N. side is late Dec., on the S. side, Perp. The side windows in the aisles are Perp., also a pair in the chancel, and the priest's door. The S. porch with parvise above is of brick (Tudor), and contains a broken stoup. In the chancel there are a double piscina (Dec.), an aumbry and two Perp. altar-tombs, of which one has the effigy of a priest, and is now placed in a recess under a Dec. arch ; also oak stalls with misereres, a good Perp. chancel screen, and two smaller screens, separating off the E. bays of the aisles as chapels. The S. chapel has a plain piscina, and a good Perp. tomb now used as an altar. The N. chapel has been made the organ-chamber. Both chapel and nave have good roofs. The pulpit, which is ancient, was presented by Captain Lindsay in 1901, in memory of Lord Wantage, his kinsman. There are a few scraps of old coloured glass.

The village contains several timber-built houses, and a larger Jacobean house, with gables and oriel windows, and the date 1631.

Swallowfield (3½ m. E. of Mortimer) has a fine park, close to which is the junction of the Loddon and the

[1] Parker believes it is the chancel arch, removed to its present position in the 14th cent.

Blackwater. Inside the church is a statement that it was built in 1256. This is refuted by the style, for the N. and S. doors, and the E. end are all Norman. There is an old wooden roof. The rest is rebuilt and quite modern. The S. porch has a good barge-board. The belfry is of timber and brick. There is a tomb to Edward Swayne (chirurgeon) (1650), and two brasses, Margaret Letterford (1450) and Christopher Lytcott (1554). The plain coffin at the W. end is said to be that of Sir John le de Spencer. In the churchyard is the tomb of Miss Mitford.

Swinford Bridge is a well-built and handsome bridge of nine arches, which carries the Oxford and Witney road over the Thames ($\frac{1}{2}$ m. S. of Eynsham). The name may indicate that it was a ford shallow enough for swine to cross (cf. *Oxford*). From the bridge there are good river views in both directions, especially eastward, where the dense Eynsham Woods climb the hill to a fir crown at the top. More W. is a bare detached hill, the top platform of which looks as if it were scarped. It is not, however, recognized by the "Victoria History" as one of the hill forts of Berkshire. From the top the view is charming, the river almost surrounding the hill in a series of snakelike loops.

Thames River. (See Introduction.)

Thatcham is a large village in the Kennet Valley, about 4 m. E. of Newbury. It has a large and open market-square, in the centre of which are the remains of the old market cross. A modern inscription refers to the ancient market, established before 1135, specially protected by Henry II. from the jealous interference of the men of Newbury, and transferred by Henry III. from Sunday to Thursday. The church is spacious and dignified, but was badly restored in 1852. The S. door is good Norman, with fish-tail mouldings. The arcades are plain Trans., but the chancel arch, also Trans. originally, is quite new. Nearly all the windows are rebuilt, but in the N. aisle there are some old Perp. windows, also a Perp. door. At the E. end of the S. aisle is the Fuller Chapel (Perp.), separated by a four-centred arch from the chancel, and containing the tombs of Sir W. Danvers (1504) and Nicholas Fuller (1620). The inscription on the restored brass to Thomas Loundye should be read. The tower has a Perp. upper story, but the W. window and door are late Dec. The font is plain Perp. At the E. end of the village is a *chantry chapel*, built in 1334, and turned into a blue-coat school by Lady Frances Winchcombe of Buckle-bury in 1707. All the windows have been altered, but it retains two Dec. canopied niches outside (W.), and a blocked Perp. door (S.). Inside there is a plain piscina, and a roof of dark timber.

Theale is a village in the Kennet Valley with a modern church. A large variety of relics have been found here, including early British urns, and Romano-British ware. The site appears to have been occupied by British, Romano-British and Saxon settlements successively.

Tidmarsh (1½ m. S. of Pangbourne) has a small but interesting church close to the little Pang. The S. door is rich Norman, and the font Trans. The bulk of the church is E.E. The unique E.E. chancel is a semi-octagonal apse, with a lancet in each face, and divided by vaulting-shafts which support a central boss. The chancel arch is probably of the same date. There are also two lancets at the E. end of the nave, and a lancet triplet (restored) at the W. end. The other windows are restored Trans. to Dec. The bell-cote is carried on an interior Perp. framework. There are brasses to (1) Margaret Woods (1499); (2) an unnamed knight (1520); (3) William Dale (1536).

Tilehurst and *Tilehurst Common* are large straggling villages on the hilly plateau in the angle between the Thames and the Kennet, and lying considerably S. of Tilehurst station. Tilehurst church is entirely new, but retains a splendid gilt and alabaster monument to Sir Peter Vanlore and wife (1627). Several children are sculptured on the tomb. Six of them have skulls in their hands, but a smaller figure has the skull under his hand. The emblem means that they died before their parents. There is also a brass to a More, wife and five children (1469).

Tubney. (See *Fyfield*.)

Twyford was made a parish in 1876. On the Bath road, which passes through it, are some almshouses endowed by Lady Frances Winchcombe (see *Thatcham*). They are of picturesque brick. Over the porch is the inscription, "*Domino et Pauperibus* 1640."

UFFINGTON lies 2 m. directly N. of *White Horse Hill* (*q.v.*). The village and the whole neighbourhood have been admirably described in the opening pages of "Tom Brown's Schooldays." Those, however, who are led by the author's enthusiasm to explore the country for themselves must remember that his archæology is not up to date. Uffington Castle and the Ridgeway are not Roman: the Great White Horse is no memorial of the battle of Ashdown, which was probably not fought here (see *Ashdown*), nor, for the matter of that, was it the great battle in which Alfred "broke the Danish power." But, with this caution, all lovers of Berkshire should reread the story of Tom Brown's childhood. The glory of Uffington is its splendid cruciform church, with a unique octagonal central tower. The building is entirely E.E., the only admixture being one reticulated window S. of the chancel. The tower rests on four splendidly moulded piers and arches, the work being considerably squinched to fit the eight sides on. The effect is rather singular than beautiful, and the upper story seems to have been badly rebuilt. Almost all the windows in the church are lancets, those in the chancel and the transepts being finely recessed beneath well-moulded arches. An upper and a lower string-course run round the whole church, both inside and out. The *chancel* has N. and S. doors, the N. one blocked. There is an arch leading into the sanctuary of a somewhat different character from the other arches. On the S. there are, in order: (1) round-headed aumbry; (2) fine canopied E.E. sedilia (restored but good) with uniform piscina; (3) a second foliated piscina. The reredos and roof are modern. In the *N. transept* there are two altar-recesses E., with trefoiled piscinæ at the side. They are recessed under beautifully moulded arches resting on columns. The lancet triplets at the back have very strange straight-sided heads. This peculiarity seems to be determined by the shape of the gables above them, which should be viewed from outside. The whole work is obviously original. The N. transept also contains an aumbry with four compartments, some good pew-backs, an old iron-bound chest, and a tomb to Edward Archer (1603). In the *S. transept* there is another altar-recess, similar to those in N. transept. One good pew-back is used to support the visitors' book. Note the following extract " from an old bible in the parish ": "Then was Uffingdon stepel beat down by a tempas, wind, thunder and liten. Dec. 2nd day 1740." This shows that the tower used to be surmounted by a spire. In the transept there is a tomb to John Saunders (1638), and below it a plate to another John Saunders (d. 1599). In the *nave* all the lancet windows have unfortunately been cut off at the top.

An inscription on N. wall states that this was done in 1678 when a flat leaden roof (since altered) was put on. The N. door is blocked, but similar to the S. door. Over it is a good circular six-foil window. The font is new. The three beautiful doorways on the S. side should be studied from without. All show excellent E.E. detail. The porch of the S. nave door is vaulted and contains a parvise, and the door has good ironwork. The pretty door in the S.E. aisle of S. transept is recessed under a fine canopy, with a sunken quatrefoil in the spandril above the arch. The S. door of chancel is also under a canopy, but not so elaborate. Below the exterior string moulding are twelve circular recesses, intended to contain brass dedication crosses.

The chalk building S. of church has the date 1617 in a sunken panel over the door. It has gable-crosses and looks very ecclesiastical. Formerly a school, it is now used as a reading-room.

UFTON COURT (about 2 m. S.E. of Aldermaston station) is one of the most picturesque old Elizabethan houses in the county. The estate was bought in 1568 by Lady Mervyn (widow of Sir John Mervyn), who built the present house, incorporating in it parts of an earlier building—*i.e.* the kitchen, buttery and portions of the S. wing. She married Richard Perkins, and died 1581. The dole of bread and flannel which she bequeathed to the poor of Ufton is still distributed from a window in the house on the Friday after the third Sunday in Lent. A similar dole to Padworth is now distributed at Padworth itself. The Perkins family, who already held the manor of Ufton, now lived in Ufton Court until 1769. In 1715 the N. part of the house was rebuilt to be a fit home for Arabella Fermor, the celebrated beauty who was the Belinda of Pope's "Rape of the Lock," and had just married

Upton Court

Francis Perkins. The interior fittings of the N. wing are still of this period, but the exterior was altered again in 1838, and made similar to the rest of the building. The house is sometimes shown, if the tenant be written to previously. It is built in the usual " E " form. In the front it shows a great deal of good timber-work and rough-cast ; at the back it is entirely old red brick. There are as many as nineteen old gables, and several massive twisted chimneys. All the windows have wooden frames and tracery. The top story overhangs all round the front, resting on massive wooden beams. In the centre is a very picturesque projecting porch of open woodwork, with a small room above it. The N. wing, which contains the drawing-room, is now shut up, and is not shown. In the S. wing there are the priest's staircase and oratory, dating from about 1500. The latter is a small panelled room. Above under the gables is the chapel, which shows no old features. The Perkins family was Roman Catholic and often harboured recusant priests. There are as many as three priest-holes in the mansion, one a well-like hole with a ladder, at the S. end of the long gallery. In this connexion it is interesting to record that early in the last century a brass crucifix of beautiful mediæval workmanship was discovered here. It has been repaired, and now stands on an altar in the chapel of St John's Hospital, Cowley (Oxford). In the central building, besides the long gallery, there are several interesting rooms. The library has an original mantel-board, with the inscription, " F. P. 1583." The hall has a stucco ceiling and marble floor. On the plaster are the initials of Lady Mervyn. There are some good doors, but the minstrels' gallery has been boarded up and turned into a bedroom. There is also a splendid old staircase. The leadwork on the roof is dated 1664.

At the back of the house is a raised terrace in bad repair, from which a flight of steps leads down to the old garden and the fishponds.

The church of *Ufton Nervet* is about ½ m. N.E. It has been rebuilt, but contains several Perkins monuments—*i.e.* to Richard Perkins (1560), Francis Perkins (1615), and two 17th-cent. brass plates. Also a brass to William Smith (1627), and a brass plate to Francis Hyde (1686).

Upton is a village under the Downs, with a small church of great age. Most of it is at least early Norman and parts may be Saxon. Restoration has partly spoilt it, but fortunately some of the ancient features have been retained unaltered. The very rude N. doorway seems to be Saxon. The S. door is early Norman. The nave contains one original round-headed window, an old wooden roof, and a plain cylindrical font, now set on a modern base. The round chancel arch is rude and massive. The E. window is new, but there are three original round-headed windows at the sides, two of which are tiny ones with deep splays, and a third one, larger, into which an old E.E. window, found at the restoration, has been inserted. Other features are modernized.

Virginia Water is a large artificial piece of water S. of Windsor Park. It is only partly in Berkshire, the county boundary here cutting straight across it. It lies among thick woods, which make the views of its banks very picturesque. On the S. bank (in Surrey) have been set up some remarkable ancient columns brought from Leptis Magna, near Tripoli, and looking strangely out of place.

Walbury Hill and Camp. (See *Inkpen Beacon*.)

WALLINGFORD is remarkable for several reasons. Its position on an important ford of the river has given

it a long connexion with English history from the
earliest times. It lies within strange earthen ramparts
of unknown antiquity. Finally Wallingford and Donnington are the only two places in Berkshire which
preserve some fragments of their vanished castles. The
ramparts are rectangular in form, and surround the
town on three sides, the river being on the fourth. In
places they are very distinct, but they can be traced all
round. The date of their formation is very uncertain.
From the large number of antiquities of the Bronze
Age found in the town it is clear that there must have
been settlers here in those early times, who possibly
built the ramparts. But it seems as obvious, from the
large number of coins discovered, that the site was also
occupied in Romano-British times. No building nor
foundation decisively Roman has, however, been discovered. The settlement was apparently non-military,
and of little account. In Saxon times a more important
town arose, which was burnt by the Danes in 1006. (See
also *Cholsey*.) A remarkable seal found in the town,
and now in the British Museum, belongs to this period.
It bears the inscription, "*Sigillum Godwini Ministri*," and
on the reverse side, "*Sigillum Godgythe monache dodate*"
(= *deodatae*). Godgytha may have been the abbess of
a monastery founded by Godwin. It is not probable
that the reference is to the great Earl Godwin. At the
time of the Conquest the leading citizen of Wallingford
was Wigod, who submitted to William I. and allowed
him to pass through Wallingford *en route* to London in
1066. William's follower, Robert D'Oilly of Oxford,
married Wigod's daughter, and either built or rebuilt
the Castle, which is so prominent in English history.
Wallingford Priory, built about the same time, has also
been assigned to Robert D'Oilly, but its real founder
was Paul, Abbot of St Alban's, of which abbey it was

a cell. It was surrendered in 1525 to provide funds
for the building of Cardinal Wolsey's college at Oxford.
After the Conquest Wallingford becomes an important
military place. During the Civil War in Stephen's
reign Earl Brian, heir of Wigod's daughter, held the
Castle successfully for Matilda. In 1139 Stephen himself attacked it without result. Here Matilda twice
fled for refuge : in 1141, after her sensational escape from
Winchester ; and in the next year, when she escaped
in equally dramatic fashion from Oxford Castle. In
1145 there was a second siege, and finally in 1152 a
third desperate attempt was made to take the town,
during which the citizens called Prince Henry to their
aid. After some more desultory fighting a compro-
mise was arranged, and in 1153 the war ended with
the *Treaty of Wallingford*, by which the succession was
secured to Henry. The loyal borough obtained a
charter, and a Parliament was soon afterwards sum-
moned to meet here. Very shortly the ownership of
the Castle fell by escheat into the hands of the King. In
Richard I.'s absence it was held by Prince John, and
was one of the centres of his treacherous designs against
his brother. In John's own reign a conference on
ecclesiastical disturbances was held here. Under
Henry III. the Castle was conferred on Richard, King of
the Romans, who was himself, with Prince Edward,
brought here as prisoner after the battle of Lewes in
1264. In Edward I.'s reign Wallingford sent two
burgesses to Parliament, a privilege it retained until
1832, when it lost one representative. The second
was only taken away in 1885. With the troubles of
Edward II.'s reign Wallingford Castle is much connected. It was given to Piers Gaveston, and at a
tournament held here in honour of his marriage with
the King's niece the insulting nicknames he gave to the

barons made many enemies. On his death Queen Isabella received the Castle, and here at Christmas 1326 she and her paramour Mortimer held high festival, after they had captured the unfortunate Edward II. In 1400 the three earls who had conspired against Henry IV. passed through Wallingford in their retreat. In the course of the next two centuries the Castle had some royal visitors, but presently fell into disrepair. In the Great Civil War it was refortified and held successfully for the King by Governor Blagge. It was the last place in Berkshire to hold out, and only surrendered to Fairfax on 27th July 1646, when the news came of Charles' surrender to the Scots. In 1652 the Castle was finally destroyed.

Considering its long history the town is rather poor in archæological remains. The ancient earthworks indeed are prominent, and can be seen at the S.W. angle, where they enclose the public recreation-ground. But the Priory has disappeared altogether, and of the great Castle very slight indications remain. The site is in private grounds, partly a garden, entered by a lodge on the Oxford road, to which the public are admitted between two and five P.M. in July and August. Just N. of the garden is the picturesque mound which marks the site of the keep. This is now planted with trees, and ascended by a winding path, but not one stone of the building remains. Farther N. is traceable the enclosure of the courtyard, on the outer wall of which are two picturesque fragments of masonry. One is set on the top of the bank which sinks sharp E. to the level of the river. It shows in front a ruined window-frame, and also a pretty E.E. piscina of white stone, which can hardly be *in situ*. The other fragment, facing N., is smaller, built of flint and beautifully covered with ivy. Beyond may be traced the lines of the moats which proved so formidable a defence to the Castle; three on the N. side, and two on the W. Within the Castle precincts is the ruined church of St Nicholas, which shows only an ivy-clad tower and a few Perp. features. There are three other churches in the town, but they are disappointing. St. Mary the More, in the market-place, has been rebuilt and completely modernized except the massive tower, which is late and debased Perp. and retains, low down on the N. side, a piece of ancient sculpture, conjectured to represent King Stephen on horseback. Close by is the town hall, a commonplace building, with an undercroft, and a gallery from which election results are returned. In the 18th cent. these scenes may have been lively, since two instances are recorded in which the Mayor, in announcing the elected candidate, quite disregarded the actual votes. St Leonard's, in the S.E. quarter of the town, is the only church of any interest. It has been much damaged at various times, and about 1850 was largely rebuilt, but it retains some old Norman and Trans. work, nearly all of which is in the chancel. There are two fine Norman arches, both covered with original diaper-work. One is the chancel arch, the other leads into the apse, now rebuilt. The S. wall of chancel is old, with original flint-work, two small lancets, and the heads of a small Norman window. The N. wall both of chancel and nave is original, showing herringbone-work. The single lancet is old; the double lancets are new, but one is set in an old frame. The font is new, but set on an old base. Nave arcade and clerestory are new, and the N. door, which was early Norman, has been rebuilt. Some authorities think that part of the early work in the church is pre-Conquest. St Peter's, as an inscription states, was rebuilt in 1769, and the tower in 1777. The curious stone spire is far too prominent, and spoils most views of the town. Of St Hallow's Church only the graveyard remains. Of the two hospitals one still exists (E. of the Reading road) and shows picturesque brick chimneys. Under a central gable is a coat-of-arms and inscription stating that it was founded " by Mr William Angier & Mary his sister A.D. 1681." The bridge over the Thames is a fine structure of fourteen arches.

Waltham St Lawrence (about 3 m. E. of Twyford) has a church partly restored, but with a good deal of old work. There are two arcades, of which the two W. arches are plain Norman, the rest of the arcades being Dec. The windows are mainly Dec., most of which have been restored, but the two E. of the nave aisles are old. The W. tower has a Geometrical W. window (heavy but good), a Perp. W. door and a Perp. upper story. There is a restored Dec. piscina, a screen embodying parts of an old Dec. screen, and a pulpit dated 1619. In the vestry is a *prie-dieu* monument to Sir Henry Neville and wife (1573). Just outside the churchyard are four trees forming a pound ; also a timber-built inn.

Waltham, White (2 m. S.W. of Maidenhead), has a rebuilt church, which, however, retains a few ancient features, principally E.E.—*i.e.* three side lancets in the chancel, and a pretty E.E. double piscina, with marble pillar and quatrefoil above. In the S. transept there is a second piscina, and another lancet, and a Dec. window at the E. end. Some other window-frames are old. Under one of them is scratched, " *Miserere I.H.S.*" At the last restoration in 1893 a group of alabaster figures was found, supposed to be part of the old reredos. N. of the church is the old timber-built manor-house, and just outside the churchyard wall are the village stocks and whipping-post.

WANTAGE is the principal market town in the Vale of the White Horse. It is famous as the birthplace of

King Alfred in 849, but the royal palace has disappeared, and there is no memorial of the King, unless it be the so-called Alfred's well, and Alfred's bath (a pool paved with brick), neither of which is of much account. In the market-place there is a statue of the King carved by Count Gleichen, and presented to the town by the late Lord Wantage. (See *Lockinge*.) The town has had no subsequent connexion with history, except that Charles I. marched through it in 1642 *en route* to intercept Essex's army at Newbury. In 1692 Bishop Butler, author of "The Analogy," was born in the town. There is a good oil-painting of him in the church vestry. The church was rebuilt late in the E.E. period (about 1260-1270), and its style may be called early Geometrical. The outside has been much altered, but the central portions are still in this style, including (1) the central tower, resting upon four massive piers and with quadripartite vaulting; (2) the fine nave arcades, of which one capital shows dog-tooth moulding; (3) two arches leading E. from S. transept. The arch leading W. from the S. transept and the lancet near it are also E.E in style, but look earlier. Could they have belonged to an earlier church? The font is also beautiful E.E., ten-sided, with three rows of dog-tooth. All other features are later. The few Dec. windows are mostly restored, but there are two excellent ones at the W. end, which show transoms. The E. window is modern, and unworthy of its architect, Street. Nearly all the windows, however, are Perp. The long row of Perp. windows in the nave aisles, with clerestory above and Perp. S. porch with parvise, gives from outside the first impression that the church is mainly in this style. Inside there are some Perp. arches—*i.e.* those leading N. and S. from the chancel, and E. and W. from the N. transept. A good Perp. door of black oak leads to the vestry. There are three foliated piscinæ, the one in the chancel being double. There is a stoup under a cinq-foiled arch on N. wall (inside), and a small stone coffin. The woodwork is excellent. There are stalls with misereres and poppy-heads, good parclose screens, and an open timber roof in the nave. In the chancel is alabaster tomb of Sir William Fitzwarren and his wife Amicia (1361). There are several brasses: (1) Sir Ivo Fitzwarren (1414); (2) inscription to Roger Merlaw (1460); (3) William Gidding (1512); (4) Walter Talbot (1522); (5) floreated cross.

The Grammar School was founded in 1597. The buildings were originally placed in the churchyard, but in 1849 they were removed to a new site. There is a tradition that the old buildings incorporated some parts of an ancient Norman church or chapel, of which the only remnant is the round arch, which was removed in 1849, and now forms the entrance of the boarders' common room. It is a very fine Norman doorway, with an outer row of thirty-two beak-heads.

The Sisterhood of St Mary's, Wantage, was founded in 1850, and has good buildings.

WARFIELD (2 m. N. of Bracknell) contains the only church of real interest in the forest region of the Bagshot Sands. The earliest work is E.E., of which traces are found only on the N. wall of the nave-aisle. One lancet remains and traces of three others, and there is also a plain door. When the arcade was altered the roof was raised, so that the present windows are larger. The existing church is mainly good Dec., but there is also a fair amount of Perp., and some features admit of doubt. The chancel with its N. aisle, including apparently the arcade between them and the chancel arch, is very beautiful and interesting late Dec. The five-light E. window has splendid flowing tracery, and some pretty old glass, showing angels swinging censers. All the side windows are two-light Dec. One on the S. has been prolonged under a transom to form a low-side window. The arcade leading to the aisle has mouldings prolonged to the ground without capitals, and hood-mouldings resting on corbel heads. In the spandrils are canopied niches (beautiful but defaced). The chancel arch is similar in character. There are several other interesting features. Behind the altar at the S.E. corner is a newel staircase with spiral above. The sedilia and piscina are very beautiful. In the spandril there is a moustachioed face with oak leaves coming from his mouth, a pattern that has been copied in the modern reredos. There are two squints, one on each side. The rood-screen (Perp.) originally stretched across both aisles and chancel. The part across the aisle still remains, though the rood-loft above has apparently been restored. The rood-loft stairs remain, N. of the aisle, and are carried in an outside bulge. Stretching across the chancel is a modern stone screen, which, however, has been copied from a little bit of panelling in S.W. corner. The stone pulpit and font are also new. The W. tower is good late Dec. with a small spire and a belfry tower at S.E. corner, but the W. window and door, near which are traces of a stoup, are Perp. The nave shows features partly Dec., partly Perp. There are two windows with late Geometrical tracery, and the arcade is also possibly Dec., though this is not certain. The rest of the windows, the S. door and roof, are Perp. The S. transept is entered by a Perp. arch, but has restored windows. There are three *prie-dieu* monuments, one to Thomas Wilkinson (1611), and the matrices of two old brasses. Several windows show bits of old glass. The church is surrounded by fine elms.

Wargrave (1½ m. N. of Twyford) is another of the

picturesque riverside villages which border the Thames. The *George and Dragon* is a well-known hostelry, the signboard of which was painted by two R.A.'s, Leslie and Broughton. The church is practically rebuilt. The only old parts are : (1) Norman doorway (N.), somewhat dilapidated ; (2) Perp. window (N.) in a sort of transept ; (3) 16th-cent. brick tower. Outside is a tomb to George Nind, killed at Trafalgar. There is some old woodwork—*i.e.* a Jacobean pew in N. transept, and a Jacobean pulpit with a coat-of-arms on each panel. In the churchyard are two ancient discarded fonts, one plain Norman, the other handsome Perp.

Wasing (2 m. S. of Midgham station) has a little church in the beautiful grounds of Wasing Place, with some fine cedars near it. The nave is 18th cent., but has a series of about ten windows with Flemish glass. The chancel was rebuilt about 1880, when two E.E. windows (a single and a double lancet) were found buried in the thickness of the wall and replaced, and the others were made E.E. to match. There is an old timber roof and a small wooden belfry. Note external inscription to a former rector.

Watchfield. (See *Shrivenham*.)

Watcombe (about 3 m. N. of West Shefford) is the site of a village which has disappeared. To reach it take the Wantage road from West Shefford for 2½ m. and then turn by a lane L. Just at the turn is a very fine group of yews, a relic of an old garden. It is sometimes called Paradise, and three of the largest yews are named Adam, Eve and the Serpent. The site of the village is now a training-stable, which practically bars access to it. Built up in one of the outhouses are some fragments of the vanished church, consisting of a few stones, some with defaced corbel heads on them, and one showing the date 1721.

Wayland Smith's Cave. (See *White Horse Hill.*)

Welford is perhaps the prettiest spot in the Lambourn Valley. (See *Lambourn River.*) The river views from the two bridges are specially delightful; and the manor-house and church stand amid a perfect bower of trees, surrounded by a magnificent deer park. The church, although largely rebuilt, contains strong points of interest. The remarkable tower has been rebuilt on original lines. The three lower stories, built of flint, are Norman and round (*cf.* Great Shefford church, also in the Lambourn Valley). Above this is a fourth (stone) story and a spire, both E.E. and octagonal. On each side of both tower and spire is a double lancet window with a quatrefoil in the head, the upper range of windows being surmounted by triangular canopies. The whole effect is rich and beautiful. The nave with its aisles is quite new, with the exception of a piece of old Norman wall on the S.W. side. The chancel is E.E., and has not been quite so ruthlessly " restored " as the nave, some of the old stones having been used in the side lancets and the priest's door (blocked). The beautiful Trans. font and E.E. sedilia still remain. There are several monuments: (1) brass to John Young (undated); (2) brass to John Westlake (1420); (3) *prie-dieu* monument to Lady Parry (1585); (4) tomb with floreated cross; (5) tombs in vestry to the Mundys, especially Elizabeth Mundy (1689). Under a cedar in the churchyard is an almost perfect cross.

Wellington College, one of the three great public schools in Berkshire, was intended to be a national memorial to the Great Duke, and was both built and endowed with the sum of £145,000, collected by subscriptions from the army and the general public. The buildings were opened by Queen Victoria in January 1859, the first headmaster being Edward Benson, afterwards

BRIDGE IN GROUNDS OF WELLINGTON COLLEGE

Archbishop. The Governing Body has for president the Duke of Connaught, and our late King Edward was one of its most active members, and always showed the greatest interest in the school. The numbers are at present about four hundred and seventy. The school is principally of a military character, and seventy of the sons of deceased officers are educated at nominal charges. The buildings are imposing, containing two good internal " quads.," a new dining-room with a gallery, and a spacious and dignified chapel. The arrangement of combining dormitories with studies will be familiar to many from the pages of " Hugh Rendall," and also the custom of naming the dormitories after celebrated military events. The grounds in which the College stands are extensive and beautiful, sweeping away on all sides deep into the fir woods, with which this part of the county is thickly planted. The nearest village is Crowthorne.

West Woodhay (3 m. S. of Kintbury) has an old manor-house, partly built by Inigo Jones, and delightfully situated under the Inkpen Beacon range. Close to it is the graveyard of the old brick church, pulled down in 1882, of which the outline is traced in box-plants. A new church has been built farther from the house.

WHITE HORSE HILL is the highest point of the Berkshire Downs (856 ft.), which, however, are not so high as the Inkpen Beacon range. Viewed from the north, it is a splendid hill, rising well above the general sky-line of the Downs, and showing a grassy side, too steep to be cultivated. It can be reached by a lane running directly S. from Uffington, or by ascending from the Port Way, which runs at its foot. The front shows a large and effective combe, into which there falls on the W. side a series of vertical hollows known as the *Manger*. The ascent is by the slope to the E. of the combe, advanced in front of which is a rounded and detached hillock. This is *Dragon Hill*—where St George, according to local tradition, both killed and buried the dragon ; if indeed the deliverer is not rather supposed to be " King Gaarge," as the Uffington poet humorously suggests.[1] On the hillside above between the great combe and another one to the E. the one chalk monument in Berkshire, the *Great White Horse*, which gives the hill its name, is cut out in the turf. The days are past when Tom Hughes and others could confidently assert that it was cut by King Alfred to commemorate his victory at Ashdown over the Danes. The monument is, with very little doubt, far older, and more probably is connected with some religious rite of the ancient Britons, if indeed it is not older still. The highly conventionalized and disjointed form of the horse, in which head, neck and body are represented by one long waving line, and the legs by single detached lines, resembles very closely the horse as depicted on British coins. The equine resemblance is certainly very faint, but there is a distinct suggestion that the animal is galloping wildly. The whole figure is 374 ft. long, and is well seen from the railway, 3 m. distant. At the top of the hill is *Uffington Castle*, another of the prehistoric forts which have so often mistakenly been called Roman. It is smaller than Letcombe Castle, but shows a fine rampart and ditch, and apparently four gateways. The view is splendid. Below is the " great vale spread out as the garden of the Lord," [2] bounded by the ridge starting from Badbury and Faringdon Clump and running E. to the Cumnor Hills. Eastward the

[1] See Meade Faulkner in Murray's " Berkshire."
[2] " Tom Brown," c. I.   (See *Uffington*.)

Dorchester Clumps stand in front of the Chilterns, which bound the view; while westward the eye ranges far into Wiltshire and Gloucestershire.

About 1½ m. S.W. along the ridge of the Downs is *Wayland Smith's Cave,* lying in a hollow surrounded by a ring of beech-trees, 50 yds. N. of the Ridgeway. It is a ruined cromlech, the largest stone of which remains *in situ,* resting on five others. The remaining stones are scattered about. The whole formed a sepulchral chamber, probably of a chieftain, and was originally covered with earth. The celebrated local legend explaining the name is that, if a traveller's horse had lost a shoe, he brought the horse to this place with a piece of money, and then departed. On his return he found the horse had been shod by an invisible smith. This is really one of the variants of a widespread legend concerning a mysterious worker in metals and forger of armour named Weland, who figures in the folk-lore of many countries. Rudyard Kipling, for instance, tells a similar tale of Sussex in the first chapter of " Puck of Pook's Hill." The story has been turned to good account by Scott in " Kenilworth." It may be noted that in his narrative the cromlech is not the cave, which is a small underground chamber close by and due to Scott's imagination. The top stone of the cromlech is " Wayland Smith's counter," on which the money had to be placed.

Wickham (1½ m. S.W. of Welford station) has a church with a Saxon tower. It is built of flint, and shows long and short work. The windows are either two-light, divided by a central baluster, or small and round-headed with a double splay. The rude octagonal font may be coeval with the tower. The church was unfortunately rebuilt about 1840 in florid Gothic of the worst type. Some of the spoils of the old church are on the rectory lawn and conservatory.

Windsor is a town almost entirely without interest apart from its Castle. It contains a few 17th-cent. houses, a town hall by Sir Christopher Wren, and a rebuilt church with one ancient monument (undated), a *prie-dieu* to Edward Jobson and wife.

WINDSOR CASTLE is so intimately connected with nearly every name in English History that to give an adequate account of it in a few pages is impossible. It must suffice to touch very lightly on the stages of its growth and the various scenes it has witnessed. The story begins with Edward the Confessor, who had a palace at Old Windsor (see later), and had given most of the Forest to the monks of Westminster. After the Conquest William I. was struck alike by the admirable situation for defence which the detached chalk hill beside the river afforded, and by the excellent hunting-grounds of the wide-spreading Forest. The monks were easily persuaded to give up the Confessor's grant in exchange for two Essex manors, and the Conqueror built the first castle on the well-known site, probably consisting of little but a keep on the central mound where the Round Tower now stands. The next step was taken by Henry I., who abandoned Old Windsor and built a palace on the S. side of what is now the Upper Ward. Of this structure portions of the masonry may still exist in the lower part of the present buildings, particularly in the Devil's Tower, at the S.W. corner of the Upper Ward. After this the principal building kings were Henry III. and Edward III. Henry III. built a second palace in the present Lower Ward, comprising a great hall, chapel and kitchen. (These were afterwards swept away to make room for St George's Chapel and the adjoining ecclesiastical buildings.) A beautiful fragment of the work remains in the E.E. arcade on the S. wall of the Dean's Cloisters. The foundations of Henry's buildings have been recently excavated, so that new light may reasonably be soon expected on the difficult and complicated story of the Castle buildings. The whole of the Lower Ward was also surrounded by Henry with a curtain wall, comprising several of the present towers, most of which, including the Salisbury and Garter towers, have been rebuilt or greatly altered, but one, the Curfew Tower, on the extreme W., still retains much of the original work. In the reign of Edward III. extensive building operations were carried out under the guidance of the celebrated William of Wykeham, and it is at this time that the Castle assumed in the main its present familiar shape. William of Wykeham himself lived in Winchester Tower (N.E. of the Lower Ward), which he himself had built, and on which may still be read the inscription, "Hoc fecit Wykeham." The story is that the King was angry at this inscription, on which the ingenious prelate explained that it meant: "This was the making of Wykeham." Exactly how much of the present castle was built at this time it is very difficult to say. A third palace was erected, on the N. side of the Upper Ward, including the magnificent St George's Hall. In the Middle Ward the familiar Round Tower was built, replacing apparently an earlier round tower due to Henry III. In the Lower Ward nearly all of Henry III.'s work was removed to make room for the newly founded College of St George, with its chapel, and houses for canons and poor knights. Of these buildings the Dean's Cloister is the most striking part which has been left unaltered. St George's Chapel was entirely rebuilt by Edward IV., who replaced it by the present structure, to which Henry VII. added the roof of the nave, and Henry VIII. the roof of the chancel. Henry VII. also built the chapel now transformed into the Albert Memorial Chapel. To recount the subsequent additions to and alterations of the pile would be tedious. Much of the original work is Tudor, much Elizabethan. In later times the whole has been rebuilt and repaired again and again, so that it is most difficult to recognize the original character of most parts. The last and worst of these alterations was under George IV., who put the whole Castle into the hands of Wyattville. The result was that much mediæval detail was effaced, and the whole surface of the building reduced to a dead level of decorous modernity. It is indeed a remarkable testimony to the grandeur and beauty of the Castle that a wholesale restoration, undertaken at such an unfortunate time, has proved quite unable to spoil it. And in one respect Wyattville was even inspired, when he raised the Round Tower 39 ft., and added the turret from which the Royal Standard waves when the sovereign is in residence. Yet perhaps the nobility of the pile is most felt when the striking sky-line is observed from a distance, or when, from a nearer point of view, the buildings majestically dominate town park and river (see Frontispiece). When close at hand there is an atmosphere of up-to-date repair about the whole, which cannot but detract from the general impression.

The events connected with the Castle concern, as a rule, the private life of our royal family, rather than the general history of England. William I., as we have seen, did not actually reside here, though he had several lodges built in the Forest for convenience of hunting. But from the time of Henry I. downward Windsor has been a royal residence. Here Henry married his second wife, Adeliza, in a chapel now vanished. During the absence of Richard I. the Castle underwent many mutations. It was seized for a while by the intriguing William Longchamps, and later by the equally intriguing Prince John, afterwards the king who left the Castle to sign Magna Charta at the neighbouring Runnymede. But the king who has most identified himself with Windsor is Edward III. He himself was born here, and lived happily here with his wife Philippa. Three of their children were born in the Castle, the Black Prince, Margaret and Thomas of Windsor, and here also the Black Prince married Joan of Kent. Still more interesting than these family details are the institutions which made Windsor the centre of the chivalry of England in Edward III.'s reign. St George's College and St George's Hall, already referred to, are connected with the recognition of St George as the patron saint of England, and the founding of the Order of the Knights of the Garter. The celebrated story of the Countess of Salisbury, including Froissart's addition of her noble repulse of the King's passion, appears to be legendary, and the origin of the Garter and its motto an unsolved puzzle. The knights were feasted by the King in the Round Tower, where the Round Table of King Arthur was revived to do them honour, and they tilted in the tournament ground beneath the N. terrace. Conspicuous among them was the King himself, who bore a shield with a white swan, and the motto :

"Hay, hay, the White Swan !
By God's Soul, I am thy man."

In 1390 Chaucer was master of the works for repairing St George's Chapel, and stayed for a year in Winchester

Tower. Richard II.'s story is also much connected with Windsor. In 1397 a Court of Chivalry was held here, in which it was determined that Mowbray and Bolingbroke should decide their quarrel in the lists at Coventry. This is the first scene of Shakespeare's *Richard II.* Two years later Richard, leaving for his ill-advised Irish expedition, took here an affecting farewell of his child-wife Isabella, a little girl of eleven. As it proved, they never met again. The scene has been described by Froissart in a beautiful passage, too long for quotation. Scarcely a year later we find Richard deposed and a prisoner, and the Earls of Kent, Salisbury and Huntingdon conspiring to murder Henry IV. at Windsor. Forewarned by Aumale, who was traitor to both sides, Henry escaped to London in time, and the Earls, after a futile attack on Windsor, found themselves committed to a hopeless resistance. The rest of their story concerns other parts of Berkshire. Henry VI. was born at Windsor, and his father is said to have foretold his destiny in the following lines :

"I, born at Monmouth, shall small time reign and much get.
Henry, born at Windsor, shall long reign and all lose."

The Tudor sovereigns may be passed over rapidly. Of Henry VIII. in Windsor we have a picture in Harrison Ainsworth's "Windsor Castle," which introduces us to every part of the building. In 1543 three martyrs were burnt in Windsor, of whom Testwood, a member of St George's Choir, was the most important. Queen Elizabeth's connexion with the place will be recalled to all by *The Merry Wives of Windsor*, written by Shakespeare at the Queen's express command, to show Falstaff in love, and played for the first time before her in the Chapter Library. In the reigns of James I. and Charles I. disputes arose between the king and the citizens concerning the right of cutting timber in the Park. This partly explains the strange fact that, when the Civil War broke out, Windsor was nearly the only part of Berkshire which proved disloyal. Soon after Charles had left the Castle in February 1642 it was occupied, apparently without resistance, by the Parliament. Essex made it his headquarters before his advance on Reading in 1643, and, at the time of the formation of the New Model, troops were drilled by Fairfax in the Park. Charles was brought back here as a prisoner in 1647, but was soon afterwards removed to Caversham. Windsor was for a while James II.'s headquarters, when William of Orange was marching on London. Then James retreated to Whitehall, and William himself occupied Windsor.

Great interest attaches to the long roll of state prisoners who have been confined in the Castle. First in order of time was Mowbray, Earl of Northumbria, imprisoned by William I. on the charge of murdering Malcolm, King of Scotland. In 1210 John is said to have revenged the rebellion of William de Braose by starving to death in his dungeons Lady de Braose and her eldest son. In Edward III.'s reign the Castle was tenanted by two captive kings, David of Scotland, captured at Neville's Cross, and John of France, captured at Poitiers. The latter's excellent taste is said to have helped Edward in building his castle. In the next century there was another royal prisoner, Prince James, afterwards James I. of Scotland, who was confined in the Devil's Tower during the whole reign of Henry V. He has described in verse in the "King's Quhair" how he fell in love with a beauteous lady whom he saw walking in the rose-garden below (*i.e.* by the fosse, E. of the Round Tower). This was Lady Jane Beaufort, who afterwards became his wife, and went back to Scotland as his queen. During the last years of Henry VIII.'s reign Earl Surrey was frequently imprisoned, and wrote some of his poems in the Castle. He was finally executed just before Henry's own death. In the Great Civil War several Cavalier prisoners were kept in the Norman Gateway, among them Sir Edmund Fortescue and Sir Francis Dodington, who have scratched their initials on the wall. The last state prisoner was Lord Feversham, who was sent by James II. with a message to William of Orange, and imprisoned in order to terrify his master.

Next in order to be described are the parts of the Castle usually seen by the visitor. The division into three wards has already been tacitly assumed. The Lower Ward is mainly given up to the ecclesiastical and military establishments and is freely open to the general public. The Middle Ward is practically the Round Tower, which can be ascended on Tuesday, Wednesday and Thursday, between eleven and four. The Upper Ward contains the royal palace, which of course is jealously guarded, though the State Apartments can be seen, in the absence of the Court, on the same days and hours as the Round Tower, at the fee of a shilling a head. The main entrance to the Lower Ward is from the S. through Henry VIII.'s Gateway. The gateway is really much older than its name implies, though it may have been refaced in the Tudor period. On entering Salisbury and Garter towers are L., and the houses of the military knights R., with the Garter Hall Tower in the centre and Henry III.'s Tower beyond. Right in front is ST GEORGE'S CHAPEL, *open from* 12.30 *to* 4 P.M. *except on Fridays*. This, as we have already stated, was built by Edward IV. on or near the site of two previous chapels, one built by Henry III. and the other by Edward III. Of the latter not a trace remains; of

WINDSOR CASTLE

the former there is only a blind arcade (E.E. restored) on the E. wall of the ambulatory, which runs round the choir. Apart from this the chapel is wholly rich late Perp. From the outside the two rows of great windows with depressed arches are very fine. The clerestory windows are separated by flying buttresses which abut on ordinary upright buttresses between the aisle windows. Inside the windows seem to fill up nearly all the walls, and flood the interior with light. All the remaining space is wholly occupied by panelling, and the ribs of the nave pillars run up into the magnificent roof, largely of fan-tracery, which was added by Henry VII. The great W. window is especially fine, and looks well from outside, with a broad flight of steps leading up to it. In it have been inserted all the fragments of old glass that could be found. From the central crossing we pass through the modern organ-screen into the Choir, of which the roof was built by Henry VIII. On either side are the stalls of the Knights of the Garter, of dark oak with tabernacle canopies, all dating from the time of Henry VII. They contain old brass plates with the names and dates of previous occupants, and are overhung with swords, helmets and banners. The stalls of the royal family are nearest the organ, and next come those of foreign kings. In the centre is a stone stating that in the vault below are buried: (1) Jane Seymour (1537); (2) Henry VIII. (1547); (3) Charles I. (1648)[1]; (4) a child of Queen Anne. Pope's lines are therefore no longer strictly true:

> "Make sacred Charles' tomb for ever known:
> Obscure the place, and uninscribed the stone."

Clarendon's eloquent description of Charles' funeral is too long for quotation, but the details will be familiar,

[1] 8th February 1649 is the actual date.

the snow that fell on the pall, the chapel "altered and transformed" by the havoc of the Puritans, the silent committal, in which Bishop Juxon's lips alone were seen to move, the Church of England service having been forbidden. A little farther L. is the entrance to a second royal vault, which extends beneath the Albert Memorial Chapel. Here are buried George III., with all his family, George IV. and William IV. Of late years only three additions have been made to the royal company, the Duke of Albany in 1884, the Duke of Clarence in 1892, and his great father, Edward VII., in 1910, a loss so recent that it can only be alluded to in reverent sorrow. Nine years before, the public funeral of Victoria the well-beloved had taken place on this same spot, but she rests, not here, but in the neighbouring mausoleum at Frogmore, beside her husband, Prince Albert, and near her mother, the Duchess of Kent, both of whom were buried there in 1861. To the solemn memories of this spot it is well to add the happier ones of the many splendid and joyful royal marriages which have been solemnized here, one of which cannot but occur to all men's hearts at the present time, the union of our late King with Princess Alexandra of Denmark in 1863.

We have now to make the round of the chapels, and observe the monuments. Most of these are in the six side chapels, the position of which will be found in the plan. We start at the N.W. corner with the Urswick Chapel (No. 1 in the plan), the original tenant of which, Dean Urswick (d. 1505), has been turned out to make room for the monument of Princess Charlotte, to which a strange effect, more suitable to a theatre than to a church, has been given by admitting light through coloured glass. Proceeding E. we next reach the Rutland Chapel (No. 2), in the centre of the N. wall. Here are brasses to Sir Thomas St Leger and his wife.

He was executed by Richard III. in 1483. Also the altar-tomb of Sir George Manners (d. 1513) and his wife, ancestors of the Rutland family. Still going E. along the ambulatory, which runs outside the choir, we reach first on the R. the Hastings Chantry, containing the tomb of Edward IV.'s minister, beheaded by Richard III., and then, a little farther on the R., the tomb of Edward IV. himself, of which the most striking part is the elaborate iron screen which separates it from the Choir, and which it is worth returning to the Choir to inspect. At the N.E. corner there is a door leading into the chapter-house, which contains the sword and a portrait of Edward III. Crossing to the S. side, we next have, at the S.E. corner, the Lincoln Chapel (No. 3), which contains the altar-tomb of the Earl of Lincoln (d. 1584). Here Edward IV. placed the bones of a popular saint, the hero of a doggerel rhyme :

> " John Shorn,
> A gentleman born
> Conjured the devil into a boot."

Of course both shrine and painted windows have long disappeared. A little farther W. a slab of black marble covers the grave of Henry VI., who was originally buried at Chertsey, but transferred hither by Richard III. His red velvet hat was popularly supposed to cure headache. The nearness of his grave to that of Edward IV. inspired Pope's well-known lines :

> " The grave unites, where even the great find rest,
> And blended lie the oppressor and the oppressed."

Farther on the R. is another black marble slab, to the memory of Charles Brandon, Duke of Suffolk, who married Henry VII.'s daughter, Mary. Still farther, also R., is the Oxenbridge Chantry, founded 1522 ; also the screen and monument to Dean Urswick removed from his chapel. Just opposite (L.) is the little Kings' Chapel (No. 4), built probably about 1500 by Oliver King, Bishop of Exeter, and later of Bath and Wells, and containing tombs of his family, also panel portraits of Edward IV., Edward V. and Henry VI. A little W. is Braye Chapel (No. 5), founded by Sir Reginald Braye (d. 1502). Here is the font, several beautiful tombs, and a memorial to the Prince Imperial, killed in the Zulu War. The Lady or Beaufort Chapel (No. 6) is at the S.W. corner, and contains the tombs of Charles Somerset, Earl of Worcester (d. 1526), and Henry, first Duke of Beaufort (d. 1699). The Marquis of Worcester, who gallantly defended Raglan Castle (d. 1646), is buried here, but has no monument.

E. of St George's Chapel is the *Albert Memorial Chapel*, originally built by Henry VII. as his burial-place. After building it, he changed his mind, and built another chapel in Westminster. Accordingly this chapel was given by Henry VIII. to Wolsey, who built for himself here a magnificent tomb, all of which disappeared during the disorderly period of the Civil War, except the black marble sarcophagus, which now covers Nelson's tomb in St Paul's. Mass was celebrated here by James II., in consequence of which the chapel was desecrated, and lay unused, until it was partly rebuilt by George III., when he built the Royal Tomb House beneath it. On Prince Albert's death Queen Victoria resolved to turn it into a memorial chapel, adorned with the most precious treasures of art and the most valuable materials. The work was carried out by Sir Gilbert Scott, but the effect is costly without being beautiful, and most visitors will be content with the view of it which may be had from the W. end doorway. In front of the altar are three monuments, to Prince Albert, the Duke of Albany, and the

Duke of Clarence, of whom the last two rest in the vault below.

N. of the Memorial Chapel are the *Dean's Cloisters*. On the S. wall is a fragment of Henry III.'s work, a very beautiful E.E. blind arcade, with door at the S.W. corner. In one panel there is a mural painting of the head of Henry III. himself. The cloisters are Edward III.'s work, and are in style Trans. to Perp., as also are the doors and vaulted S. porch at the N.W. corner. Still farther N. are the *Canons' Cloisters*, which are of picturesque timber and communicate with the ascent to the Castle known as the Hundred Steps. To the E. of the cloisters lies the *Deanery*, on the wall of which is an inscription with a coat-of-arms stating that Christopher Urswick, Dean, with whose tomb we have already met, built the Deanery in 1500. To the W. we pass by the Canons' Houses to the *Horseshoe Cloisters*, at the W. end of St George's Chapel. These are timber-built houses erected by Sir Gilbert Scott in Tudor style, and, apart from their obvious modernity, are successful. A little farther we reach the W. extremity of the Castle at *Curfew* or *Clewer Tower*. Although this has often been refaced, and an incongruous belfry was placed upon it in 1872, yet it is the tower which shows most clearly the genuine work of Henry III. Inside should be noticed the thick walls of hard chalk, in which were formed little chambers, where prisoners are said to have been confined. There is a trap door, supposed to lead to an underground passage, by which Ainsworth makes Herne the Hunter enter the Castle. The oak timbers supporting the belfry are old. In the belfry there is an old gun, said to have been pointed by Cromwell to command the bridge over the Thames, and near it is a cell, where Henry VIII. is said to have imprisoned a butcher for speaking against Anne Boleyn.

BERKSHIRE

Returning to the front quadrangle, we may now pass on to the *Middle Ward* and ascend the *Round Tower*. The entrance is on the N. side, through what is known as the Norman Gateway, though it has been twice rebuilt, and shows no Norman feature. Inside there is nothing to see except a huge bell, brought from Sebastopol in 1855. The top is worth ascending for the magnificent view. The foreground is especially rich in trees, a detail which is always effective. Note the fine appearance of Eton Chapel, the windings of the Thames above Windsor, and the Long Avenue of the Park, which stretches away straight for nearly three miles. It will be observed that when raising the walls of the tower (see *ante*) Wyattville did not also raise the interior buildings, which makes the effect from above curious. After descending, turn first L. and then R. to the *North Terrace*. This is also famous for its view, which is similar to, but not so commanding as, that from the Round Tower. At the W. end is *Winchester Tower*, which has been inhabited in turn by Wykeham, Chaucer and Wyattville (see *ante*). If the Eastern and Southern terraces are also to be seen, which is occasionally the case, they should not be missed. The three together form a promenade hardly to be equalled, and were a favourite walk of Elizabeth, Charles I., Charles II. and George III.

From near the E. end of the North Terrace a doorway leads into the *State Apartments*, which are in the N. wing of the Upper Ward. (*Tickets must be previously obtained from the Lord Chamberlain's Office in the Lower Ward.*) First the Grand Staircase is ascended, where is the famous shield, doubtfully attributed to Benvenuto Cellinio, which was given to Henry VIII. by Francis I. on the Field of the Cloth of Gold. Sixteen rooms in all are shown, always in the same order. The *State*

Ante-room (1) has a painted ceiling by Verrio and fine carvings by Grinling Gibbons. The next six rooms contain a succession of fine pictures, many of them by celebrated masters. The *King's Drawing-room* (2) is entirely filled with a splendid collection of Rubens' works. In the *Council Chamber* (3) note two views by Canaletto and a "St Sebastian" by Guido Reni; in the *King's Closet* (4), landscapes by Teniers and two more works of Canaletto, and in the *Queen's Closet* (5) scenes by Claude and Poussin and portraits by Lely and Holbein. The *Picture Gallery* (6) contains four more portraits by Holbein, and amongst other fine pictures works by Correggio, Andrea del Sarto, Claude, Canaletto, Titian and Rembrandt. Note also the remarkable picture, usually called "The Misers," by Quentin Matsys, who is said to have been a smith, and to have won his wife, an artist's daughter, by showing himself able to paint this picture. The *Van-dyke Room* (7), contains a unique collection of twenty-two portraits by this master, including the celebrated picture of Charles I. on horseback, and several of Henrietta Maria. The next two rooms, the *Audience Chamber* (8) and the *Presence Chamber* (9), have ceilings by Verrio, and Gobelin tapestry representing the history of Esther. Both have several portraits, and in (8) their frames are carved by Grinling Gibbons. The *Guard Room* (10) shows in the centre the armour worn by Dymoke, the King's Champion, at the coronation of George IV. Armour is displayed in abundance, and a case with the swords of Charles I., John Hampden and Marlborough. Also there are busts of Marlborough and Wellington. *St George's Hall* (11) is perhaps the most interesting of all. It is decorated with the coats-of-arms of all the Knights of the Garter, while the banners of the twenty-five original knights are hung along the top of the walls. Ranged round the room are several suits of armour, and there are full-length portraits of the English kings from James I. to George IV., all by celebrated artists. The *Grand Reception-room* (12) has splendid Gobelin tapestry, and a malachite vase, the gift of Nicholas I. to Queen Victoria. The *Throne-room* (13) is where the ceremony of investiture of Knights of the Garter takes place, and is appropriately ornamented with Garter blue velvet. The silver-gilt throne formerly belonged to the Kings of Kandy. The room also contains several royal portraits. Next come the *Ante-Throne-room* (14), and then the *Waterloo Chamber* (15), which contains portraits of all sovereigns, generals and ministers who took part in the Congress of Vienna. Most are painted by Sir Thomas Lawrence. Note also the carvings by Grinling Gibbons. When a play is acted before the Court, this room is used as the theatre. In the last room, the *Grand Vestibule* (16), there is a fine statue of Queen Victoria, and the footstool of Tippoo Sahib, a gold tiger-head with crystal teeth. From this point the visitors are again conducted down the Grand Staircase.

The *Upper Ward* contains the private residence of the sovereign. With the Round Tower it forms a quadrangle, of which the buildings on the N. are mainly the State Apartments just visited, but also include the Royal Private Library (not shown), which is full of beautiful pictures. On the E. are the private apartments of the sovereign, and on the S. the visitors' apartments. In the quadrangle there is a statue of Charles II., the main interest of which lies in the pedestal, on which are carved fruit, etc., by Grinling Gibbons.

The *Home Park*, enclosed by William III., is quite close to the Castle walls. It used to contain Herne's Oak, connected with the legend of Herne the Hunter, which is familiar from the last act of *The Merry Wives of Windsor* and the diablerie in Harrison Ainsworth's "Windsor Castle." The oak in question, which was of doubtful identity, was blown down in 1863, but an oak sapling was planted on the site. To the S. of the Home Park is *Frogmore House*, in the grounds of which are the two mausoleums, one to the Duchess of Kent, the other containing the tombs of Queen Victoria and Prince Albert. They are never shown. Southwards *Windsor Great Park* stretches for mile on mile. When, on the S., the limits of the Park are reached, much of the continuous forests adjoining are still royal land. The *Long Walk*, planted by Charles II. and William III., is a magnificent double avenue of elms, stretching for about 2½ m. from the Castle to the mound called Snow Hill, where there is a colossal equestrian statue of George III. The Park is traversed by two or three public roads. It is full of deer, and shows many scattered groups of oak and elm trees. In the N. part it is flat, but as we proceed southward it becomes gracefully undulating, the trees at the same time becoming thicker.

Old Windsor (2 m. S.E.) is reached by a road across the Park. Here there was a palace of Edward the Confessor, where he miraculously restored to sight a blind woodcutter named Wulwin, from whose eyes there dropped blood, as he exclaimed with rapture, "I see you, O king! I see you, O king!" Here too tradition recounts that Harold and Tostig had an unbrotherly fight, and that Earl Godwin died suddenly, choked by the piece of bread he had impiously prayed might be his last, if he were guilty of the death of the King's brother Alfred. Really these stories are wicked Norman slanders, intended to blacken the fame of the great Saxon family that opposed the Conqueror.

Godwin in fact died at Winchester, and the only foundation for the above story is that he was stricken with illness when dining at the King's table there. The palace continued till the reign of Henry I. It has now vanished, but its site was probably between the church and the river. The rectangular church was originally E.E., in which style the tower and the chancel still remain, though partly restored. The side windows are all Dec. insertions, and similar in pattern—*i.e.* square-headed and filled with Geometrical tracery, the effect of which is graceful. There is a double piscina, and a square aumbry on either side of the altar. One window shows a little old glass, three pairs of birds with intertwined necks. There is a curious tomb to Humphrey Michell (d. 1598), also to his wife, and another of his family.

Winkfield (about 3½ m. N. of Ascot or N.E. of Bracknell) is a very extensive parish, including Winkfield Street and Winkfield Row. The church is practically rebuilt. One window only may be old, a double foliated lancet W. of the aisle. The tower is curious 17th-cent. brick. There is an Elizabethan arcade of oak running down the centre of the church. At one point are the initials E.R. and the date 1592. At another, where it has been repaired, are the initials V.R. and the date 1887. There is a curious brass to Thomas Montagu (d. 1630), and the monument of Lord Metcalfe (d. 1846), with an epitaph by Macaulay.

Winterbourne (2 m. E. of Boxford) has an E.E. church, rebuilt in 1854. One original lancet survives, S. of chancel. The E. window is good Dec. In the S. aisle is an old ruined piscina. The tower is brick, dated 1739. In the vestry is a marble tomb, dated 1729.

Wittenham, Little (3½ m. S.E. of Culham station), is a

small picturesque village close to the Thames (here
crossed by Day's Lock and a wooden bridge) and
resting under the Dorchester or Wittenham Clumps
(v. *Sinodun*). The church has been rebuilt, all but the
tower, of which the lower part is Dec. and the upper
Perp. It has a strange belfry tower. The font is
Perp. There are several monuments and brasses,
mostly to the Dunches, a family now extinct, who once
held the manor. Most are under the tower, where
note especially the effigies of Sir William Dunch and his
wife (1611), and brass to William Dunch (1597). In
the chancel is a 15th-cent. altar-tomb. Note also a
brass to an infant a year old, Anne Dunch. An ancient
bronze shield, found in the bed of the river here, is now
in the British Museum.

WITTENHAM, LONG (2 m. S.E. of Culham station),
is on the broad flat plain of the Gault, just S. of the
Thames, which here sweeps round in a graceful curve
to Clifton Hampden weir, while a straight cut on the
far side leads to the lock. The village, true to its
name, stretches in a long line, parallel to the river,
but turning its back upon it. There are several half-
timbered houses, including the Plough Inn, and a striking
house near the church, with a projecting upper story
propped on huge beams. At the S. end is a fine restored
village cross with several steps. The *church* is most
attractive, both inside and outside. Of the original
Norman building (about 1120-1140) there remain the
chancel arch, which shows arabesque capitals, and a
small recessed window in the chancel. Early in the 13th
cent. the chancel was rebuilt, all the windows but one
being changed to lancets. Of the same date are the
priest's door and the three piscinæ, two of which
are in the sill of a lancet window. At the same time
the S. aisle was thrown out, with its E.E. arcade, which

shows good stiff-stalk foliage of a somewhat early pattern. About 1280 the long S. transeptal chapel was built, the Geometrical window on the S. being its principal feature. The piscina below is of the same date and quite unique, for in front of the drain there lies the small effigy of a knight in armour, very probably the founder of the chapel. Above is a canopy on which are carved two angels. At the same time the pair of early. Dec. windows was inserted W. of the chancel, and prolonged to form low-side windows. Their tracery resembles that of a window in the S. chapel. Soon after the church was acquired by Exeter College, Oxford, in 1322, a fourth set of changes took place. The N. arcade and aisle were thrown out, and the windows of the S. aisle altered, so that all the aisle windows, together with N. and S. doors, are Curvilinear. Near the W. respond of the N. arcade is a small Dec. pillar piscina, with a Dec. niche near it. The tower is Perp. and built of beautiful grey stone. The clerestory is late Perp. In 1850 the chancel was restored, so that the lancets look new. Also the present E. and W. windows were inserted. All other windows are old and good. There is a remarkable leaden font of Trans. date, obviously from the same hand as those of the adjoining Oxfordshire churches of Dorchester and Warborough. A curious squint seems intended to give a view of the S. chapel altar from the body of the church. The woodwork is good. There is a pretty timber porch, and some old pews. The pulpit, S. chapel screen, and font-cover are Jacobean ; also some stall-work with poppy-heads, which was brought from Exeter College. The parish has been rich in archæological finds. In the field called " Free Acre," just S. of the village, and bounded by the Wallingford road, an important Anglo-Saxon cemetery

The Church Porch: Long Wittenham:

was excavated in 1859-1860. Of the objects found, now in the British Museum, the most interesting was a sort of beaker with bronze panels, showing Christian subjects. It is supposed to have contained holy water. In 1893 a British and Romano-British settlement was discovered near Northfield Farm, which lies about 1 m. N. of the village, in the great loop formed by the Thames. The settlement seems to have consisted wholly of wattle-work and mud. It has been carefully examined by Dr Haverfield.

Wokingham is a pleasant town with a largish market-place, but with little to show the visitor. A charter was granted to it by Queen Elizabeth in 1583, and confirmed by James I. in 1612. The outside of the parish church has been made entirely new, but inside there are two lofty and dignified Perp. arcades, and a good roof resting on corbel heads. There is a beautiful Perp. font, with a pedestal showing a strange sort of cable moulding ; also a curious brass with two kneeling figures, which is set in a stone frame. At the *Rose Inn* in Wokingham it is stated that there were composed the verses to " Molly Mog," which will be found among Gay's poems. The story is that " three men of Art "— *i.e.* Gay, Swift and Pope—beguiled a wet day at the inn by writing the song in praise of the landlady's pretty daughter. As, however, Swift afterwards refers to the ballad as Gay's, it may be considered that poet's own composition. The main object seems to have been to get as many rhymes as possible to " Mog." For a sample we may take the following verse :—

" A letter when I am inditing,
  Comes Cupid and gives me a jog,
And fills all the paper with writing
  Of nothing but sweet Molly Mog."

BERKSHIRE

A mile S. of the town, at Chapel Green, are some almshouses founded in 1665.

Woolhampton (close to Midgham station) is a village in the Kennet Valley. The church, which is quite new, is ¾ m. to the S., at the top of the hill, which commands fine views over the valley. The old church, described by Parker, was destroyed in 1860, when a Norman stone font, with remarkable leaden figures, was discarded, and buried beneath the present church.

Woolley Park. (See *Chaddleworth.*)

Woolstone (2½ m. S. of Uffington station) is a pretty little village lying close under *White Horse Hill.* The interesting church is of hard chalk, and is in style Trans. with some Dec. alterations. As is the case in many Trans. churches, there is some doubt about the exact date of the details. The N. door is good Norman, without Trans. details, and the S. door is also plain Norman. The font, one of the three leaden ones in Berkshire, shows E.E. details, but is set on a Norman base. The chancel arch and the arch leading to the S. transeptal chapel are more decidedly Trans. There are two plain recessed lancets in the nave. The walls of the chancel, including the window-frames, are also Trans. There are two inserted Geometrical windows, one in the S. transept, the other N. of nave; and four later Dec. windows, two N. and two S. of the chancel. There is a Dec. piscina, a sill-sedile and a square aumbry. The E. end is brick and dated 1760, but the E. window is modern. The W. window is church-warden and there is a modern bell-cote.

Wootton (3 m. N. of Abingdon) is a straggling village partly built on the S. side of Boar's Hill. The church is plain rectangular, with a Dec. chancel, and a late Perp. nave. It is nicely kept, but of very little interest. Note a Dec. piscina and the stump of an old cross.

Wytham (about 3½ m. N.W. of Oxford) is the most northern village in Berkshire. It lies between the Thames Valley and the Wytham Hills, here covered with beautiful hanging woods, which reach as far as Swinford Bridge, near which they are sometimes called the Eynsham Woods. They are in the estate of the Earl of Abingdon, and kept strictly private. The village itself is highly picturesque, consisting of well-built stone cottages lying amongst well-kept gardens, where strawberries are largely grown. At the end of June all Oxford comes here to eat strawberries. The usual route is up the river and then by the pleasant field-track from Godstow Bridge (about ½ m.).

Wytham Place, the seat of the Earl of Abingdon, is a late Perp. mansion, built when the Harcourts held the manor, and partly altered in Elizabeth's reign. About the beginning of the 19th cent. the third Earl of Abingdon destroyed Rycote Place (see "Little Guide Book to Oxfordshire "), and transported some of the doors and windows to Wytham Place. The house, which is not shown, has a fine front, the gatehouse in the centre being particularly good original work. The *church* is said to have been built about 1480 by the Abingdon monks. But in 1814 the third Earl of Abingdon repeated his act of vandalism at Rycote, by destroying Cumnor Place (*q.v.*) to rebuild the church with the materials. Accordingly the whole interest of the present edifice lies in the doors and windows which come from Cumnor. The churchyard is entered on the N. by a square-headed gate bearing the inscription, " *Janua vitæ verbum domini.*" Just before passing it, another doorway may be seen on the L., with the date 1372. Both of these, together with the strange debased porch, and the door under the tower (N.), are part of the Cumnor spoils. Inside, the principal features brought from Cumnor are three remarkable late Dec.. windows, with beautiful tracery, two of which show the approach of Perp. by the stiffening of the mullions. The E. window is traditionally that of the chamber in which Amy Robsart slept just before her death. Whether the early Perp. window N. of the nave, or the corbel heads supporting the roof, one of which represents a man playing on the bagpipes, also came from Cumnor, there seems no evidence. The tower apparently belongs to the old Perp. church. There is some curious Dutch glass in the chancel windows, and some older-looking medallions in two of the nave windows. There are three memorial stones, dated 1617, 1624 and 1634, and two old defaced brasses on the floor, supposed to be of the date 1455.

Yattendon (2 m. S.E. of Hampstead Norris) is a cheerful, well-built village surrounded by fine trees. The church is entirely Perp. (about 1450), but the windows have been restored, so that it looks new. All is uniform, the five-light E. window and the S. door being especially good work. The rood-stairs remain, carried in an outside buttress-turret; also part of the original rood-screen, a Jacobean pulpit and a fine timber roof. There is a large monument to Sir John Norreys (d. 1597), who was favoured by Queen Elizabeth, because his father had been unjustly executed for alleged intimacy with Anne Boleyn. The church is rather well known for its singing. It uses a special hymn-book, with the object of reviving old melodies, which is dedicated to Robert Bridges and H. Ellis Woolridge. There are elaborate stalls for the choir and a very large organ.